The language of architecture

For Elisabeth, who shared all the troubles and few of the pleasures

Niels Luning Prak

The language of architecture
A contribution to architectural theory

Mouton - The Hague - Paris

THIS BOOK WAS PUBLISHED WITH THE AID OF THE NETHERLANDS
ORGANISATION FOR THE ADVANCEMENT OF PURE RESEARCH (Z.W.O.)

© MOUTON & CO 1968
Printed in the Netherlands by Koninklijke Drukkerij G. J. Thieme N.V. Nijmegen

Preface

1. Summary

This book is about the theory of architecture. It is in particular an attempt to find some consistent pattern of relations between architectural aesthetics and social history.

The first part makes a plea for a general aesthetics free from values and embracing the particular theories advanced by Le Corbusier, Van Doesburg, Team Ten, or by Alberti, Laugier, Pugin and Viollet-le-Duc. Parts of these theories deal with purely formal problems, other parts with the significance of forms. General aesthetics is therefore split into formal and symbolic aesthetics. Formal aesthetics probably depends upon the Gestalt laws of perception.

Part of the confusion in architectural writing arises from the assumption that architectural space is a simple visible object. Arguments are advanced for distinguishing at least three kinds of space: the physical (the volume of air of the heating engineers), the conceptual (the space we see or visualize) and the behavioral. In construction too it is useful to make a distinction between physical (calculated) and phenomenal structure.

This discussion is followed by an enumeration of formal categories which are used in the subsequent historical analysis.

The historical part tries to connect the forms of a building, as far as they are due to art and not to practical necessities, with the society in which it arose. It 'explains' architecture in terms of social change. The gradually worsening conditions in the declining Roman Empire may have been conducive to the spread of Christianity and have promoted an 'introverted' architecture. The insecurity of the Age of the Great Migrations may have led to the concept of the Romanesque church as a 'sacred fortress', a bulwark against evil, and have caused an outspoken timidity in construction. Conversely, when conditions improved in the Later Middle Ages, constructions became gradually more daring, and churches lighter and more festive, more 'optimistic'. Medieval society was static and collectivistic; ours is dynamic and individualistic. Medieval society was threatened by *outside* forces of destruction; ours is on the contrary threatened by internal dissension. The change started with the Renaissance, and was accompanied by a change in symbolism.

Architecture began to symbolize an ideal world, to which man ought to aspire, a dreamland. Three different forms of dreamland were tried out: Classicism (Renaissance, Mannerism and Baroque), Eclecticism and finally Modern Architecture. Each began with 'pure' and simple forms, representing a harmonic cosmos in contrast to the real world. As the divergent processes in society spread inexorably, architectural forms became more involved. An agressive plasticity tries to force the spectator to believe in architectural dreamland, both in the Baroque and in our architecture of today.

Architectural dreamland is a figment of the imagination and therefore far removed from the practical problems of building. This is perhaps one of the causes of the gradually widening gap between architecture and engineering, leading finally to the still widely admired structural nonsense of Niemeyer's Presidential Palace in Brasilia or Utzon's unrealizable shells in the Sydney Opera House.

The historical analysis shows the possibilities of this kind of approach. The number of examples has been gradually increased towards the end, because the goal was an interpretation of modern architecture. It shows that the Modern Movement can be viewed as part and parcel of a consistent development, instead of as an isolated phenomenon. Chapter V (The overall pattern) gives a more extensive summary of the historical part of the book.

2. The question of truth

A book like this is bound to receive a lot of adverse criticism. The author is well aware that he has stuck his neck out. The historical facts adduced in support of the theory may contain some errors and omissions, but are based in the main on recent literature and will probably not be called in question. The weak spot lies in the connection between historical social conditions and the architecture of the period.

The supposition is that the architectural aesthetics are a subconscious emotional reaction to the social conditions. This is entirely a hypothetical construction; its very nature precludes a direct proof, which could be tested for instance in a crucial experiment. Even if we still could get Brunelleschi to lie down on the analyst's couch, it seems doubtful whether we would get much out of him. All the 'evidence' offered consists therefore of a brief analysis of what I believe to be the relevant conditions and a contemporaneous piece of writing which sets the mood. It would be easy to counter such examples with others, breathing optimism in a time of hardship (Bede, for instance), or pessimism in a happier period.

Also, if the supposed connection holds, this theory is not exempt from the influence of its historical setting. It is therefore neither the only, nor the final word about architectural aesthetics. The best I can hope for is that it becomes a link in a chain. Perhaps its most valuable aspect is the *kind* of approach; that, I believe, will stand, even when the interpretation itself has been changed or rejected.

It is hoped that this book will influence architectural criticism. It makes it possible to distinguish between formal and symbolic statements, and to indicate why certain solutions may have been preferred to others. It may show why an architect builds as he does, why he writes as he does and how the two are interrelated. And it could do so even for one who finds the particular explanations offered in Part II unacceptable.

3. Sources and acknowledgements

The idea that works of art are symbols of emotions has been taken from two books by Susanne Langer, *Philosophy in a New Key* (1942) and *Feeling and Form* (1953). Her philosophy of art stems from the work of E. Cassirer, *Die Philosophie der Symbolischen Formen* (1923–1929). The idea is much older though: in Jouffroy, *Cours d'esthétique* (1845, p. 175) we find: '...can anyone doubt that the symbolic aspect of objects or their qualities is a source of aesthetic emotions?'

That emotions symbolized in art may arise from social conditions was the thesis of Walter Abell in *The Collective Dream in Art* (1957). The third part of my book is a sequel to his. His book deals with the general outline of the doctrine; it is of necessity rather abstract and vague. I have tried on the contrary to be as concrete and specific as possible. He built the general frame of reference; I have attempted to fill it in with the reality of actual buildings. The tracing of emotions to outward circumstances goes back to Freud, and the view that social conditions are reflected in the movement of ideas stems, of course, from Marx. A connection between abstract art and anxiety and between realism and a sense of well-being is also found in Wilhelm Worringer's *Abstraktion und Einfühlung* (1908).

The breakdown of architecture into form-aspects 9 believe to be—to some extent—a contribution of my own. It has been influenced by the 'Bauhaus Vorkurs' of J. Itten and (later) L. Moholy-Nagy. The closest parallel to my classification of form-aspects is a table in L. Moholy-Nagy, *Von Material zu Architektur* (1929). My classification is more complete, I think, and more useful for the analysis of buildings. The insistence on the relativity of contrasts and the co-ordinate system of the aspects seems to me also an innovation, at least in architectural theory.

That architecture can be interpreted as a symbolic language with a definite iconographical meaning is a fairly recent discovery of art-history.*

An important part of the art-historical material has been culled from the books and articles of the following art-historians: M. Aubert, R. Banham, H. Beseler, R. Branner, W. Buchowiecki, K. J. Conant, F. W. Deichmann, P. Frankl, A. Grabar, H. L. C. Jaffé, E. Kaufmann, F. van der Meer, W. and E. Paatz, E. Panofsky, H. R.

---

* The following articles and books deal with this subject:
E. Baldwin Smith, *The Dome*, Princeton, 1950.
—, *Architectural Symbolism of Imperial Rome and the Middle Ages*, Princeton, 1956.
G. Bandmann, *Mittelalterliche Architektur als Bedeutungsträger*, Berlin, 1951.
R. Banham, *Theory and Design in the First Machine Age*, London, 1960.
L. Hautecoeur, *Mystique et architecture. Symbolisme du cercle et de la coupole*, Paris, 1954.
R. Krautheimer, 'Introduction to an Iconography of Mediaeval Architecture' *Journal of the Warburg and Courtauld Institutes*, Vol. V, 1942, pp. 1 f.
—, 'The Carolingian Revival of Early Christian Architecture' *Art Bulletin*. Vol. XXIV, 1942. pp. 1 f.
H. Sedlmayr, 'Architektur als abbildende Kunst', *Österreichische Akademie der Wissenschaften*, Phil. Hist. Klasse, Vol. 225, Part 3, Vienna, 1948.
R. Wittkower, *Architectural Principles in the Age of Humanism*, London, 1952.
C. Heitz, *Recherches sur les rapports entre architecture et liturgie à l'époque carolingienne*, Paris, 1963.

Hitchcock and A. Schmidt. The socio-psychological interpretation of each of the nine historical buildings is of necessity original. It is only this interpretation that matters here; by its juxtaposition with the other art-historical material I have tried to show that the theory is in agreement with accepted knowledge. It might perhaps even be regarded as the logical conclusion of the normal art-historical interpretations.

I have been influenced by the writings of the sociologists G. Friedmann, G. Gurvitch, G. C. Homans, R. K. Merton, W. F. Ogburn, T. Parsons, D. Riesman and M. Weber and the psychologists F. H. Allport, R. Arnheim, O. Klineberg, K. Koffka, W. Köhler, K. Lewin, C. E. Osgood and M. Wertheimer.

I am deeply indebted to F. van der Meer for his kind but incisive criticism of the whole book. His advice has greatly reduced its length and thereby increased its readability. J. J. Terwen provided me originally with the measurements of the Pazzi Chapel. F. J. Tichelman translated several Latin texts for me. P. Singolonberg and the late P. Frankl advised on several technical points. Mrs. A. B. Oosterlee-Hewson kindly and patiently helped me to eliminate the most striking offenses against English usage.

Delft, July 1966 N.L.P.

Copyright acknowledgements

For permission to quote from the volumes and articles listed below, grateful acknowledgement is made to the following authors and publishers:

W. Abell, *The collective Dream in Art*, Harvard University Press, 1957
Th. Brown, *The Work of G. Rietveld, Architect*, A. W. Bruna & Sons, Utrecht, 1958
B. Brownell, F. L. Wright, *Architecture and modern Life*, Harper & Brothers, 1938
W. Gropius, *Scope of total Architecture*, Harper & Brothers, 1955
M. Hadas, *A History of Rome*, Doubleday & Co., 1956
Ph. Johnson, 'A house in New Canaan', *Architectural Review*, Vol. 106, Sept. 1950
The Odyssey, translated by E. V. Rieu, Penguin Books, 1948
E. Panofsky, 'The History of Art as a Humanistic Discipline', *The Meaning of the Humanities*, edited by T. M. Greene, Princeton University Press, 1940
—, Das Erste Blatt aus dem 'Libro' Giorgio Vasari's... *Städel Jahrbuch*, VI, 1930
—, *Abbot Suger on the Abbey Church of St Denis*, Princeton University Press, 1946
The Renaissance Philosophy of Man, edited by E. Cassirer, P. O. Kristeller and J. H. Randall, University of Chicago Press, 1950
H. E. Winlock, *The Temple of Ramesses I at Abydos*, The Metropolitan Museum of Art, 1937

Contents

Preface
Summary v; The question of truth vi; Sources and acknowledgements vii v

List of plates xiii

Part I: analytical

I Formal and symbolic aesthetics 3
The Vitruvian subdivision 3; Aesthetics 4; The psychology of perception 7; Space 11

II Symbolism 14
The language of architecture 14; The art of words 16; The roots of emotion in art 19

III Basic concepts in architecture 24
Place 24; Space 26; Structure 29

IV Classification of forms 32
The dimensions of architectural form 32; Structure 35; Typology of spatial composition 36

Part II: historical

V The overall pattern 41
Levels of meaning 41; All in the same boat 43; Divided against itself 44; Construction and art 49

VI Santa Costanza, Rome 51
Description 51; Analysis 59

VII St Michael, Hildesheim 61
Description 61; Analysis 67

VIII Notre Dame of Amiens 76
Description 76; Analysis 88

IX Pazzi Chapel, Florence 100
Description 100; Analysis 110

X	Imperial Library, Vienna	117
	Historical setting 117; Description 119; Iconographical program 126; Analysis 132	
XI	Westminster New Palace, Londen	137
	Description 137; Analysis 145	
XII	Amsterdam Exchange	152
	Description 152; Analysis 156	
XIII	Johnson House, New Canaan	162
	Description 162; Analysis 163	
XIV	Notre Dame du Haut, Ronchamp	170
	Description 170; Analysis 173	
XV	Recent developments	178

Appendices

A	An analysis of Van Doesburg's sixteen points	182
B	Categories of criticism	187
Notes		189

List of plates

I. Santa Costanza, Rome, exterior. (Photo, Deutsches Archäologisches Institut, Rome.)
II. Santa Costanza, Rome, interior. (Photo, Deutsches Archäologisches Institut, Rome.)
III. Exterior of St Michael, Hildesheim. (Photo, Mrs. Dorothea Lax, Hildesheim.)
IV. Interior of the southern aisle of St Michael, Hildesheim. (Photo, Marburg Photo.)
V. Exterior of Amiens cathedral. (Photo, Sofer, St Maur.)
VI. Interior of Amiens cathedral. (Photo, Marburg Photo.)
VII. Amiens cathedral: southern aisle with part of radiant chapel in the left. (Photo, H. Sibbelee, Maartensdijk.)
VIII. Amiens cathedral: longitudinal section through the chancel and the Lady Chapel.
IX. Exterior of the Pazzi Chapel, Florence. (Photo, N. Luning Prak, Rotterdam.)
X. Interior of the Pazzi Chapel, Florence. (Photo, Alinari, Florence.)
XI. Exterior of the Imperial Library in Vienna in 1780, after a watercolour by Carl Schütz.
XII. Interior of the Imperial Library. (Photo, Österreichische Nationalbibliothek, Vienna.)
XIII. Imperial Library in Vienna: detail of ceiling-paintings. (Photo, Österreichische Nationalbibliothek, Vienna.)
XIV. Central hall of the Imperial Library, Vienna, after a perspective drawing by S. Kleiner.
XV. View of Westminster New Palace, London. (Photo, Valentine's Postcards, London.)
XVI. Westminster Hall, interior.
XVII. The lower part of Victoria Tower, Westminster New Palace.
XVIII. The interior of the Peer's Lobby in Westminster New Palace.
XIX. Exterior of the northern end of the Amsterdam Exchange. (Photo, Publieke Werken, Amsterdam.)
XX. Detail of the interior elevation of the main hall in the Amsterdam Exchange. (Photo, N. Luning Prak, Rotterdam.)
XXI. Exterior of the Johnson house, New Canaan. (Photo, N. Luning Prak, Rotterdam.)
XXII. Section of the competition project for the replanning of the railway station at Ludwigshafen by Van den Broek and Bakema.
XXIII. Exterior of N. Dame du Haut, Ronchamp. (Photo, L. Vos de Wael.)
XXIV. Interior of N. Dame du Haut, Ronchamp. (Photo, F. Keuzenkamp, Pijnacker.)

Part one: analytical

Formal and symbolic aesthetics

1. The Vitruvian subdivision

Leonardo Benevolo in his *Storia dell' architettura moderna* confronts some of the well-known old photographs of key monuments with pictures taken at a more recent date. These illustrations confirm what many already knew or guessed: many famous modern buildings have not stood up well to the test of time. Most extant medieval churches are in a better state of preservation than the early villas of Le Corbusier, the Dessau Bauhaus or Duiker's Zonnestraalbuilding. Recently the Weissenhofsiedlung at Stuttgart has been extensively restored, less than forty years after its completion.

The rapid deterioration is partly due to changes in function, partly to indifference, but certainly also to a makeshift construction. Alfred Roth's Dolderthal flats in Zürich are still as good as new, mainly because of their impeccable technical detailing.

This shows that the Vitruvian subdivision into function, construction and aesthetics (Wotton's commodity, firmness and delight)[1] is more than an abstract aid to thought. Artistic excellence is neither a guarantee for constructive soundness, nor does it vouchsafe a maximum in comfort and practically.

Indeed why should it? A building of note creates an image, a view on a world of space till then unknown. The image of Mies' Barcelona pavilion is still with us, although nobody of the present generation of architects has seen it in reality. Little does it matter now if the actual building was solid and practical or not.

Each of the three aspects is a world in itself. In its function, a building is merely an outsize tool, in the same way as stoves, cars and refrigerators or the machinery which Le Corbusier adduced are. Technically a building can be regarded in the same class as large immobile constructions, such as canals, roads, docks and bridges. Its preoccupation with visual form connects architecture with sculpture and painting. Taken by themselves, these different worlds are unrelated. They only meet in a work of architecture. The bond has to be created, it cannot be taken for granted.

Different and often conflicting demands are made upon the architect from the three realms. In normal praxis, the result is usually a compromise: sometimes form is sacrificed to function, in other parts of the design the roles are reversed. The ideal remains a building in which the three aspects go hand in hand and each receives its due; but many architects get no further than an uneasy truce. Mies and Le Corbusier have always let form prevail over practicality and construction. Strict functionalism, which ostensibly puts aesthetics in the last place, has rarely received more than lip-service. Nor was Gothic architecture primarily glorified construction, as Viollet-le-Duc and Pugin would have it.[2]

On the whole, the Vitruvian division is both necessary and sufficient for our purpose. However, our main topic aesthetics, has to be subdivided once again.

2. Aesthetics

It is usually easy to reach agreement on the functional or constructional merits or defects of a particular building. But the aesthetic evaluation is a different matter altogether. Not only do we find a variety of opinion among critics, but their judgments seem also to vary according to which age they belonged. Whole periods have been accused of producing nothing of architectural value. Baroque was considered a debased style at the turn of the century; we are slowly retracting our wholesale condemnation of nineteenth century eclecticism.

For instance: Palladio wrote about a group of Bolognese clients who wanted to finish the Gothic church of San Petronio with a Gothic facade: 'I do not know in what German author they have ever read a definition of architecture, which is nothing but a symmetry of the members within a body, each being so well proportioned and so concordant with the others and vice versa that by their harmony they give the impression of majesty and decorum; the Gothic style, however, should be called confusion and not architecture. ...'[3]

In his *Four Books on Architecture*, Palladio gives a specific instance of the concordance of members within a body: 'I have made the frontispiece in the fore-front in all the fabrics for villas... because such frontispieces shew off the entrance of the house and add very much to the grandeur and magnificence of the work, the front being thus made more eminent than the rest. ... And the parts on the right correspond with those on the left.'[4] The same principle of the dominant middle is advocated by Ruskin: 'In fine west fronts (of churches), the centre is always the principal mass... the purer method is, to keep them (i.e. the towers of the façade) down in due relation to the centre and to throw up the pediment in a steep connecting mass, drawing the eye to it by rich tracery. ...'[5] Ruskin abhorred the classical style practised by Palladio; he admired Gothic, in particular Venetian Gothic, which must have been the Gothic with which Palladio was most familiar. Thus we have the curious result that conformity in rules does not at all imply conformity in judgment.

This contradiction disappears if a distinction is made between formal and symbolic aesthetics. Palladio and Ruskin agree on the *formal* principle, but disagree on the style in which this principle should be expressed. For Palladio Gothic is a foreign style of barbarian origins, which emerged from a dark era in which true—i.e. ancient culture degenerated. Classical architecture is pagan architecture for Ruskin, whilst Gothic on the contrary is connected with the greatest age of Christianity. This latter kind of aesthetic evaluation concerns itself with the *meaning* of forms, and not with their composition. This meaning may have gradually become associated with the forms under review, or consciously intended from the start; it may be different for the architect, for a contemporary observer and for a later one. Certainly Ruskin's interpretation of Gothic architecture was widely different from both that of fourteenth century man and from our own. As this variety of meanings is irrelevant to the main theme of this book, all types will be subsumed under the generic term: *symbolism*.

Formal aesthetics deals with proportions, rhythm, repetition, formal cohesion, consistency, etc. Symbolic aesthetics on the contrary employs such epithets as 'honest', 'truly modern'; or, in the case of Palladio 'barbarian' versus 'good'; or, again with Ruskin and Pugin: 'pagan' versus 'Christian'.

A distinction between these two classes has the advantage of solving some other aesthetic problems. With its help we are free to admire the work of Royal Barry Wills, Edwin Lutyens, Herbert Baker, Cass Gilbert, John Russell Pope and Paul Schmitthenner on formal grounds, whilst we deplore their use of an obsolete symbolism. Without the slightest notion of their symbolic meaning, we may still appreciate the Taj Mahal or the Katsura Palace on formal grounds.

The example of non-Western architecture, as well as the principle described by Palladio and Ruskin show that formal appreciation is far more general and constant than the symbolic. The formal aspects can therefore probably be identified with the 'eternal beauty' in art. We recognize it in historical buildings, in Cape Cod cottages, in Swiss chalets, in Pueblo Indian villages; in the bridges of Maillart, the shells of Candela, and the structures of Nervi; in Negro masks and Polynesian shields, and in all types of ornaments. Formal aesthetics is rooted in our psychological structure.

The symbolic mode of evaluation is heuristic. It is rooted in the meaning which particular forms have acquired for a certain society at a particular time. Ruskin's love of Gothic for instance is connected with religious reforms in Victorian England: the Cambridge Camden Society and the Oxford Movement. These again have to do with a growing awareness of the ills of the Early Industrial Revolution. The study of this pattern of relations between social conditions, the world of ideas, and the symbols used by architects is the main theme of this book.

The distinction between formal and symbolic aesthetics is not at all as obvious as it might seem. Books on architectural aesthetics, such as the works of Vitruvius, Alberti, Viollet-le-Duc, or Le Corbusier usually present an apparently coherent system of norms in which the two classes are blended. For instance, in Le Corbusier's *Vers une architecture*, the chapter on 'Volume' (Mass) opens with: 'Our eyes are made to see forms in light. The primary forms are beautiful forms because they are clearly readable. The architects of today no longer build simple forms. The engineers, working with calculations, use geometrical forms, which satisfy our eyes by geometry and our spirit by mathematics; their creations are becoming great art.'[6] The Phileban solids are advocated both on formal grounds (readability, beauty) and on symbolic ones, as is shown by the reference to engineering.

In practice, architectural aesthetics is always of this type: a more or less coherent system of criteria which are formal and symbolic at the same time. It is nearly always possible to find examples from the history of architecture which employ the same formal devices as those advocated by the author (this shows again the universality of formal aesthetics); thus most writers 'prove' that their theory is universally valid with the help of the Parthenon (Le Corbusier), Rheims cathedral, the pyramids, etc. If the theories could indeed lay a claim to universal validity, architectural aesthetics would have shown a consistent development over the centuries, comparable to physics or biology! But the authors have an axe to grind; they want us to accept their values and their philosophy. This philosophy is rooted in a particular society (or group in society) at a certain point in its historical development. Objective, scientific validity is therefore obviously ruled out for such theories.

However, it is possible that the pattern of relations between a society, its 'Weltanschauung' and its aesthetics is a regular one, recurrent in more or less the same form over the centuries. This leads to the notion of a general aesthetics, which embraces the particular ones of Vitruvius, Perret or Le Corbusier. Such a general aesthetics would be free from values; it would not condemn or praise, but show only a pattern. The normal, particular aesthetics would exemplify the 'laws' of the general type. Again, this general aesthetics would have to be divided in a formal and a symbolic branch; the latter concerned with the heuristic symbolism, the former with the more enduring questions of proportions, harmony and contrast, etc. To this last type we turn now.

3. The psychology of perception

There exists an intimate relation between the psychology of perception and art, as has been remarked by various authors.[1] In particular the laws of configuration of Gestalt psychology have a great deal in common with some formal criteria, culled from various aesthetic treatises.

Normal visual perception is so clearly consistent with what is experienced as 'the outside world', and of such apparent simplicity, that perception was originally seen as a completely passive process. By confronting test persons with ambiguous figures, it was shown that this naïve view is false. The images received on the

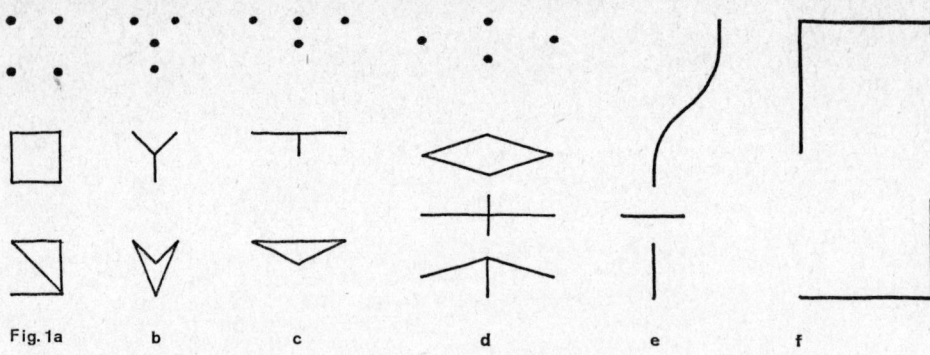

Fig. 1a   b   c   d   e   f

retinas of our eyes are organized into meaningful patterns; this organization, when faced with a choice, shows a preference for one type of perception over another. Thus perception is a dynamic process, in which we actively participate.

These preferences can be grouped under four headings:[8]

1. Proximity
Objects which are close to each other in the retinal image tend to be seen as a group. For example: the stars of the constellations in the sky look as if they are near each other, though they may be only nearly behind each other and yet still very far apart.

2. Repetition
We are inclined to perceive equalities even where they do not exist. Two glowing points in a dark room at equal distance from the observer, but of unequal brightness, look like two equally bright points at unequal distances. Two vertical lines (in a homogeneous visual field) at equal distance and of unequal lengths, are perceived as lines of equal length but at different distances.[9]

3. Simplest and largest figure
We perceive the simplest and the largest forms possible. The point configurations of Figure 1 for instance are perceived as the line figures in the row just below them. Only with an effort can they be seen as the figures of the bottom row. Perception therefore follows the outline of the figure, i.e. the largest possible form, in Figures 1a and 1d. Proximity between the points in the centre cause the Figures 1b and 1c to be seen as Y and T rather than in full outline. Symmetry along the horizontal axis causes Figure 1d to be seen as a rhomb, notwithstanding the proximity between the two points in the middle and its resemblance to Figure 1c. It depends upon the circumstances which tendency prevails. Simple figures like rectangles or circles are easier to 'read' (just as Le Corbusier said) than complex figures. Symmetry is simpler in this sense than asymmetry.

The basic regular forms of Euclidean geometry are thus the 'language of visual perception'.

4. Continuity and closure

Lines tend to run on beyond their end points; planes beyond their edges. The curved line of Figure 1 e is perceived as continuing beyond the interruption. The lines of Figure 1 f are seen as parts of the outline of a rectangle, rather than as separate figures (closure).

The forces of perceptual dynamics operate in the artist as much as in the spectator. The artist uses these forces to bring coherence in his work. Examples of such coherence are: the repetition in ornament or in curtain walls; the use of large, simple blocks (the 'prisme pur') for offices; and the alignment of detached houses in modern estates (continuity).

The Greek requirement that a work of art be such 'that nothing can be added or taken away'[10] can be interpreted as a version of the Gestalt demand for simple forms. Plato particularly mentions figures made with ruler and compass as 'absolutely beautiful'[11] (just as Le Corbusier did). Simple overall forms and repetition of elements are the expected things. By using the forces at work in perceptual dynamics, the artist makes it easy for his public; he creates a maximum of harmony, a work which can be recognized at a glance. Such work offers little of interest, because one knows what is coming next. The gratification of the perceptual mechanism runs the danger of becoming exceedingly dull.

Therefore, the story is not finished with the enumeration of the Gestalt laws of perception. Opposed to the tendency to see repetition and simple forms is the need for variety, to see something of visual interest.[12] A work of art which only skilfully integrated what was already expected from the point of view of perceptual psychology would lack all individual character. The majority of commercial buildings are just such nondescript monuments to boredom; one cannot object to them on formal grounds, and yet, because of their utter lack of expression, one cannot love them either.

The opposite of visual harmony is visual *contrast*. Contrast disturbs the harmonious pattern of expected, 'normal' forms. Because of the existence of a norm in all of us, it becomes possible to surprise us by a deviation from it. Often the artists are quite conscious of such deviations: 'The new architecture is *anti-cubic*, that is to say, it does not try to freeze the different functional space-cells in one closed cube. Rather *it throws the functional space-cells* (as well as overhanging planes, balcony volumes, etc.) centrifugally from the *core of the cube*, and through this means height, width, depth + time approach a totally new plastic expression in open spaces. In this way architecture gets (in so far as this is possible from a constructional point of view—task of the engineers!) a more or less floating aspect that, so to speak, works against the gravitational forces of nature.'[13] (Van Doesburg) The closed cube is of course the simple Phileban solid which is expected in perception; by going against this expectation, the 'new architecture' is able to achieve an impression of floating in the air. Contrast is a means of expression, presupposing norms against which such contrast can be made.

Most well-known Western architecture follows the precepts of perceptual psychology on some points, and flaunts them, often deliberately, on others. Whilst the contrasts individualize the building and express the intentions of its architect, the use of perceptually expected forms (such as repetition, simple overall form, continuity, etc.) serves to *compensate* for the disruption caused by the contrasts and gives the required formal unity. The strong contrasts between verticals and horizontals in Greek temples is offset by their simple overall form and their use of repetitive elements. The spatial complexity and the strongly contrasting proportions of Amiens cathedral are compensated for by the continuity of members (arches continuing in wall-shafts), the parallelism of all sub-spaces and the endless repetition of elements.

The necessary coherence between the many disparate elements of Le Corbusier's church in Ronchamp is attained by two devices: sub-spaces, such as the three side-chapels, are not articulated separate compartments, but merge with the nave, resulting in a single, undulating interior; and nearly the whole area is brought under the large unbroken membrane of the overhanging roof.

Architects employ different methods to create a formal unity between the elements of their designs, as these examples show. In Amiens such unity depends primarily on repetition, in Ronchamp on the use of a single indivisible mass. Perception of unity does not require a strict adherence to all Gestalt laws at the same time; a contrast in one area (which goes *against* perceptual expectations and therefore disrupts the unity) may be compensated for by a harmony in another. Architects are thus at liberty to choose from a (limited) range of formally unifying devices. There-

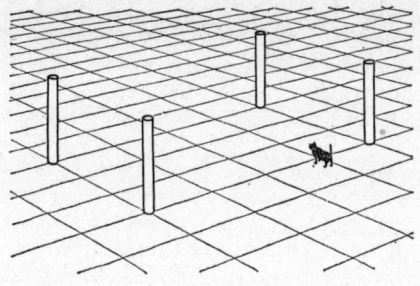 

Figure 2a. Conceptual forms of space   2b.

fore, although formal architectural principles show a far greater consistency over the centuries than symbolic ones, they are not always the same principles, in spite of their common psychological roots. The choice of formal principles depends on the symbolic apparatus used for expression; the two must be compatible.

The *degree* of formal coherence varies also; it is much higher in Amiens than in Ronchamp. This variable is an extremely significant one, as will be shown in the historical part of this book. Nineteenth and twentieth century architecture have a preference for contrast over harmony in common; on the other hand, Renaissance and Gothic architecture show a marked inclination towards formal harmony, in spite of their different symbolism. The classification into harmonious and expressionistic corresponds to Nietzsche's subdivision into Apollonian and Dionysian art. An excess of contrasts leads in the end to visual chaos, whilst an excess of harmony results in ornament or in the dull monotony of most commercial buildings.

Modern critics often use the criteria of 'clarity' and 'consistency'. Clarity requires strong contrasts in some aspects of the design, compensated for by equally marked harmonies (following Gestalt laws) in other aspects. The opposite is a more mellow blend of both. A design which uses the *same* contrasts and harmonies in every part is called 'consistent'.

The work of Mies van der Rohe exhibits both qualities to perfection: contrasts in proportions and in open and closed parts of the spatial envelope, united by a strict adherence to rectangularity and repetition. Nineteenth century architecture, as well as a good deal of Hindu architecture is 'confused' (as opposed to 'clear') and therefore deprecated. These criteria are evidently not universal (even though they can be applied to a good deal of historical architecture), but peculiar to our time. They belong to particular, not to general aesthetics.

4. Space

Just as easily as we complete the area between four dots to a square or a rhomb (Figures 1a and 1d), we can also imagine a rectangular volume between the four poles of Figure 2a. Although we have no certainty in this respect, it seems doubtful whether a cat would perceive this space in a similar way. The cat is probably more of a realist than we are. The illusion of a clearly defined space increases when we add a roof, as in Figure 2b.

This sort of space must be distinguished from the space of physics. In a physical sense there is no clearly defined spatial volume in Figure 2a; there are no more than four poles standing on a tiled floor. I propose to call the rectangular blocks of air between the four poles of Figures 2a and 2b *conceptual space*, to indicate that they are figments of the imagination. Conceptual space is a product of the Gestalt laws of perception; it is the space we see. Physical space is independent of psychology; it follows that it is not co-extensive with conceptual space. Physical space can be described and measured in the terms of Euclidean geometry, hyperbolic geometry or elliptical geometry; this is a matter of convenience. For celestial space, non-Euclidean geometry is more convenient than Euclidean. Conceptual space, because it uses the Phileban solids as its basic categories, is always Euclidean.

Physical and conceptual space coincide more often than not—which is why it requires an effort to think of them as different. When I sit in my study, the physical volume of air has the same dimensions as the conceptual space I perceive.

A bee crawls along the window-sill; I open the window to let it out. At this moment I change the physical space of the room; it now communicates freely with infinite space of the universe, as the bee shows when it happily flies away. But my room has not suddenly taken on infinite dimensions; it looks much the same as before. Conceptual space has not changed.

The heating engineer is exclusively concerned with physical space. If you keep your windows open all the time, he would find it difficult to keep you warm and he would warn you that you would be 'heating the universe'. The architect has to deal with conceptual space, but also with physical space, as he must build rooms which can be heated.

There is yet another type of space. Let us suppose that there is something wrong with the electrical conduits under the floor of my study. The electrician has to saw a large hole four by five feet in the floor, before he has located the source of the troubles. Unfortunately he cannot finish the job on the Friday on which he starts, so he tacks a neat piece of transparent plastic foil over the opening.

Neither physical nor conceptual space have changed. But during the entire weekend I have to move my chair very gingerly in order not to drop one of the legs into the hole and I have to make a considerable detour if I want to reach the door. Instead of a simple room in which I could walk up and down, I have now a sort of corridor around the hole. This O-shaped room is what is left of the *behavioral space* of my study.

Which type is the 'real' or 'true' space is a moot question; the answer depends on how one defines reality. It is more fruitful to define space as a set of relations. Exact descriptions and calculations of physical events, such as eclipses or the launching of rockets, take account of physical relations and have therefore to be done in physical space. Taking my own movements as a starting point, I have to use behavioral space as a medium. Shifting my attention to relations between sense-data, to the space I see or visualize, I am obliged to use conceptual space.

The foundation of our naïve notions of space is certainly the space we see, perceptual space. This is a sub-category of conceptual space. In a book about architecture it is convenient to add to it the space visualized by the architect when he draws a plan, or by the reader when he studies the drawings and photographs of this book, and call this combination: conceptual space.

Symbolism

1. The language of architecture

'If we worshipped Jupiter or were votaries of Juggernaut, we should raise a temple or erect a pagoda. If we believed in Mahomet, we should mount the crescent, and raise a mosque. If we burnt our dead, and offered animals to gods, we should use cinerary urns, and carve sacrificial friezes of bulls and goats. If we denied Christ, we should reject his Cross. For all these would be natural consequences; but in the name of common sense, whilst we profess the creed of Christians, whilst we glory in being Englishmen, let us have an architecture, the arrangement and details of which will alike remind us of our faith and our country,—an architecture whose beauties we may claim as our own, whose symbols have originated in our religion and our customs. Such an architecture is to be found in the works of our great ancestors, whose noble conceptions and mighty works were originated and perfected under a faith and system, for the most part common with our own.'[1] Thus August Welby Pugin pleaded eloquently for the exclusive use of Neo-Gothic architecture.

Architects use forms and materials as symbols. Gothic was specifically English and Christian for Pugin, just as bare geometrical forms, a stress on horizontals, and the use of much glass and concrete seem particularly modern to us. There is a remarkable consistency in nearly all the architecture of a region during a period; upon this hinges the notion of a particular style. The same forms are used over and over again, in ever different combinations; apparently they meant the same thing to everybody. A free choice between different forms, such as the eclecticism against which Pugin argues so fervently, is the exception; stylistic consistency is the rule. As the studies of Wittkower, Hautecoeur, Baldwin Smith or Banham have shown, symbolism is the reason behind it.[2]

What makes up a style? It must be something more than pediments or pointed arches. Neo-Gothic architects took great pains to copy Gothic details faithfully; but the composition of their designs betrays their Victorian origin. Composition is as characteristic of a style as its details; it unites the details in a system which may, with a stretch of the imagination, be compared to a language. The 'words' of such a language are the elementary and characteristic forms, such as columns, pilasters, entablatures and mouldings; composition is its 'grammar'.[3] Both the details and the composition carry a meaning. The different styles are different languages, often as hard to understand for a modern spectator as a foreign tongue.

The semantic analysis of verbal utterances is much easier to do than that of buildings; that is the main advantage of the comparison. The symbolic mechanism is the same.

The simplest form of this mechanism[4] consists of three terms: a symbol (1) represents some object (the denotatum, 2) for somebody (the interpreter, 3). For example: 'Martin' (1) is for me (3) the name of my son (2), or in a different field, I (3) can recognize a photograph (1) as the portrait of Abraham Lincoln (2). The verbal form of this symbolism can be understood by our dog, for he pricks up his ears when you tell him: 'the Master!' But we part company with the animal kingdom at the next stage of symbolization. Hearing a proper name such as 'John' spoken by somebody does not induce me to expect seeing John the next minute; it only makes me think of John. This form of symbolism consists of four terms: a symbol refers for me as interpreter to a concept which in its turn may be connected with an object. This object is now the connotation of the symbol, whilst it was its denotation in the three-termed, relation. Rough precast concrete slabs used as a facing on a cast-in-situ concrete column denote that column and connote (in their deliberate use of rough concrete, instead of stone) the modern era.

The classical orders symbolized the culture of Antiquity for Palladio and the power of the State for the architects of the Third Reich. The same form can carry different meanings, dependent on the context in which they are used; just as 'bright' means something else in 'a bright boy' than in 'a bright colour'. If it has been used frequently enough, part of the meaning of the context sticks to the form, even when it is seen apart from its context. Thus the depreciation of much Neo-Baroque architecture of around 1900 led to a repugnance to the original style; for many Europeans, giant columns in front of buildings have become associated with the fascist regimes. It also happens with words: some of Keats' rapture rings on in 'a thing of beauty', some of Anthony's irony still clings to 'an honourable man'. Often quoted lines are *dominant contexts*, influencing in particular the emotional side of meaning.

The words 'repose' and 'rest', or 'steed' and 'horse' have the same meaning. The first of each pair is rather stilted, the second is the usual word. Because of their emotional overtones, the first words are used only in flowery language or ironically; but these contexts reinforce in turn the original stilted meaning. The interaction between context and symbol is a circular process.

The emotional overtones of a word are not the same for everyone. A rather clinical definition of 'love' as 'the libidinous attraction between two people of different sex' would undoubtedly raise objections in some quarters. 'That is not love, that's lust!' they may exclaim. For them the dominant context of 'love' is religious or platonic; hence they feel that the word is debased by its use in such a lowly sense. For the same reason Palladio thought 'architecture' too good a term to apply to Gothic buildings.

2. The art of words

Of all the varied uses that are made of language, the artistic is the most interesting for our purpose. Poetry and drama may provide us with another clue to the riddles of art in general. I will start with the comparison between two short passages.

'At a moderate distance from the harbour on their coast lies an island, inhabited by many wild goats. Most of its area is wooded; there are also some mountains and some natural pastures. All vegetation is natural, for the island has not yet been visited by man...'

'Not very far from the harbour on their coast, and not so near either, there lies a luxuriant island, covered with woods, which is the home of innumerable goats. The goats are wild, for man has made no pathways that might frighten them off, nor do hunters visit the island with their hounds to rough it in the forests and to range the mountain tops. Used neither for grazing nor for ploughing, it lies forever unsown and untilled; and this land where no man goes makes a happy pasture for the bleating goats.' (*The Odyssey*, Book IX)[5]

The last passage is Odysseus' description of his initial landing-place when he visited the land of the Cyclops. It is a prelude to the tale of his stay in the cave of Polyphemus, who ate some of his companions and was blinded by Odysseus with a glowing stake. The approaching drama in the story is announced by a somewhat ominous description of an island which is otherwise of no importance. How this sense of impending danger is conveyed by the narrative becomes evident from a comparison of the two paragraphs.

Both describe the same island and contain the same factual information. But whereas the first contains nothing more than that information, the second paragraph suggests utter desolation and the approach of some calamity in addition. In its choice of words and its syntactical construction the second passage carries an atmosphere which the first lacks entirely.

The words of the *Odyssey* are 'evocative'; they have those emotional overtones mentioned before ('luxuriant, innumerable, frighten, to rough it, to range'). Hence the passage is emotionally coloured too. The Homeric lines describe the island as the very opposite of an inhabited and cultivated area. The whole piece is one long string of negations ('not far, not near, no pathways, nor do hunters, neither grazing, nor ploughing, unsown, untilled, no man ...'), which result in a negative attitude of the reader (or listener): it might be better not to go ashore at all. The first passage designates an island; the second designates the same island plus an emotion.

Emotion is a general characteristic of art. Shakespeare's Henry the Fifth is a far more attractive figure than the king from the history books, just as his Richard the Third is more repellent than he was in reality. We may be enthralled by a painted portrait, but not by a passport-photograph. The world of fiction is distinguished from the world of fact by its emotive qualities. The meaning of art is primarily one of feeling: *the works of art are symbols of emotions.*[6]

A work of art, just as a word, symbolizes the *concept* of an emotion, and through that concept the emotion itself. That is why we can admire a picture with a repulsive subject, such as Picasso's Guernica, or the demoniacal figures of Jerome Bosch. Most people are able to applaud an actor who plays a villainous part well. Children often want to kill the villain of the piece, because their concepts are still closely interlocked with reality. And even we, are we not sometimes moved to tears or roused to indignation by a novel? We know of course that the characters are 'not real', the events imaginary. Logically, the emotion and its concept are separate, but this dichotomy is much harder to perform in the realm of feeling than in the impassioned world of logic itself.

Let us revert for a moment to the passage from the *Odyssey*. All its adjectives and all its negations contribute to the foreboding of doom. Nowhere does the narrator fall back on the matter-of-fact terminology which characterises the first clause; nor does he strike at any place a lighter vein. It is *consistent* in its use of emotive words and constructions, and this in particular makes it a work of art. Through consistency a unified picture is built up. The efficient use of emotional meanings in language distinguishes poetry from doggerel.

A work of art should 'do' something to us, it should strike a chord. Not all art does that to all people. Many think Picasso only 'weird' and Faulkner 'dirty'. Their work has no meaning for them, and therefore, indeed, to them it is not art. But it is a long way from a personal to a general lack of understanding: others may still be able to decode Picasso's message and be moved by his work. Vincent van Gogh was misunderstood by nearly all his contemporaries; we, who are accustomed to his visions, can admire his paintings.

The amount of emotionality contained in the meaning of a poem, a sentence or even a single word varies a great deal. It ranges from the faded colours of the cliché to the harsh language of Osborn. Even a simple metaphor has an emotional tinge; can it be a work of art? Yes, for there is no sharp boundary between art and non-art. 'Therefore', writes Panofsky, 'one cannot, and should not, attempt to define the precise moment at which a vehicle of communication or an apparatus begins to be a work of art. If I write to a friend to ask him for dinner, my letter is primarily a communication. But the more I shift the emphasis to the form of my script, the more nearly does it become a work of calligraphy, and the more I emphasize the form of my language (I could even go so far as to invite him by a sonnet), the more nearly does it become a work of literature or poetry.'[7]

3. The roots of emotion in art

A symbolic language with an emotional meaning; is that a satisfactory explanation of art? It hardly seems so. For even if emotions govern a large part of our lives and especially our most important decisions, such as the choice of a mate or a career, we are interested in the actual emotions themselves and not in the faint images given in art. If we want to know what to do when we are irresistibly attracted by an unsuitable person, we may immerse ourselves in books on psychology or in the marriage-counselling columns in a ladies' weekly, but what help can Robert Burns or D. H. Lawrence provide in such a case? Seeing the pangs of Othello might make a man realize the bliss of a happy marriage, but the example of his bickering neighbours does that even more forcibly. Emotions as portrayed in art may ring a bell of recognition, may even lead to some deeper understanding of our own emotional life, but that is not a sufficient cause for art. Why spend large sums on the reproduction of such repulsive themes as are given in Ibsen's *Ghosts*, the plays of Strindberg or Tennessee Williams, if it is only to deepen understanding? The question: 'Why art?' has not been fully answered yet.

If the works of art are rooted in emotion, it is natural to look to psychology for an answer. Modern psychology has been interested in art and expressed its views at length. Psycho-analysts, soon after Freud's epoch-making work on the symbolism of dreams, were quick to see the connection between dream-symbols and art-symbols.[8]

Psycho-analytical views on art have been elaborated by Ehrenzweig and Neumann,[9] to mention only two. Though their work has clarified many important points, it does not go beyond details; the overall view is still lacking. From clinical experience they know that art is intimately related with their science, and that they hold a clue, perhaps *the* clue to its riddles. But the question is which clue? The position is stated by Baudoin: 'It is now easy to conceive art as a dream and a sort of game with the same function for humanity as a whole, as dreaming and playing have for the individual. Art is not only an outlet for unutilized drives; it is also a form of playing, an exercise in which these drives look for new objects and imagine the various possibilities for their future evolution. And could high art not be defined as the dream of orientation of a humanity in search of its soul?'[10]

The possibilities suggested by Baudoin have found a superb expression in *The Collective Dream in Art* by Walter Abell.[11] Taking full advantage of all that psychology, economics, history and sociology have to offer him, Abell unfolds a background as rich in perspectives for art, as psycho-analysis for dreams or as anthropology for understanding human culture. His theory draws a parallel between the emotional attitudes of an individual and those of society as a whole. He thinks that similar effects may have similar causes—and indeed he finds rather plausible explanations for phenomena which have been incomprehensible up till now.

Abell starts with a question which was often put to him as a teacher of art-history. 'What can be the meaning', his students asked, 'of the gargoyles on Gothic churches?' The gargoyles have an ancestry: monsters occur in Romanesque churches like Vézelay or Cluny on the capitals of the nave, therefore on a much more prominent point than the gargoyles on the roof. Morphologically the monsters are copies from imported Near-Eastern examples on cloth. The *fact* of copying does not of course provide an explanation for the *act* of copying. Digging somewhat deeper in the art-historical material, one is soon surrounded by a host of medieval griffins, lions, dragons, demons, serpents; briefly, by monstrous beasts of all shapes and kinds. They are spread all over Europe, occurring in France, Germany, Italy, Spain, Scandinavia and the British Isles. Comparing the various items in this collection, a curious circumstance emerges. Often a monster and a man engaged in combat are depicted on the same relief. On the earlier reliefs the monsters are as large as their human opponents and the fight is a very ferocious one, but in the later presentations the men grow bigger and stronger and the monsters correspondingly submit more and more to their domination. Finally, in Gothic times the monsters are brought entirely under human control; they occur under the feet of the 'Beau Dieu' (Christ) of Chartres, and are made fun of in having to serve as waterspouts. One could dismiss this as a charming folkloristic trait in medieval culture, which gradually disappeared as people became more sophisticated. But if the dragons descend from Near-Eastern examples they can hardly be called folklore. Nor does it seem realistic to explain them as reproducing the temptations of the celibate monks.[12] For medieval secular literature like Beowulf, Tristan or the Volsung Saga also abounds with monsters. 'Naturally few heroes in any early romance have escaped combat with a monster', Sampson writes in the Concise Cambridge

History of English Literature. And again, there is the same tendency: the earlier the description of any fight with a monster, the more formidable the monster becomes.

In early tales (Volsung Saga) the human hero loses from the monster, just as in some of the early reliefs (St. Trophime, Arles) the combatant is eaten by the dragon.

Looking beyond the domain of art-history, we see that the decline of the monsters in myth and art is accompanied by a marked change in the social conditions. The first centuries after Christ were centuries of great upheaval: barbaric tribes invaded the Roman empire. It was the age of the great European migrations; each wave of settlers was pushed further West by its successors. Then we get the invasion of the Huns and in the Dark Ages (about 500-1000), the raids of the Norsemen and the spread of Islam through Spain to France, until the Muslims were stopped by Charles Martel (732). In these unsettled conditions there was no time for the development of agriculture or the improvement of social institutions. Famines and plagues ravaged the hardpressed population. If we add to these material troubles the conflict between the heathen creeds of the invaders and the Christian faith and the internal conflicts of the Church, we get a rather gloomy picture of that time.

Abell connects these circumstances with the monsters appearing in art and myth. The circumstances produced in society the emotions of fear, despair and frustration. And the monster images are the symbolic representations in art of these emotions; they are the collective dream of society. Just as an individual, society has its bad dreams when it is in a difficult situation, but also, like a person, it can grow out of this condition. The migrations of tribes lessened, the immigrants settled down, and agriculture gradually advanced. The social conditions improved, the church matured into an established institution and inventions lightened the burdens of life. Better methods of farming freed hands for other work than agriculture, cities started to grow and trade spread its net over Europe.

'As an individual experiences elation when he achieves a long sought success, as he sighs with relief when he escapes from long-feared dangers, so Gothic society experienced elation and relief in the degree to which it had attained well-being and security, had emerged from inherited mental conflicts and had bulwarked itself against existing dangers.'[13] This elation was symbolically expressed in poking fun at the monsters: now the demons were boiled in a pot or ridden by a man. Medieval man, first picturing himself in hopeless, heroic combat with the evils of his time.

now felt he had laid the ghosts. They had not disappeared from his consciousness, but he is no longer afraid. In the struggle between the forces of good and evil, God had vanquished the demons. Again the confidence was expressed not only in the statuary, but in the contemporaneous accounts as well, which speak of 'beautitude', the 'great joy', the 'joys of God'.

One more aspect stands out from the collection of monster-sculptures in medieval art. The earlier sculptures are much more schematic than the later ones. This is not restricted to the representations of monsters, for all natural (or supernatural) themes are depicted in a more realistic manner in the later Middle Ages than in Romanesque art. It has sometimes been explained by technical inability of the artists: they strove for a naturalistic representation, but did not know how to attain it. Yet it seems hardly probable that tenth century Europeans, having still a wealth of classical examples at their disposal, would be unable to attain the technical mastery of the Magdalenian (Paleolithic) art of Lascaux or the naturalism of the Ife portraits of Gold Coast Negro art.[14] Nor is the assumption of such clumsiness warranted by the technical mastery they showed in building the Carolingian Church at Aix-la-Chapelle, the Ottonian churches at Gernrode and Hildesheim, or the perfection of stone-cutting in Vézelay and Cluny. On the contrary, we may assume that the abstraction of Romanesque art is an (unconscious) artistic intention, and has been caused by the same emotional attitude that produced the monsters. For, when the social and material conditions are grim and unpleasant, there seems hardly any reason for depicting reality with loving care. Abstraction could then be seen as a Freudian *repression* of reality, a turning away from the outside world. As that world gained in attractiveness, artists turned with increasing attention towards its appearance, finally producing such naturalistic art as the statuary on Rheims Cathedral.[15]

If this interpretation is tenable, it should be possible to extend it to other periods and societies. Abell traces the evolution of abstraction and realism in some primitive cultures—and it turns out that such art prevails where-ever the material circumstances are precarious and the world looks a grim place to live in. But it is not a general law that *all* primitive cultures have an abstract art. On the contrary, Paleolithic society was certainly primitive and produced also very naturalistic art, witness the paintings in Altamira and Lascaux. In its terminal periods however, it turned more and more towards abstraction and schematization. This turning away from reality may have been caused by the retreat of the glaciers of the Ice-age, northward, and the change in fauna, flora and climate accompanying that phenomenon. The circumstances to which late Paleolithic society had been adapted, the hunting and food-gathering on which subsistence itself depended, changed enormously, and man had to readapt himself.[16]

In our time art is again in full retreat from realism. Impressionism, expressionism, cubism, symbolism and finally the abstract art of today show a progressive estrangement between nature and art. The pendulum of realism versus abstraction, starting from the ornamental art of the Alans, Teutons and Visigoths swung gradually out to the intense realism of the High Renaissance and is now going back to abstraction. Is not our epoch a rather uneasy one too? The daily bread seems threatened, as automation proceeds in industry; existence itself is endangered by atomic bombs carried in rockets. Once more we have to face a change in the very order of existence and adapt ourselves to a new world. Such changes are perhaps due to a change in the means of subsistence: in the last hundred years we have been switching over from an economy dominated by agriculture to an economy dominated by technology. The process has not yet ended and the upheavals in society may be a painful by-product. Amidst such insecurity, we project our uneasiness into the material world, we tend to shut ourselves off, and realism once more disappears from art. And the monsters have returned, in the chilling pictures of surrealism.

Art shows then, not 'the appearance of things', but their 'true nature'; Abell's theory is a sort of extension of this homely old saw. The way a thing is depicted, is, according to Abell, a symbol for an attitude towards reality, caused by external social circumstances. Things are painted rosy or black depending on whether the circumstances are experienced collectively as good or bad[17].

Basic concepts in architecture

1. Place

'And Jacob went out from Beersheba, and went toward Haran. And he lighted upon a certain place, and tarried there all night, because the sun was set; and he took of the stones of that place, and put them for his pillows, and lay down in that place to sleep. And he dreamed, and behold a ladder set up on the earth, and the top of it reached to heaven: and behold the angels of God ascending and descending on it. And behold, the Lord stood above it and said: "I am the Lord God of Abraham thy father, and the God of Isaac: the land whereon thou liest, to thee will I give it, and to thy seed ..."

'And Jacob awaked out of his sleep, and he said, Surely the Lord is in this place; and I knew it not. And he was afraid, and said, How dreadful is this place! this is none other but the house of God, and this is the gate of heaven. And Jacob rose up early in the morning, and took the stone that he had put for his pillows, and set it up for a pillar, and poured oil on top of it.' (Genesis 28: 10–18)

This passage contains the germ of everything architectural. Any monument, like Jacobs stone at Bethel or the pyramid commemorating Napoleon's battle at Austerlitz, any building like a garage, a townhall or a library, determines a certain place singling it out from all other places.

The home is 'our place', the one place we can call our own. The office is a place to work in, the church a place to worship in, the football-field a place to play on and the road a place to drive along. All these, and buildings foremost among them, are specific, definite and separate places, or in the words of Susanne Langer: 'ethnic domains'.[1]

In a building, part of the available undifferentiated space around us is set aside for one or more specific functions. The various functions differ in their practical

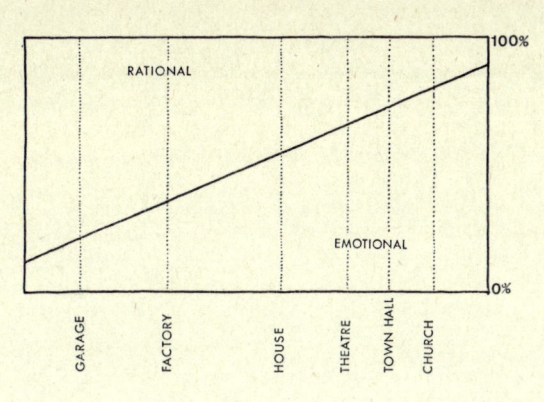

Figure 3. Rational versus emotional factors in architecture

requirements but also in their emotional significance. The 'places' of these functions have to correspond with such differences. The function of a building determines its form in a double sense. In a purely rational sense by requiring that it will be practical and will work; in an aesthetic sense by demanding that the felt, emotional importance of the function finds some expression in the architecture. If 'function' is so defined as to cover both the rational and emotional requirements of a certain purpose, then all architecture is 'functional'. The rational demand made of a townhall is that it serves as an efficient office building for the administration of the city; the aesthetic demand may be that it shows the dignity of the municipality.

Rational and emotional factors vary in the proportion of their influence on the design. The different types of buildings can be plotted on a graph, showing this variation (Figure 3). This graph, which we owe to Le Corbusier,[2] expresses more clearly than a description, that in a factory aesthetics are sacrificed to usefulness and cost, and that in a church often good acoustics or efficient circulation are sacrificed to aesthetics. The group of buildings on the right side of the graph is from an artistic point of view the most interesting one. That is why the history of architecture is primarily the history of public and religious buildings, and pays little attention to the development of housing.

Like most schemes, the graph compresses a complex reality into a manageable but oversimplified abstraction; it is an aid to thought rather than a statistical representation of reality. The types of buildings have no fixed percentage of the rational over the emotional factor. The town hall for instance is losing its glamour; from a magnificent expression of the power and glory of the city it is becoming more and more a workaday office building, in keeping with the fading importance of municipal government. The factory on the contrary is getting ever more aesthetic attention; its emotional factor is on the increase. In terms of the graph we may say that the town hall is moving to the left and the factory to the right.

The intimate connection between function and art in architecture points to a fundamental difference between architecture and the other visual arts. This difference can best be demonstrated with an example. Around 1315 B.C. the Egyptian pharaoh Sethy built a commemorative temple for his father Rameses I at Abydos. Inside the temple stood a statue of Rameses; the walls were covered with dedicatory inscriptions, containing such invocations as 'The king of Upper and Lower Egypt, the son of Re, Sethy Mer-en-Pthah says: O Good God! Mayest thou occupy the seat which I have made for thee and view thy mortuary temple. I am thy son; I did those things which were beneficial to thee when I built a temple to thy kâ, and when I caused that thy statue should rest within it; food, drink and every offering being established every day, as is done for all Gods.' And Sethy asks the August God Wen-Nufer to 'eternally protect his (Rameses) dwelling'.[3] The statue of Rameses I is the seat for the 'kâ', and the temple is the house for the seat for the 'kâ'. The erection of the statue is an expression of the reverence felt for Rameses, but the temple is an expression of the reverence felt for the holy place around the statue. The temple as an art-form is therefore only a *mediate* symbol for the respect felt for Rameses, whilst the statue is a *direct* symbol of such respect. The same thing occurs in the churches of to-day. The piety felt for a saint is *directly* expressed in an inscription, a psalm, a mass, or in his statue; because the saint is venerable, the place where he is honoured is venerable too, and that emotion is expressed in the architecture. Pictures and statues are direct symbols, a building is a mediate one, connected with the feeling for a 'thing' only through the feeling for its place.

2. Space

The 'place' of Jacob's dream was a point only, and a single stone sufficed to mark it. The place of the frontier between two countries is no more than a line, but most things require a surface or even a three-dimensional space, like the statue of Rameses.

The space allotted to storage, to living, or to working has to be free of obstructions and easily accessible. It has to be 'open', so it takes the form of a room enclosed by walls, a floor and a ceiling and is accessible through a door. For indicating the location of Jacob's vision, such a room is not necessary. There is no need to create a free area; the space which he wanted to dedicate to his dream was entirely filled up by the stone. If some activity is located in a certain space it needs free air to be performed in. But if a *concept* is allotted some space there is no need for air; the space of the concept may be taken up by solid masonry.

Many funerary monuments such as the Egyptian pyramids, the tombs of Hadrian and Caecilia Metella in Rome or the Etruscan tumuli are such solid or practically solid buildings. The importance of the persons buried in or under them required the erection of a large mausoleum; as it was not necessary to do anything inside the building, it could be filled up entirely with brick, earth or stone.

Thus we have some spaces in architecture which can be used and entered (our living room), and some which cannot (the pyramids). The difficulties raised by this paradox vanish if we apply the distinction between the three types of space described in Chapter I. The pyramids have no behavioral space on the inside; only a physical and a conceptual one. As noted before, the three types of space are relatively independent.

The space of the art of architecture is conceptual space. The physical spaces of any New England common, of Rockefeller Plaza or inside Lincoln Memorial are in open connection with the space of the universe and therefore unbounded; but their conceptual spaces are clearly delimited. The crossing in the church can be envisaged as an intersection between the spaces of the nave and the transept; this is only possible in conceptual space. Physically the space of the church is cruciform, because physical space is one and indivisible. Nor do we find any difference in our behavioral space between the crossing and the chancel, except that we have more directions in which to go. The conceptual spaces of the nave and the transept however can be easily distinguished.

The conceptual space of the crossing can be considered as a part of the nave, or a part of the transept, or both, or as a separate spatial unit. Apparently the same (physical) constructions may evoke several conceptual spaces, just as a word may have several meanings.

Conceptual spaces can also enclose one another. To get at the living quarters of Harlech Castle, we have to cross the moat (1) pass through the outer curtain (2) and the main gate (3) before we finally see the residence (4). The hall is part of a larger space which is again a part of a still larger space. It is singled out from an area already set apart. It might be called 'multiply-determined space', because its space is also (partly) determined by all the larger spatial concepts of which it forms a segment.

The conceptual spaces of a complex building, such as the Capitol in Washington, cannot immediately be apprehended. We must walk around the building, go inside and visit all the main rooms and halls; briefly, we have to experience architecture. From this multitude of impressions we build up, part by part, a concept of the total spatial structure. Architects can also form this concept from the plans and sections, just as a musician reads a score. The concept arising from the plans however is but a weak substitute for the real thing: it lacks scale, the colour and texture of the materials, the effects of natural and artificial lighting, and, above all, the *ambiential* qualities of the building itself.

The link between physical and conceptual space can now be elucidated. Spatial concepts may be constructed from plans, sections and photographs; but to savour a piece of architecture to the full extent we need the building itself. Only there do we get a correct impression of the size, the handling of materials, the play of light and shadow or the relation to its site. The physical building is the mainspring of its conceptual space.[4] The architecture of the building may be dull or exciting; the physical building is just so much concrete, steel, glass, stone, etc. The physical building can leak or rot; its architecture is impervious to water.

Conceptual space is a product of our mental make-up and obeys the Gestalt laws of perception. Hence the preference for the simpler Euclidean volumes, the Phileban solids which we find in most architectural theory and practice. Spaces of rectangular, cylindrical or spherical form are easy to conceive: therefore they are so often used in design. Rectangular forms in particular are found in architecture all over the world: in Chinese or Aztec temples, Papuan men's halls or Babylonian ziggurats. Part of this preference for rectangularity is undoubtedly due to expedience. Rectangular rooms can be subdivided into rectangular rooms; it is easier to build walls with rectangular bricks than with any other shape. The average length of available trees leads naturally to rafters of the same size and hence to rectangular or circular houses. Part of this preference must be ascribed to the Gestalt laws; a cube is the simplest solid in Cartesian co-ordinates. It also seems possible that this psychological preference is rooted in our biological constitution. Because of our symmetry, the position of our eyes, and our way of moving around, we naturally differentiate between 'before' and 'behind', 'right' and 'left'. The gravitational field causes an asymmetry in our physical world, from which results the distinction between 'above' and 'below'. These directions may have created a kind of built-in Cartesian co-ordinate system, with which we orient ourselves in the

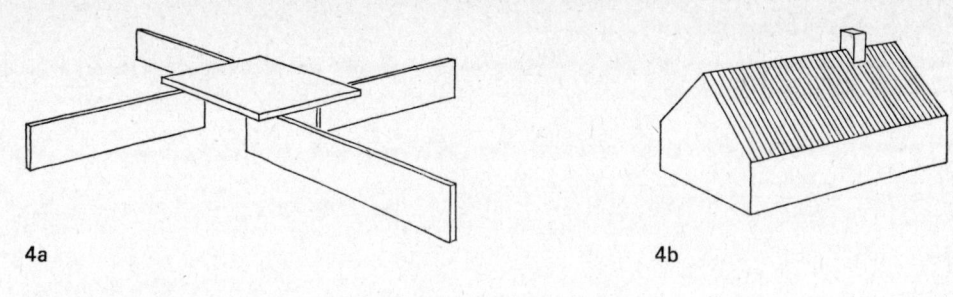

Figure 4. Free-flowing space in comparison with a normal house

world. The well-known perception of trapezoïdal rooms as rectangular is due to this instinct for rectangularity.

The Phileban solids contrast sharply with the forms of Nature. Therefore an architect may create a symbol for Nature by preventing the formation of crystalline spatial concepts: witness the architecture of Gaudí, of Art Nouveau and Le Corbusier's chapel in Ronchamp. Such 'organic' architecture uses undulating walls, slanting roofs, broken surfaces and sinuous, irregular curves; its conceptual spaces are vague instead of clear-cut.

Another way of preventing the formation of a definite Gestalt, a clear-cut conceptual space, is the jutting out of walls, balconies and roof-planes. Figure 4a illustrates the form of space which occurred for instance in Mies' Barcelona pavilion, in Rietveld's Sonsbeek pavilion or in the houses of Neutra. It is the anti cubic architecture which Van Doesburg referred to (page 10). It is intended as the antipode of the type of Figure 4b. The ordinary cottage stands in contrast to the space of the universe; this modern form is meant to be a part of it.

Brick or stone walls going through a glass-front create a bond between the finite inside and the cosmos outside; they suggest that they could go on to infinity. Though physically of course as finite as the cottage and only a little harder to heat, this type of house is conceptually infinite. It does not cut a definite chunk out of cosmic space, but merely 'densifies' space.

3. Structure

'Right' and 'left', 'before' and 'behind' are interchangeable; one has only to turn around. 'Above' and 'below' are not interchangeable. Physical and behavioral space are anisotropic; their structure is determined by gravity.

Conceptual space, as Piaget and Inhelder have shown, is a product of interaction of a child with its environment.[5] In all motor-activity, such as learning to walk, building with blocks, climbing a tree, riding a bicycle or jumping a fence, gravity looms large. Therefore conceptual space is also anisotropic.

The constant battle with gravity puts a negative emotional value on the downward direction and a positive value on the upward one. The evaluation shows clearly in such metaphors as: 'a heavy penalty', ' a light comedy', ' a rising young executive', 'falling from the narrow path', 'going downhill', etc.

Motor activity furnishes us with a common-sense 'understanding' of the world around us. Part of this understanding applies to architectural constructions. We 'see' the columns of a structural frame supporting the beams. In reality, part of the load on the beams is absorbed by the rigid connections of the beams to the columns. We 'understand' a bridge with three shallow arches as an arched bridge, such as a Roman aqueduct, even if we know that it is a continuous prestressed concrete beam with a varying cross-section. Evidently there is a difference between physical, calculated structure, and the structure as 'understood' by common sense. There is need for a distinction between *physical structure* and *phenomenal structure*, analogous to the distinction between physical and conceptual space.

Phenomenal and physical structure need not correspond. Their difference may even fool the professional. The Dutch architect Duiker was once constructing a block of flats in The Hague, when the municipal inspector of Public Works came to see the job and objected to the slender columns and large overhangs of the floors, even though the calculations of the reinforced concrete had been approved by his department. Duiker invited him to stay for a trial of the construction. To prove his own confidence in his design, he sat down with a box of cigars beside him under the doubtful looking floor, whilst workmen piled sandbags on top till two times the specified load of the building code had been reached. The inspector, notwithstanding his belief in calculation, thought the thing looked hazardous and could only be convinced by such a demonstration.

As a student I walked once on the parapet of the cathedral of Beauvais, 160 feet above the ground, with a group of friends. Suddenly a young lady hesitated to go on: was not this church renowned for the many times its vaults had collapsed? And was it not (again) in the scaffolds for a much needed restoration after the war? To reassure her, one of us pushed against a solid looking pinnacle on a flying buttress; the seven foot long block, weighing something like 2000 pounds, swayed perceptibly! Duikers apartments were more solid than they looked, but this pinnacle looked more solid than it was.

The emotive evaluation of the battle with gravity causes architects and their public to take an interest in structure, an interest far exceeding that in heating or acoustics. Hence the efforts to influence phenomenal structure by the use of specific architectural elements. Paul Rudolph wrote: 'Mies has handled the steel frame more eloquently than anyone else in this country. The integral part, the steel frame, is usually not exposed, but only an exterior symbol of structure, because he has no way of doing it otherwise. He has to put concrete around the structural frame, and besides, the structural steel is possibly far too large for the desired visual effect. He super-imposes another steel structure, very slender, which seems quite justifiable. The symbol of structure rather than the structure itself is perhaps something which we don't understand as well as we might."[6]

Following Rudolph, we may call this *symbolic structure:* forms which evoke a phenomenal structure in the spectator, and which are not—or not entirely—necessary for the physical structure. The device is quite old: the Gothic system of ribs and shafts is largely such a symbolic structure.

The modern demand for 'honesty' in construction requires that physical and phenomenal structure coincide. Symbolic structure too must correspond to the physical structure, because it is the origin of the phenomenal. But in a great many famous buildings they differ, often considerably. The columns of Greek temples were carefully joined and plastered to make them look monolithic. Le Corbusier's chapel in Ronchamp has a full-blown concrete skeleton hidden in its phenomenally solid walls.

Classification of forms

1. The dimensions of architectural form

One of the sights that is often urged on the weary tourist dutifully visiting a medieval cathedral is the view from the tower. Induced by the lure of seeing a similar tower twenty miles away, or simply by the mountaineering challenge of scaling its 300 feet, he starts to climb its narrow winding stairs. Halfway up he begins to doubt the wisdom of such an undertaking at the end of a day already full of plodding past things-he-must-see; he could have sat down in the square and enjoyed a glass of wine. The sound of shuffling feet above and below keeps him going. But when he finally pushes open the shaky door and stoops to get out on the roof, he is rewarded by a sight that momentarily blots out even his sense of sporting achievement. There, all around him, lies the city! Cars push slowly through its streets, the tinkle of the bell of the tram is very faintly heard. What a concentration of human ingenuity in such a small area! What a jumble of forms of buildings! He tries to find his hotel, but cannot recall whether it had a pitched roof or a flat one. What can that large building over there be? He does not remember having seen it before. And if he is of a systematic turn of mind, he wonders how it would be possible to find some sense in all these architectural shapes. Should they be catalogued by age, on 'stylistic' marks, or by purpose, putting all shops in one class and all churches in another, or by form, collecting round buildings, rectangular ones, flat roofs, pitched roofs, etc.?

It is evident that all these methods of ordering can be applied to the same collection of buildings. Each method orders buildings according to a certain *aspect* of that building, and the method chosen depends on the goal one has in mind. The classification proposed here is based on formal criteria. A building, or part of a building is broken down into the formal aspects of conceptual space or phenomenal structure.[1] The aspects can be arranged in antithetical pairs (or triads, quartets,

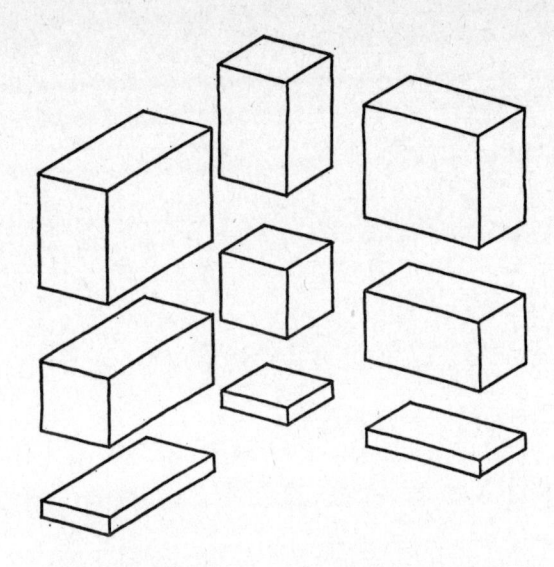

Figure 5. Proportion

etc.). An antithetical pair can be imagined as representing two extreme points on a linear co-ordinate.[2] For instance a square and a set of parallel lines occupy such points on a co-ordinate of proportion in the plane: the first of the proportion 1:1, the second of 1:∞. Any rectangle can be plotted on this co-ordinate, once its proportion of length to width is known. Other forms can be mapped on this co-ordinate too: a circle in comparison to an ellipse for instance. The co-ordinate system shows the gradual transition from one form to another and would allow exact, measurable comparison. The two main classes used are those of form and of structure. It is possible to construct a third class, of surface (colour, texture), which, since it is not used in the rest of the book, will not be described.

FORM
Proportion (Figure 5)
Classification of forms (spaces, volumes, members) according to their relations of length to width to height. Mathematically the set l:w:h contains only two independent proportions (l:w and l:h) and could therefore be plotted on a two dimensional, plane co-ordinate system. The anisotropy of space and the evaluative difference between shallow and wide spaces (the foyer of a cinema) on one hand and narrow and deep spaces (the nave of a church) on the other makes a three-dimensional co-ordinate system necessary. Size is not under review: a building and its model occupy the same point in the co-ordinate system.

Size
A classification by height. The co-ordinate is linear, terminating in zero at one end. A building and its model occupy different points. The height of the spectator is the origin of the co-ordinate system: I can look over the fence, but not over the gardenwall.

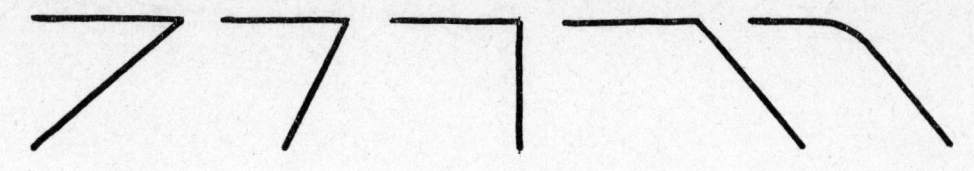

Figure 6. Angularity

Angularity (Figure 6)
From the viewpoint of Gestalt-psychology, an angle is a discontinuity in a contour or a surface. Its phenomenal opposite is therefore continuity, i.e. roundness. A very obtuse angle of for instance 170° is closer to the full continuity of 180° than an acute one of 30°. Phenomenal angularity increases therefore with the decrease of the angle. The origin of the linear co-ordinate-system lies at the right angle.

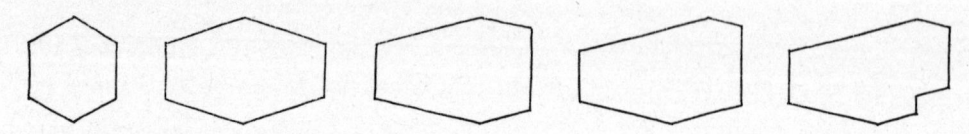

Figure 7. Regularity

Regularity (Figure 7)
This aspect is rooted in the Gestalt-psychological law of simple figures. The hallmark of regularity is the possession of one or more planes of symmetry; the sphere is thus the most regular form and occupies the extreme end of the linear co-ordinate. The antithetical concept is asymmetry. The mathematical distinction is quite clear: a figure or volume is either perfectly symmetrical, or it is not. Phenomenally, however, there are intermediate forms, as Figure 7 shows.

Plasticity
A wall covered with a panoply of shafts is called 'plastic'; a flat wall is 'smooth'.

Isolation (Figure 8)
The degree to which a space is open towards adjacent spaces is another aspect which can be classified. Such a class shows the difference between a prison-cell and a glassed-in telephone booth. In the examples, I have used two formulas to determine the degree of isolation: 1. The area of the openings as a percentage of the total outside surface; 2. the percentage of the total surface of the plan occupied by solids (walls, columns, pillars, etc.).

The classification is simple for rectangular spaces. As 'openness' can occur in three directions, we get a three-dimensional co-ordinate system. However, the

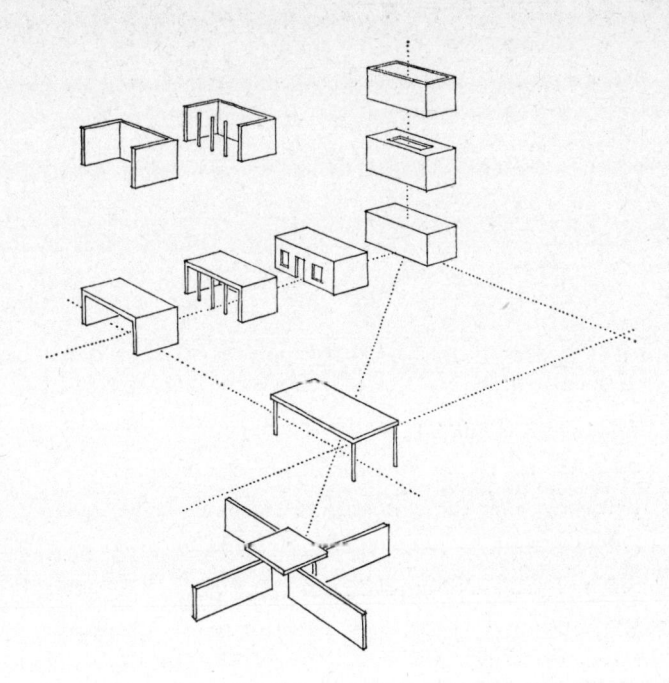

Figure 8. Isolation

simplicity ends where the boundaries of conceptual space itself are broken through. With 'free-flowing' 'densified' spaces (the Barcelona pavilion) one can no longer speak about an enveloping surface. Such spaces deliberately go against the perceptual tendency to conceive a space as a distinct, separate part of surrounding space. They have therefore to be classified as phenomenally less isolated than the other forms, and stand beyond them in the co-ordinate system.

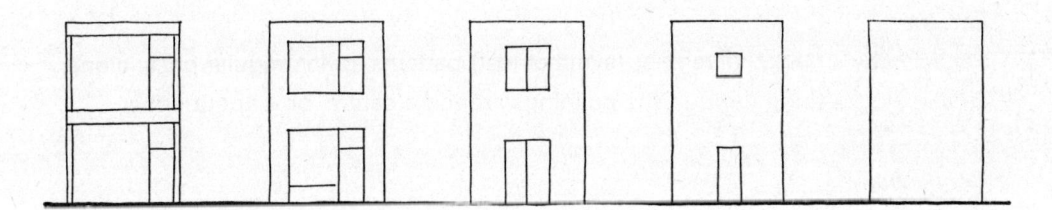

Figure 9. Homogeneity

STRUCTURE
Homogeneity (Figure 9)
If a wall appears to carry a load over its whole area, it is called *homogeneous;* if it appears that the load is carried by structural members such as columns and beams, it is said to be of *concentrated* structure. A visible concrete skeleton with brick infills is phenomenally concentrated; the same physical construction with the skeleton hidden behind the brick is homogeneous. Concentration or homogeneity is a matter of degree. The ratio between the size of the (phenomenal) load-bearing members and the size of the inert mass in between determines the degree of homogeneity.

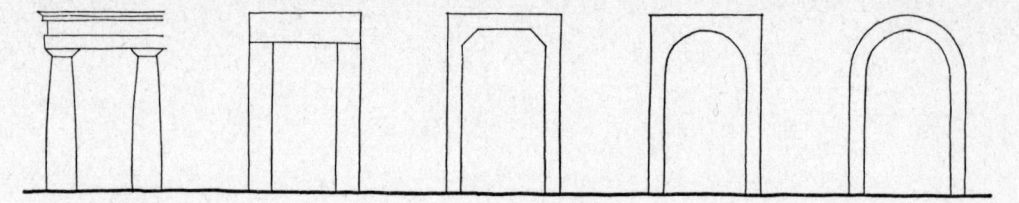

Figure 10. Continuity

Continuity (Figure 10)
A structural part is phenomenally continuous if it is not possible to distinguish parts: for example a parabolic arch without imposts or marked keystone.[3] Two columns under a beam are discontinuous at the supports. Homogeneity and continuity have linear co-ordinate systems.

2. Typology of spatial compositions

Complex buildings may be broken down into a set of irreducible sub-spaces (called *parts* hereafter), which may be related in various ways. We distinguish between two major classes of relations between parts: their position in space in relation to one another, and their formal similarity or contrast.

POSITION
Location
Parts can be arranged in regular (symmetrical) patterns, or in irregular ones; along an axis (e.g. a route through the building) around a centre, or without either.

Connection
One part can enclose another, adjoin another or intersect with another.

SIMILARITY
Similar spatial forms occupy neighbouring points in the systems of co-ordinates of the preceding paragraph. Contrast is represented by points far apart. The most significant aspects are: proportion, size and form as characterized by angularity and regularity.

Some examples
S. Costanza has a regular central plan; its main parts are of similar form and one encloses the other; Amiens cathedral has a regular axial plan with adjoining parts of similar form; Rudolph's Yale School of Architecture has an irregular central plan

with intersecting similar parts; Le Corbusier's Visual Arts Center at Harvard has an irregular axial plan with intersecting parts of contrasting form.

Formal cohesion between the parts varies a great deal between the different types of composition. It is largest with symmetrical compositions of similar parts (Amiens, Vierzehnheiligen) and at a minimum with asymmetrical compositions of contrasting parts (Visual Arts Center, Harvard). Coherence is weakened if the parts are 'good', closed Gestalts, (Phileban solids, as in Hildesheim), strengthened if the parts are of a more complex form (Amiens, Imperial Library), so that their closure towards each other is diminished.

An important feature of composition is the use of pathways through the building. The simplest form is a concatenation of equal parts: the bays in Amiens cathedral. If the parts are more isolated from each other, and dissimilar in form and/or proportion, we get a *spatial sequence*. Such sequences are particularly effective for reaching a spatial climax; they are used to that end in the Vienna Imperial library, in Westminster New Palace, and in Aalto's Saynätsalo town hall.

Part two: historical

The overall pattern

1. Levels of meaning

We are now able to trace in broad outline the pattern of relations between architecture and social conditions in Western history. The details of the picture will be filled in with the analyses of nine sample buildings in the following chapters.

The first and obvious subdivision of the mass of factors which influence architectural design is the Vitruvian triad: function, construction and aesthetics. Each of these is of course historically determined. Palaces and castles played a predominant rôle in eighteenth century architecture; there is no room for such a type of building in our more egalitarian age. The available techniques of construction put a limit to the possibilities of design. If glass can only be made in small panes, the architect must think in leaded or mullioned windows.

The aesthetic factor operates on three different levels of meaning.[1] The first is that of the parallel: monasticism flourished in the Early Middle Ages, and many abbey-churches were landmarks in architectural history. Obviously, this level is the corollary of the functional factor: the architecture of a period consists primarily of the buildings around such activities as were then considered important. The second level is that of iconology, of manifest symbolism. A dome usually represents the sky and most historical domed buildings were microcosms. Renaissance decoration was a conscious and intended reference to the great age of Rome, just as the Gothic Revival symbolized and therefore imitated the Middle Ages. The third level is that of the unconscious, latent symbolism of Abell's theory. Social conditions are supposed to induce an attitude towards what is experienced as 'the outside world'. This attitude is described in the philosophy, the *Weltanschauung* of the period, and its emotional connotation is symbolized in art and architecture. Social conditions are of course not objectively given. Nobody possesses a yard-stick against which he can measure his time as absolutely good or bad. The only possible point of reference is the past, in particular the immediate past. Therefore, when conditions improve, they may give rise to an attitude of hope, or conversely when deteriorating, they may create a feeling of despondence. In contrast to the previous two levels of meaning, this one can only be inferred. Its very nature precludes a direct proof from documentary evidence.

Symbolism (of the second and third level) decides which architectural forms will be used and how they will be brought into play by contrasting one against the other. The integration between the elements of architecture into a coherent building is the job of formal aesthetics. The symbolically necessary contrasts are compensated for by closure, repetition, simplicity of overall mass, symmetry, etc. The symbolic aesthetics of a period defines the area of freedom for its corollary, formal aesthetics.

Abell has shown how the perception of the outside world is influenced by social conditions, producing abstract and schematic art in periods of stress and naturalism in happier times. 'The world' as seen in art is the deposit of the world as emotionally apprehended. The emotive effect of the social conditions percolates through to formal aesthetics. In a prosperous time, the world is perceived as harmonious; architecture, as a part of that world, has to correspond to this harmony and show a strong degree of formal cohesion. Conversely, a world seen as full of conflict allows a far greater tolerance for contrasts, and correspondingly less coherent design.

Second and third-level symbolism do not affect the entire field of architecture. Simple utilitarian buildings and all vernacular architecture remain untouched by it. And even many forms of architecture with a capital 'A' have hardly any symbolic meaning attached. Forms which do not need to be changed simply persist. When you ask any child in the Western world to draw a church, he will produce the familiar image of the high, long building with the steeple in front. The basilical part of that scheme goes back to the 4th century and is only now in the process of being radically altered. The architect is a creature of habit as much as anybody else.

2. All in the same boat

The past two thousand years may be roughly divided into three periods: the Later Roman Empire, the Middle Ages, and Modern Times starting with the Renaissance.

Of the life of the Romans during the Decline of the Empire, historians draw a gloomy picture.[2] Overburdened by taxation, with a stagnant economy and a corrupt government, with any effort towards more freedom sternly repressed, their bondage must have seemed eternal. Does it not seem possible that they were beset by despair? Religions which promised justice and a better life in the hereafter—Christianity and the cults of Isis and Mithras—spread rapidly among the lower classes.[3] Architecture symbolized the turning-away from this world. The early Christian churches are plain barns on the outside; all the decorations are on the interior, in contrast to Antique temples. The plasticity characteristic of pagan Roman interiors was replaced by smooth walls covered with mosaics, incrustations and paintings. Isolation of interior versus exterior space increased.

The weakness of the Roman Empire opened the door to the great Migrations. From the fourth to the tenth century Europe is the scene of tumultuous warfare, wave after wave of invaders overrunning the continent.[4] Insecurity characterizes the social conditions, and if any mood predominated in that period, it was probably fear.

People appealed to saints and relics for protection and entrenched themselves in defensive-looking buildings. Architecture became a protective shell, standing between man and the dangerous world outside. With its heavy walls and tiny windows, it was even more isolated than in the preceding age. The perception of conflict affected formal aesthetics: parts contrast strongly and many seem only stuck onto the body of a building, with little attempt at making them blend with the rest of the design. Distrust of the outside world is reflected in schematic paintings and sculpture. As gravity is a phenomenon of the outside world, it may also have been looked upon with misgivings. Physical construction is timid at any rate: very heavy walls are put below light timber roofs; vaults are small in span. Smooth walls, and panelled ceilings display a lack of interest in symbolic structure.

Gothic architecture contrasts sharply in every one of the enumerated characteristics with Romanesque. The social conditions contrast too. In the face of the common danger of the Migratory Period, people had drawn together. A closed feudal society had been forged on the anvil of incessant strife. The emerging cooperation yielded results: government grew steadily in power, disorder subsided, larger harvests through crop-rotation fed an increasing population, cities grew and prospered. In comparison to the preceding age, the later Middle Ages give the impression of having been a happy period, in which people felt bound to each other by a common lot and looked with confidence towards the future.

Ample corroboration for a feeling of confidence and a trust in the outside world can be found in Gothic architecture. Never before or after were vaults of plain masonry raised to such heights on such slender supports. Gravity was no longer feared, it was experimented upon. A strong interest in structure is shown in the explicit symbolic system of shafts, ribs and flying buttresses and in the proud carpentry of the hammerbeam roofs.

Huge windows let in floods of daylight, isolation is at a minimum. Also on the inside, for the Gothic interior is one vast space, whereas the early Romanesque interior consisted of a series of separate rooms communicating with each other through fairly narrow openings.

A harmonic perception of the world may have acted on formal aesthetics. The contrasting spaces of Romanesque have been replaced by regularity. Nearly all parts of a High Gothic church are of equal form; the same structure and the same details are used throughout. Repetition causes a strong formal coherence.

3. Divided against itself

Medieval society was static and collectivistic.[5] Everyone knew where he belonged: he was born a serf, fuller or lord. There was no room for careers or social change; competition was at a minimum. Values were absolute. Legend merged with history and knowledge with myth. Many traditional cultures in Africa and Asia still show this same close-knit pattern of relations.

To such an integrated society, threats come truly from outside. It apprehends its problems in the form of an opposition between 'us' and 'the hostile world', and meets them with a mixture of religion and practical knowledge. Its symbolism is an effective means of defense. Architecture stands *between* society and the outside world. It is, also in the symbolical sense, a shelter in which one can take refuge, as in the Early Middle Ages, or a light and festive 'heavenly mansion', when people feel at ease.

Our society is dynamic and individualistic. 'All men are created equal'; what you are depends on achievement, not on birth.

Success is measured in terms of social change: to start as an errand boy and end as a millionaire is more respectable than to be born a millionaire. Competition is at a maximum. Our values are pluralistic and relative. The spectacular rise of science has been made possible only by its divorce from religion. Society is divided against itself.

Our present plight of maximum social segregation evolved but slowly. Common danger had led to a closing of the ranks in the Early Middle Ages; as the danger passed, social controls were relaxed and the divergence began. In the Renaissance it affected only the upper classes.[6] Religious unity went by the board in the Reformation; science struck out on its own in the seventeenth century, followed by the Industrial Revolution and the sharp division of labour. Feudalism waned as the divergence increased. Marxism can be seen as a final revolt against the feudal system by a reversal of its values: the class that has always been below should now be on top. Hence its appeal to societies which were still feudal: Russia, China and the Far East.

Medieval society was beset by *external* dangers. We suffer on the contrary from *internal* insecurity. In such a situation architecture ceases to be a shelter. It cannot be put as a protective carapace between society and the outside world, for the threat lies in our midst. The outside world is not perceived as hostile at all; on the contrary, it looks like a haven of peace. Architectural space, which is a little world to its inhabitants, is idealized. It becomes a symbol for the perfect, harmonious and unified cosmos surrounding rapacious mankind. A person who knows that the road to a certain highly desirable goal is blocked, turns to wish-fulfilment in dreams. Analogously, the architecture of a society divided against itself becomes a dreamland, an image of the state desired.

Three different types of dreamland were tried out one after the other: Classicism, Eclecticism and Modern Architecture. The evolution runs a similar course in each of them. It begins with the image of a harmonic cosmos, symbolized by the 'absolute' forms of the Phileban solids and simple figures. As the dream does not come true, an effort is made to overcome its unreality by the use of violent forms and optical tricks which would thrust belief down the throat of the spectator, and by an extension of the action-radius of the symbol. When this is seen not to work either, the symbolic apparatus is exchanged for another and the whole process starts anew.

The harmonic cosmos of the Renaissance was based on Neo-Platonic philosophy. As Wittkower has shown, the image of the 'Harmonia Mundi' is the root of the Renaissance preference for central plans and for a 'musical scale' of proportions. 'It is manifest that Nature delights principally in round Figures, since we find that most things which are generated, made or directed by Nature are round. Why need I instance the Stars, Trees, Animals, the Nests of Birds or the like Parts of Creation, which she has chosen to make generally Round?' wrote Alberti.[7]

Moreover, the dream was no mere flight of fancy. The Pax Romana showed that people could live in peace with each other. The paradise of Rome had been lost, but the ample remains still testified to its reality. With the adoption of Antique culture it might perhaps be regained.

But posing the ideal in the realm of art did not solve the problems. Divergence increased and the conviction of the symbolism started to wear off. The simple serenity of the early Renaissance made way for the uneasiness of Mannerism, soon to be followed by Baroque. The visitor to a Baroque building is carefully led through a spatial sequence (the 'enfilade' in the palace) to a climax. Huge and heavy masses, violent movement and optical tricks ought to convince him of the reality of the symbolic world. Imposing sites such as that of Stift Melk or of the Superga near Turin, try to overpower his doubts.

Renaissance buildings are usually independent of their sites; the Baroque aims at integration of building and landscape in one vast composition. The integration strengthens the reality of dreamland by its size, but may symbolize also the desired unity in the social field. The subordination of Bernini's square to St. Peter corresponds to the ideal of a unified Christendom subordinated to the pope. Park and town of Versailles are centered on the palace, just as the French nation ought to rally round the throne. The Revolution showed up the unreality of that ideal.

Interior spaces are also integrated, and supposedly for the same reasons. The parts of the church of Vierzehnheiligen are welded together in one undulating movement: the fused space so similar to that of modern times, as Giedion has pointed out.

But the classical dream continued to lose in persuasiveness. Its illusory character shone through, ever more clearly.

Exasperated by its shamming, perceptive theorists formulated the doctrines of 'honesty' and 'functionalism': 'In architecture only that shall show that has a definite function and which derives from the strictest necessity. ... Architecture must conform to the nature of materials,' Lodoli[8] is reported to have said about 1760.

The failing strength of the classical symbolism necessitated a change. There is first the return to more fundamental categories. Greek culture was the fountainhead of Rome, therefore a Greek Revival might perhaps be considered more convincing than its Roman derivative. The change in symbolic apparatus is accompanied by a cultivation of the absolute forms of the Phileban solids in the designs of Ledoux and Boullée. Even the justification is the same as in the Renaissance: 'Everything is circular in nature. ... The form of the cube is the symbol of immutability.'[9] (Ledoux) 'From all these observations, it follows that the spherical body is, on all accounts, the image of perfection. ... It has thus been shown that proportion and the harmony of volumes are established by Nature.'[10] (Boullée)

The concept of Nature underwent a change too. For Alberti and Palladio it embraced both the geometrical order of the starry heavens and organic life on earth. At the end of the eighteenth century this bond began to dissolve. There turned out to be two kinds of Nature: the Geometrical, to which Boullée appealed and which Newton investigated, and the 'picturesque' variety.[11] That last, the original garden of Eden, was also a paradise lost and differed considerably from the shorn hedges of the Baroque park. It was the domain of the 'noble savage', the playground of natural man. Rousseau cultivated it in writing; Pater, Watteau, Claude and Gilpin painted Arcady, and Capability Brown actually remade it in his English gardens.

In Versailles the landscape had been subordinated to the buildings; with the cult of natural man, the buildings were adapted to the landscape. Rigorous symmetry was abandoned for picturesque asymmetrical massing (Downton Castle, Strawberry Hill, Fonthill Abbey). The object is the same as in the Baroque: a unity between landscape and architecture, symbolizing a harmonic cosmos.

The power of make-believe to convince diminished as the social disintegration gained a faster pace through the Industrial Revolution. All during the nineteenth century architects continued a frantic search for a really valid symbolism, rooted in a historical reality. Different dreamlands vied with each other and thereby mutually detracted from their persuasiveness. The avowed preference for elevated sites continued, just as the love for composition in spatial sequences involving the spectator did. The doubts about the reality of the dream remained: 'Every building that is treated naturally, without disguise or concealment, cannot fail to look well... there should be no features about a building which are not necessary for convenience, construction or propriety. ... What I mean by propriety is this, that the external and internal appearance of an edifice should be illustrative of, and in accordance with, the purpose for which it is designed.'[12] (Pugin, 1841 and 1843) And so on to Sullivan.

Honesty and functionalism[13] are supposed to counteract the illusory character of architectural dreamland. Because the construction is frankly shown and the architecture follows the requirements of the programme, the building is *real* and belongs to this world, not to the realm of fantasy. The dream ought therefore to be a reality too, by implication.

But eclectic dreamland failed to convince, as the classical had failed before. The fault was sought in the historical connotations. The same invective which Pugin had once poured upon classical architecture was now levelled against all stylistic imitation. Mackintosh, Voysey, Richardson and Berlage stripped dreamland of its historical trappings. It gained thereby in honesty, but lost also its last moorings in a historical reality. It now became irrevocably a never-never land.

Once more we return to the abstract simplicity of geometry with the white cubes, the 'prismes purs' of the twenties. Their aesthetic defense is also reminiscent of Alberti, Ledoux and Boullée. Mondriaan wrote: 'Immutable harmony is reached with the relations of position and depicted by straight lines in their principal, i.e. rectangular opposition. ... In architecture, exact expression of the cosmic harmony is shown by vertical and horizontal planes. ... And man? He must be nothing by himself, and only a part of the whole. When he thus no longer feels his individuality, he will be happy in the earthly paradise created by himself.'[14]

The sphere, that 'perfect' form of Alberti and Boullée, is neither mentioned nor used; at most one finds half cylinders as in the work of Oud, Chiattone and Mendelsohn. Its unassailable round form stands aloof from surrounding space, and is therefore incompatible with the modern effort towards spatial unification. Picturesque asymmetry had loosened the architectural box at its contours. The informal plans of the 1890's led to the concept of free-flowing space and the open plan of today. Like the culture of glass, it intends to create a symbol for a unified cosmos. The correspondence with Baroque spatial fusion is rooted in a common principle.

Arcady is also still with us. The line leads from Morris's flowered wallpapers and Walter Crane's nature studies over Art Nouveau and Wright's organic architecture to Aalto, Ronchamp and the Yale Skating Rink. Its philosophy is behind the cult of materials in the raw. Rudolf Steiner turned the scattered thoughts on the subject into the coherent doctrine of anthroposophy.

But the doubts set in, even sooner than before. Recourse was had to similar means as in the eighteenth century. We are amazed that the balconies of Wright's Falling Waters remain hovering in mid-air, and that the wings of the T.W.A. building nearly seem to flap. If *that* can be true, the dream must be true too. Violent, angular forms hit out at us in Le Corbusier's Visual Arts Center at Harvard or Rudolph's School of Architecture at Yale. The modern love of concrete in the raw is a related shock-therapy to cure us from our disbelief in architectural dreamland.

4. Construction and art

The symbolic world of architecture stood between man and the outside world in the Middle Ages. Gravitation belonged to that world. Consequently an architect approached structural problems with the same attitude as he worked on symbolism: with mistrust in a period of strain and with confidence in a period of hope.

The Renaissance exploded this unified approach. Its harmonic cosmos was immutable and absolute in contrast to the ever-changing world of reality. In such a cosmos there is no day or night, no rain or frost, and also no gravitation. It is far removed from the practical problems of life.

As a result, construction was divorced from architecture as an art. It became a means to an end and not an end in itself. The separation between the skill of engineering and the art of architecture parallels the divorce between science and religion.

Inventions in building were henceforth rarely made by architects. Philibert de l'Orme and Wright are exceptions; most architects are content to use the possibilities proffered by engineers, but show little inclination to use their imagination on structural problems. Paxton, Eiffel, Freyssinet, Magnel, Nervi, Torroja and Buckminster Fuller; those names come to mind and none of them is an architect. Brunelleschi stands at the watershed. He builds an enormous semi-Gothic dome with a spectacular display of technical inventiveness, which fails to show up in any of his later Classical work.

The attitude is reflected in the architectural treatises. Gothic writing concerns itself exclusively with the practical problems of building: geometry, measuring and rules of thumb for statics.[15] Only Suger, a patron and not an architect, wrote something about aesthetics. The Renaissance treatises of Alberti and Palladio are neatly divided into two parts: one concerned with architecture as an art, and another with building as a practical skill. One finds hardly any cross-reference from one part to the other. The separate spheres are indicated in the text: 'We consider that an Edifice is a kind of Body consisting, like all other Bodies, of Design and Matter; the first is produced by the Thought, the other by Nature... We can in our Thought and Imagination contrive perfect Forms of Buildings entirely separate from Matter.'[16] (Alberti)

Later treatises, such as Guarini's *Architettura Civile* (1737) drop the technical part entirely. Boullée clearly expresses his disdain for the inferior skills of practice: 'What is architecture? Shall I define it, with Vitruvius, as the art of building? No. There is in this definition a gross error. Vitruvius takes the effect for the cause.

It is necessary to conceive in order to create. Our forefathers built their huts only after conceiving an image of them. It is this creation of the spirit that constitutes architecture, which we can consequently define as the art of producing and bringing to perfection any Edifice. The art of building is therefore only a secondary art, which it seems fitting to us to call the scientific part of architecture.'[17]

The Industrial Revolution brought technology to the foreground. This, and the desire to appear 'real' and inclusive of all aspects of human culture, has somewhat checked the growing divergence between the art and the skill of building. Still, most modern writing on architecture (Wright, Le Corbusier, Norberg-Schultz) pays but cursory attention to structural problems. The two belong to different worlds.

Santa Costanza
Rome   337–350

1. Description

This little church on the outskirts of Rome is the best preserved of all the many foundations of the Constantinian house. Built by Constantina, daughter of the great emperor, as a mausoleum for herself, it is one of the earliest buildings of imperially sanctioned Christianity. It carries over some of the splendid heritage of antiquity into the Christian future.

The mausoleum was built as an annex to the church of St. Agnes, also founded by Constantina and already in ruins in the sixth century. The lower part of the exterior wall of this church is still standing today.[1] Constantina's church had been erected in the vicinity of the catacombs containing the remains of the martyred Agnes; a seventh century church now stands above the saint's grave.

Constantina was not alone in her last resting place. The floor of the original St. Agnes was covered with graves, probably right from the beginning. The princess and the commoners were all buried in the vicinity of the martyr, in the belief that the saint would carry those physically near to her with her to heaven on the day of the Last Judgment.[2] Though this belief lacks all scriptural foundation, it was common throughout early Christianity and the Middle Ages. The cemetery around old St. Peter's was cluttered up with funerary buildings; Constantine himself was buried among such remains as he could collect of the Apostles.

The mausoleum was accessible only from the western aisle of St. Agnes. A vestibule (now demolished) connected church and tomb; the original outside portico (gone too, today) was inaccessible from inside.

Originally the building consisted of three vaulted spaces inside one another: the barrel-vaulted portico, the equally barrel-vaulted ambulatory and inside that

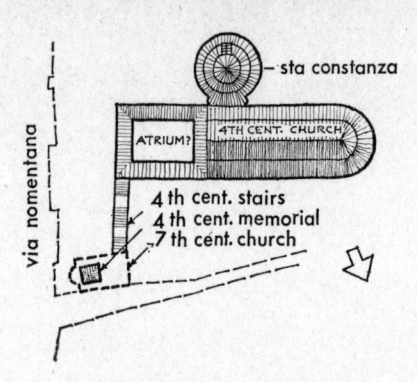

Figure 11. S. Costanza, site

the domed central hall. Opposite the entrance the barrel vault of the ambulatory is interrupted by a vaulted lantern. The vestibule was also barrel-vaulted. Thus all spaces have the same cross-section, i.e. a rectangle capped by the half circle of the arch.

Ambulatory and central hall communicate through arched openings, the arches resting on twelve pairs of columns. Mediating between the composite Corinthian capitals on the columns and the arches is a rather 'unclassical' entablature. A shallow moulding frames the entrance; a meagre cornice runs around the edge of the roof; these details and the interior colonnade are today the only sculptural ones. The rest of the walls is quite smooth. Originally there were also the outside colonnade and some shallow rims and mouldings in the marble wainscoting of the interior; but no coffers or ribs ever interrupted the smoothness of the vaults. Sculpturally the building is and was rather bare, both outside and inside; it contrasts sharply in this with the architecture of only fifty years before. There either outside or inside, or both, were richly decorated with heavy mouldings, sculptured friezes, tympans, and entablatures, leaving only rectangular panels on the walls to receive murals or incrustations.

Much more in accordance with previous Roman practice are the heavy proportions: the interior height is half the exterior diameter of the building. The columns of the interior arcade are as high as the ambulatory is wide; Vitruvius prescribes this proportion for the aisles of basilicas.

The columns of the interior arcade vary in their proportions. Their length is between seven and nine times their lower diameter (d), for, though all are cut to the same length, they are not equal in thickness. This is again without antique precedent, for whatever might be arbitrary and variable about antique monuments, it was not the proportions of the columns! In every respectable classical edifice, all columns of one set are perfectly equal, with a rigorously prescribed ratio between the lower diameter, the height of the column, the height of the capital and the entablature. Here the columns are treated indifferently; they have been taken from other antique buildings and they match only approximately. Equally 'unantique' is the treatment of the capitals on the columns. The interior ones were specially cut for the building and are all alike, but those of the exterior row (on the side of the ambulatory) are spoils again.

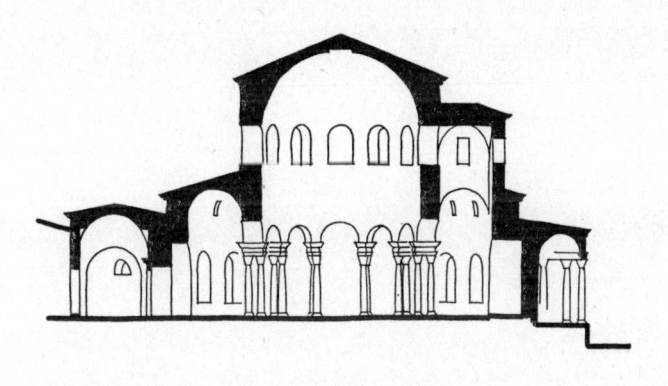

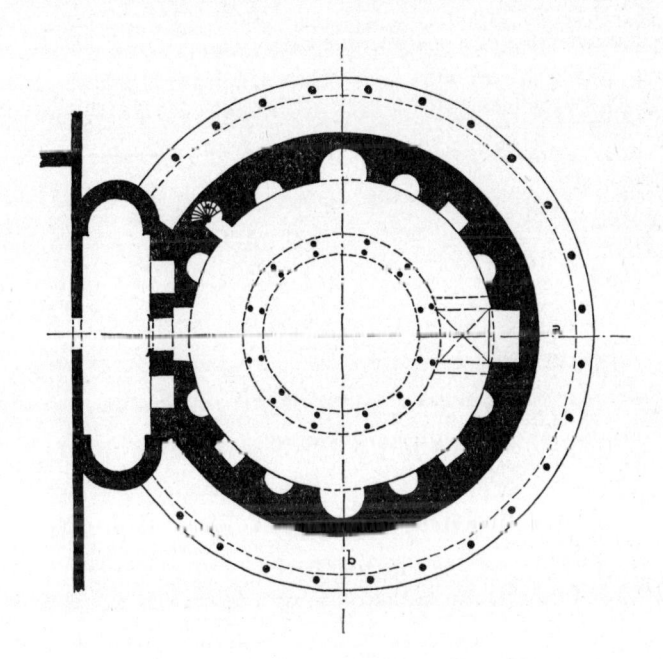

Figure 12. Santa Costanza; elevation, section and plan (after Stettler)

Central hall and ambulatory communicate easily through the large openings of the arcade. In our terminology, they are little isolated from each other: only 36% of the common wall between aisle and domed centre is taken up by columns, arches and wall area; the rest is open. By contrast, the building is very much isolated from the outside world. The heavy exterior wall occupies approximately 40% of the total floor area. Tiny slits in the tunnelvault of the ambulatory throw some light on the extant ceiling mosaics. The main source of daylight is the row of windows in the clerestory above the colonnade; here the inside opens towards the sky. Though the lighting is quite sufficient, no more than 2.3% of the total outside surface (walls and roofs) is taken up by these windows.

The heavy outside wall is probably due in the first place to the Roman practice of counteracting the horizontal thrust of vaults by great masses of masonry. Niches for cult statues, thrones, altars or the like were dug into the depth of the wall: so in S. Costanza, and so, too, in the Pantheon, or in the so-called temple of Minerva Medica. It is the opposite of the medieval practice: there the wall was buttressed from the outside, here the wall was buttressed from the inside, by the piers between the niches.

Structurally, the building is practically completely homogeneous and continuous, with the exception of the colonnades. They provide a sort of link with the past, for neither (symbolic) homogeneity nor continuity was usual for Roman architecture. On the contrary, in most monumental architecture, like Diocletian's palace in Split or his Thermae in Rome, the great vaults appear to rest on columns (hence 'concentrated'), and the continuity is broken by cornices.

As a composition of spatial elements, the building is a nearly pure example of the ring-type, with its two galleries encircling a central hall. That domed hall dominates over the surrounding rings in height and in interior width; the building descends in stages from the cupola to the ground. Though a careless look at the plan might give the impression that there are twelve planes of symmetry (disregarding the vestibule) there is actually only one true axis, going through vestibule and the niche opposite (a). In that axis lies the one large rectangular niche, originally containing the sarcophagus, and over it stands the lantern. This axis and the one perpendicular to it are indicated in the arcade by a slightly wider spacing of the columns. The niches too distinguish these axes of symmetry, the larger niches going down to the floor on the two axes (a and b), and the smaller ones with sills in between.[3]

Today, the plain exterior is matched by a nearly equally plain white interior (Plate 2). But originally all the vaults were covered by mosaics and the interior wall of the drum carried a marble incrustation. Only the mosaics of the ambulatory have remained more or less intact. Old drawings and a careful description, all of the sixteenth century, permit a partial reconstruction of the original interior.[4]

In the main, the mausoleum was decorated in the traditional Roman manner, with a lavishness due to a member of the Imperial House. The ambulatory vaults still show the type: geometrical patterns of medallions, imitations of coffervaults and intertwining vines alternate with floral motifs. Cupids, peacocks and dolphins fill up many of the geometrical frames and are strewn liberally throughout the more irregular compartments. Pagan scenes have been avoided, but the decorations strike a worldly note, with their motifs taken straight from the triclinium floor. In two compartments cupids are shown harvesting and pressing grapes. Similar scenes occur on the porphyry sarcophagus (now in the Vatican museum). The marble incrustations on the drum consisted of registers of panels and a row of pilasters framing the windows.

The framing of the scenes in the cupola mosaic was also of this type. A river filled with dolphins, ducks and fishing cupids ran along its lower rim. Twelve caryatids flanked by lions rose from little rocks in the water to divide the cupola in twelve sections. Dolphins with interlaced tails divided the surface horizontally into two registers. The lower twelve compartments contained probably only scenes from the Old Testament, the upper from the New Testament. On the left-hand wall of the lantern, directly above the sarcophagus, was a mosaic with a haloed sheep amidst drinking jars identified by Stern as the marriage of Cana.

Striking is the lack of decorations on the exterior. The outside walls are, and probably always were, of plain brickwork. Normally, an Imperial mausoleum makes some display on the exterior, to betoken the importance of the near-divine body lying there. Not in S. Costanza; all decorations are concentrated on the inside—with the exception of the exterior colonnade. It looks as if the building had turned 'introvert' in comparison with the opulent, 'extraverted' mausolea of the pagan emperors.

2. Analysis

And now the Gordian knot of meanings: how did this little tomb get its form? Though the social conditions in the Roman Empire influenced the architecture of S. Costanza, there are other influences as well. We must expect a tangle of customs and innovation merging entirely in the building and in the mind of the anonymous designer. We can only try to unravel part of this web, destroying the superb unity for the sake of clarification.

Very little is due to function, in the restricted modern sense; and whatever may be due to it, eludes us today. Perhaps the ambulatory accomodated some sort of procession and was therefore a requirement—but we do not know it.

The commemorative meal, held according to antique and early Christian custom in honour of the dead princess, probably took place at a table immediately before the apsis.[5]

More is known about structural influences. The use of vaulting and of heavy walls to counteract a horizontal thrust has been mentioned already as current Roman practice. Thus the extremely heavy outside wall and the resulting isolation become understandable, at least in part.[6]

Habitual is also the use of the classical orders (columns and entablatures) for the outside and inside colonnades, and the Roman custom of throwing arches on entablatures over the columns. New is on the contrary the 'unclassical' re-use of existing columns and capitals.

We must largely ascribe the whole composition to habit: the central plan, the cupola over the main area and the outside arcade. Mausolea with a central plan are very common in antiquity and have a long history behind them. For a larger memorial structure it may be said to be the normal type. The Mycenean treasury of Atreus of 1350 B.C. is one of the older examples. The Etruscan tumuli are round (conical) burial places. Nearer in time to S. Costanza are the mausolea of Augustus, of Cecilia Metella, of Hadrian (the present Castel Sant' Angelo) and of Diocletian in Spalato. The latter in particular has many features in common with S. Costanza: an outside colonnade, a cupola resting on a heavy wall, and an alternating system of rectangular and semicircular niches on the inside of that wall. They are examples of the antique heroon, shown in such great variety in the seventeenth century plans

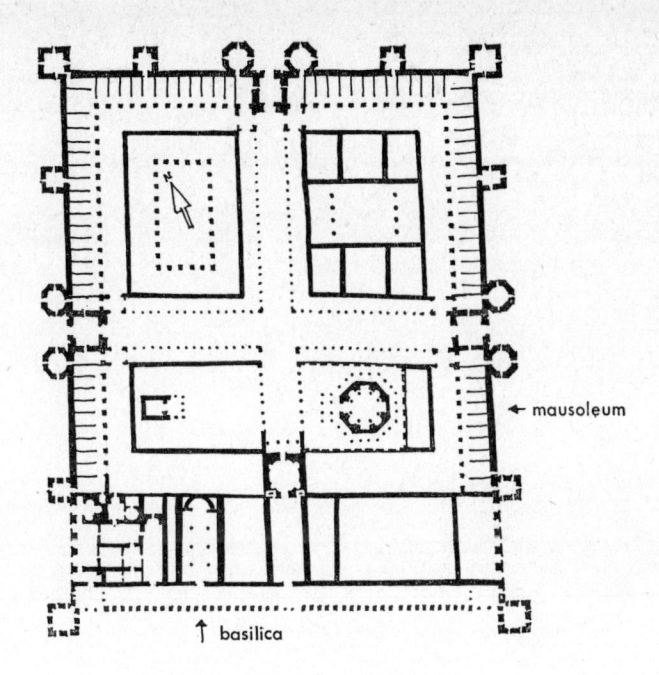

Figure 13. Diocletian's palace in Split

of Montano. The heroon stands as a monument over the grave of a hero or demi-god.

The cardinal feature of the heroon and the cause of the central plan was the dome. The dome of heaven was the dwelling-place of the elect; its earthly replica signified that the person buried under it belonged to that company. When the Roman emperors put on semi-divine or divine airs, they built themselves domed throne-rooms, as for instance the Domus Aurea of Nero. The celestial significance of the dome is the reason for its use in apses, both pagan and Christian.[7] As a tomb for an Imperial princess, S. Costanza simply had to have a dome, and therefore a central plan.

Traditional too is the decorative embellishment, with the exception of the few Christian scenes. A Christian form of decoration of sufficient splendour for an imperial mausoleum had not yet been developed, and thus the decorators fell back on the well-known motifs.

But if the general scheme is traditional and the majority of details have an honest antique past, there are also some new features. For instance the plainness outside, and the (original) decorative splendour inside is an innovation. Not in every respect though, for the great Roman baths were quite plain on the outside and decorated only on the inside; but new for an Imperial mausoleum. Mausolea, like that of Diocletian at Spalato, were intended as much for their outside impressiveness as temples or triumphal arches.

New also is the lack of plasticity. Roman architecture is associated with heavy decorations, an abundance of mouldings, and sculpture; if anything, too much for modern taste. We find none of this ostentation in S. Costanza: great restraint reigns throughout; all surfaces are as smooth as in modern architecture.

But the most conspicuous innovation is the addition of an ambulatory, opening with an arcade onto the central space. In cross-section Santa Costanza resembles the contemporary Constantinian basilicas. In both a high nave is accompanied by lower aisles; both are lit through the clerestory, the aisles being usually quite dark. Even the proportions are similar; the nave of S. Maria Maggiore is also half the total width between the outside walls, and the width of the aisles of St. John in the Lateran is approximately half that of the nave. The 'normal' cross-section of a three-aisled early Christian basilica, turned on its vertical axis, fitted with vaults and an extra row of columns to support them,[8] results in something quite similar to S. Costanza. One half of the plan is provided by the tradition of centralizing domed mausolea, and the other half seems to go back to the Early Christian Church.

But S. Costanza is practically contemporaneous with the earliest basilicas. When it was built, the peace of the church was barely forty years old, and the Lateran church, the first Christian basilica, was brand-new. Therefore it is not a question of influence, but rather one of the simultaneous development of the same motif—a nave accompanied by lower aisles—on two building types: the basilica and the mausoleum.[9] The basilicas too lacked cult-statues, borrowed their columns and capitals right and left from other antique buildings; they too had smooth walls, decorated with marble incrustations and mosaics inside and were left bare or simply plastered on the outside. In the same sense as the Christian basilica contrasts with the antique temple with all its exterior display, classically correct details and plasticity, S. Costanza contrasts with the preceding mausolea.

It is tempting to attribute all of these innovations to the same (complex) 'cause', i.e. the social conditions of the time.

The empire was sliding downhill. Despotic rule with forced labour and serfdom had followed on the anarchy of the third century. The Christian writer Lactantius is understandably biased against the persecutor Diocletian; but most of his facts stand unchallenged:

'Diocletian, that inventor of crime and contriver of wickedness, ruined everything and did not spare God himself. Partly through avarice and partly through timidity he overturned the Roman empire. He chose three men to share his government, and while the empire was quartered, armies were multiplied. Each of the four rulers desired to keep a larger army than any single emperor had done in the

I. Santa Costanza, Rome, exterior. In the foreground the wall of the apse of the ruined 4th century church of St Agnes

II. Santa Costanza, interior. Practically all daylight comes from above, through the clerestory windows

past. There were fewer people to pay than there were to receive. Farmers were impoverished by huge exactions, farms were abandoned, tilth degenerated to woodland. To saturate every corner with terror the provinces were divided into fragments, each of which and almost every town had a host of officials great and small to oppress it. There were hierarchies of bailiffs and deputies of the administrators. Very few civil cases came before them, but people were condemned every day and their property confiscated. There were countless taxes on commodities, repeated over and over and running continuously, and imposts were unendurable.'[10] Does it not seem likely that the slow decay of the empire reflected on the minds of the Romans? May it not have pervaded them with a sense of gloom and an inclination to escape from this hopeless world? Gone were the carefree attitude towards the gods and the jaunty certainty of all that Roman power could do; gone too were the golden days of Republic and Early Empire. The cultivated minds tried to accept the incorrigible evils of the time with stoic resignation; but many Romans sought refuge in esoteric cults, such as those of Mithras or Isis, or in mystic Neo-Platonism.

Christianity, more than any of the other cults, provided an answer to the search for higher, more enduring values. It negated the importance of the events in this world and stressed those in the next. It found its adherents primarily among the lower classes, which suffered most from injustice, forced labour and taxation. It promised true justice and a deliverance from hardship in the Kingdom of Heaven. 'In Pace' we read on the graves in the Roman catacombs.

The social conditions had prepared many people for a ready acceptance of the Christian creed. In the combination of these two factors, Christianity and the conditions of the time, we may find perhaps an explanation of the novel architectural features of S. Costanza.

By its very nature, Early Christianity scorned the outward pomp of pagan temples and the veneration of cult statues. The exterior of buildings, even and especially religious ones, did not matter; for was not the garb but a poor thing compared to the body it clothed, and that body again far inferior to the immortal soul that inhabited it? The mausoleum shut itself off from the outside world, but opened up inside: hence the heavy walls, the tiny windows and the easy communication between ambulatory and central space. Even the windows in the clerestory, only admitting light from above, may perhaps have been connected with the idea of salvation—the Light—descending from heaven.

With such an 'unworldly' atmosphere, it matters but little that the columns do not match or that the detailing is not everywhere as careful as it had been in an earlier era.

To turn away from this world and towards the next was a natural reaction to its unpleasantness, and this reaction was sanctioned, even advocated by the church. Such a rejection of the world implied a lack of interest in its realistic, three-dimensional appearance. To that we may ascribe perhaps the paucity of sculptural detail in S. Costanza and the Early Christian churches; decoration retreats more and more in the glossy unreal world of mosaics and painting.

At the second level of meaning we have the cosmic significance of the cupola. The interpretation of S. Costanza as an 'introverted', and in comparison to the architecture of the third century: 'unclassical' building, influenced by Christian precepts and social adversity, lies on the third level of meaning.

St. Michael
Hildesheim   1010–1033

1. Description

Many a Christian, when he has scored some success dear to his heart, puts a little extra money on the collection plate at the Sunday church service. Almost every church owns some piece of furniture or decoration given by a pious member, as a tangible expression of his gratitude to the Lord. In exactly the same sense we have to understand the foundation of the monastery of St. Michael at Hildesheim.

Bernward, bishop of Hildesheim from 993 to 1022, was a successful man.[1] As a youthful cleric he became the tutor of the later German Emperor, Otto the Third. In the company of his princely pupil he travelled through the empire and met the outstanding men of his time. His association with the court secured him the nomination to the see of Hildesheim and afforded him imperial protection which stood him in good stead during a conflict with the powerful bishop of Mainz. As a token of his friendship, Otto gave Bernward a splinter of the True Cross. Bernward had this priceless relic enshrined in a monumental bronze cross, and founded in 996 a small monastery in Hildesheim for its care and veneration.

Later he endowed this community with all his private possessions and built for it the church of St. Michael. First of all, this magnificent gesture has to be seen as a votive offering to God, the ultimate source of all our blessings.

The foundation of a church entitled its founder to several privileges. The most important of these was the stipulation that the clergy attached to the church were to read masses for the benefit of his soul.[2] Also, a great and costly gift usually creates a feeling of obligation in the receiver; for that reason the Ottonian emperors donated large tracts of land to their vassals. Medieval man hoped to influence God in the same way; by a large gift he more or less put God under an obligation to admit him to paradise. In the words of the foundation charter of St. Michael: 'Considering this, I, Bernward, named bishop through Divine predestination and not through my own deserts, have long thought by which building constructed through my merits (meritorum architectura), by what precious goods I might gain Heaven.'

Finally, like many founders of churches, Bernward lies buried in his building, surrounded by relics which were certain to go to paradise on the day of Judgment and might carry him with them.

Michael the Archangel,[3] to whom the building is consecrated, would weigh the souls at the Last Judgment and carry them to Heaven. He is the special protector of the church and the protector against evil in general; the Apocalyps describes him as the leader of the heavenly host in the final battle with the devil. The traditional representation of St. Michael standing on a dragon which he kills with a lance is based on this passage.

Evil, in medieval theology and also in modern usage is associated with darkness; salvation on the other hand with light. Hence the normal orientation of churches is towards the east, the direction from which the sun comes into the world every day. The west, the direction of sundown, is by contrast associated with darkness, evil and death. Here lies the origin of the representations of the Last Judgment above the entrance portals of Romanesque and Gothic churches: going through the door into the church is analogous to going through death and Judgment to Heaven.

St. Michael's sanctuary is always at the western end of a medieval church;[4] there he stands as a guardian against the forces of evil in the front line. St. Michael was believed to have made two miraculous appearances: once on the Monte Gargano and once on top of Hadrian's mausoleum in Rome, henceforth called Castel Sant' Angelo. According to Mâle,[5] the Archangel inherited the functions of heavenly messenger and carrier of souls from Mercury, who had always been venerated on hills and mountains in antiquity. For these reasons, and perhaps also because angels are more 'heavenly' than mortal saints, St. Michael has his altar always in a more elevated part of the building.

Bernward's church[6] was considerably altered in the seventeenth and eighteenth centuries; a bombardment in the last days of the Second World War set it on fire and left only the heavy walls upright. Recently it has been reconstructed in the original form. The towers over the crossings, the three eastern apses, the tops of the staircase towers and the roofs are therefore modern work.

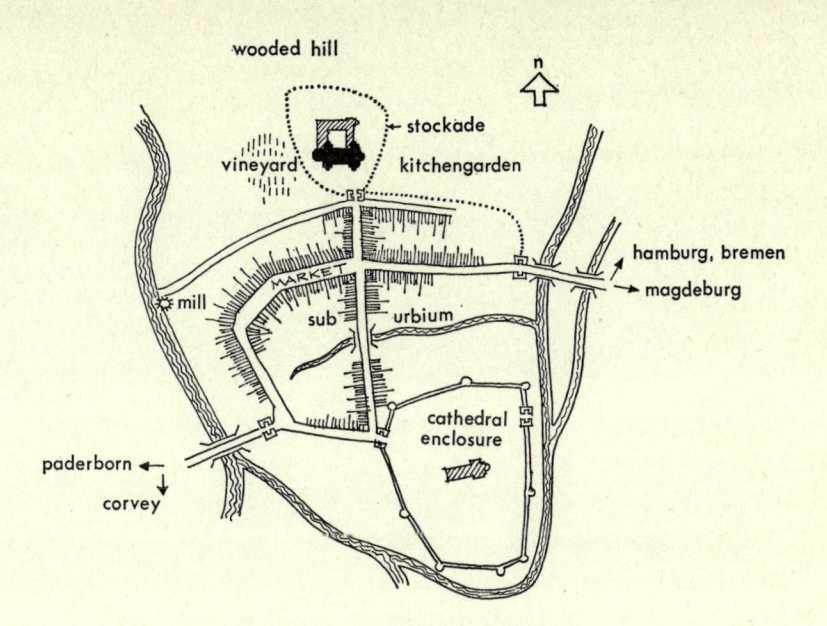

Figure 14. St. Michael; site (after Beseler-Roggenkamp)

St. Michael is a basilica; but how far more complicated in structure it is than the simple barn of the Early Christian Church! Five centuries of development of Christian forms of worship have left their mark. The building reflects the complications which had grown onto the liturgy.

The church is, in Conant's phrase,[7] a double-ender. It has a transept and three apses on the eastern side, and a perfectly equal transept with one large and deep chancel at the western end. The transepts have three-storied galleries at each extremity, reached from octagonal staircase towers on the outside. Larger square towers stand over the two crossings. The floor of the western apse is raised; below it lies a spacious crypt, surrounded by a corridor which runs along the outside wall of crypt and apse. In the centre of the crypt lies a stone sarcophagus with nine angels depicted on its lid in which Bernward was enshrined.

The Early Christian Church had but one altar; St. Michael on the contrary had a multitude. Altars stood in each of the three apses, the central altar being consecrated to St. John the Baptist. The two upper stories of the transept galleries housed altars consecrated to angels. The altar of the Cross (with the reliquary Cross above it) stood in the nave; add to this the main altar in the western apse and an altar for Mary just below it in the crypt, and it makes thirteen altars at least.[8] All the altars stood at the eastern ends of the subspaces.

There are several reasons for this multiplication of altars. First of all, the increase of the cult of relics.[9] An important relic required a separate altar, such as for instance the altar of the Cross. Soon after the completion of the church an All-Saints altar was put up in the crypt, in honour of the sixty-six minor relics collected by Bernward and built into the walls there.

Also, a sizeable proportion of the monks of tenth century monasteries were ordained. In the ninth century it became usual for every cleric to read mass daily,[10] and such services could obviously not be performed at a single altar.

Finally, a church like St. Michael has to be seen as the result of a long process of growth. At the beginning stands the 'family of churches', to which Lehmann[11] has drawn attention, consisting of two full-fledged basilicas and a baptistery. Each of these churches fulfilled probably a special function (as the baptismal chapel still does). Later, the separated churches became united in a single building; at first rather clumsily, as in Centula (790–799) or still in St. Benigne in Dijon (1001–1018); but also, after some time, with more success, as for instance in Tournus (after 950) or in Gernrode (after 961). The usual combination consists of a building of central or centralizing plan, the so-called 'Westwork', stuck to the western end of a basilica. This set may reproduce, as Heitz holds,[12] the scheme of the Holy Sepulchre. The Westwork was often added afterwards to an existing building (in Corvey, Werden, St. Benoît-sur-Loire). The single spacious interior of the Early Christian basilica had been replaced by a complicated set of interlocking cubicles.

Religious service had grown more complex too. In seventh century Rome a procession was instituted on special Feastdays, on which the pope went from one church to another, and mass was read at each 'Station'.[13] The services in the Carolingian empire were modelled on the Roman example. Divine services in the monasteries became reduced copies of this form of worship. The procession went from altar to altar instead of from church to church, the abbot taking the place of the bishop of Rome.

Processional services of this kind were probably held in St. Michael. Normal daily offices were stationary, of course. Judging from the plan of the building, it seems likely that they were held in the western chancel; it is the only place large enough to hold the entire monastic community, and it corresponds with the normal eastern apses of contemporary abbey-churches. Also, the north-western transept-arm adjoined the dormitories. Monastic dormitories were, whenever possible, laid out in the closest proximity to the main sanctuary, to facilitate the shuttling back and forth of the brethren for nocturnal prayers. The main chancel was laid at the western end because of the dedication to St. Michael.[14] The three eastern apses are customary.

The functional analysis being exhausted—perhaps even carried beyond the

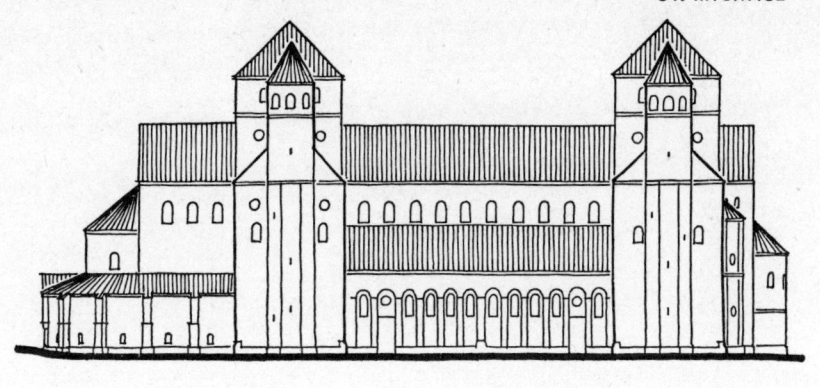

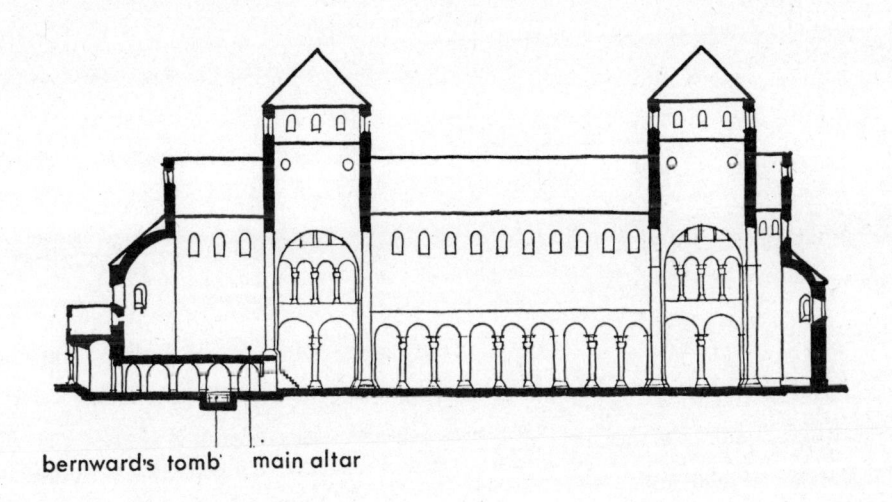

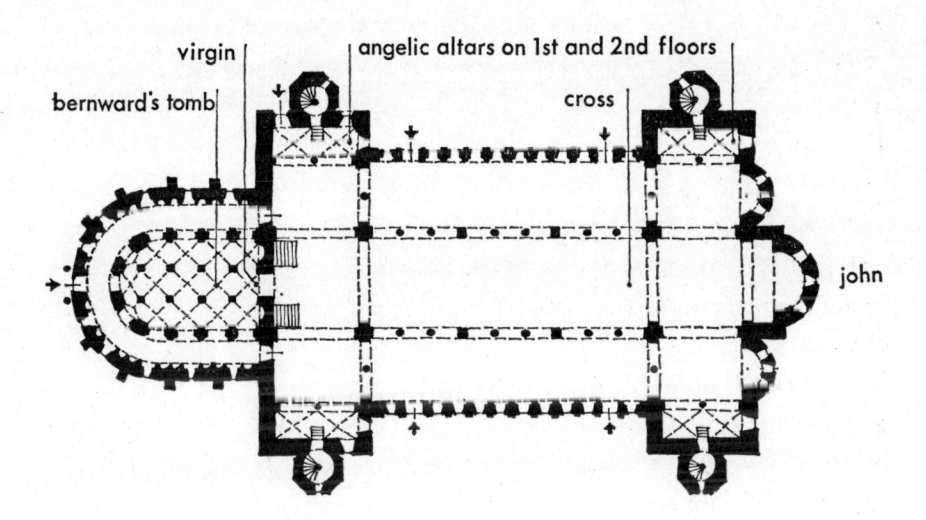

Figure 15. St. Michael; elevation, section, plan (after Beseler-Roggenkamp)

bounds of prudence—we may turn to the construction. The most conspicuous structural feature of St. Michael is the heavy outside wall; no less than five foot three inches! (160 cm). These walls have stood the building in good stead.

Any innovator or modernizer was faced with the choice of taking them down, or cutting his new windows, doors, etc. in them; the latter course was always chosen (with the exception of the western apse), as it was so much easier. And through sheer bulk they also survived two medieval fires and the bombs and conflagration of the Second World War. On their outside they are faced with ashlar, their inside is constructed of rubble, and a mixture of mortar and rubble is poured in between. The inside was of course plastered.

Surprisingly, these heavy walls supported no more than a light wooden roof, its trusses probably hidden by panelling. Only the apses, the crypt with its ambulatory, the staircase towers and the lower floors of the galleries were vaulted.

From construction we turn to form. To an architect of today there is something agreeably familiar in St. Michael's; one is tempted to say something 'modern'. No doubt this is due to its apparent simplicity. All volumes are clearcut geometrical shapes (Phileban solids), all spaces inside are of the simplest form. No profusion of ornament distracts from this simplicity; most walls are plain and smooth. Windows are simply dug into the mass of the wall, without any moulding surrounding them. Only the walls of the aisles, of the ambulatory and of two apses carried some decoration in the form of pilasters, those on the ambulatory necessitated by the outward thrust of the vault. Equal simplicity and smoothness reigns inside; the only 'plastic' details are the niches in the ambulatory wall and in the side walls of the western apse, and the columns. But even they participate in the prevailing simplicity; their block capitals (an inverted half sphere with its top and four sides sliced off) are as mathematical and abstract as the rest.

Heavy walls and tiny windows are the characteristics of strongly isolated buildings in our nomenclature. No less than 19% of the total floor area (including outside walls) is taken up by solids, and no more than 2.8% of the total outside surface is 'open', either as a window or as a door.

Structure, in the sense of symbolic structure, is played down practically to non-existence. Of course the church looks what it is, i.e. a solid masonry building covered with wooden roofs and so it satisfies the modern demand for 'honest

III. A sacred fortress. Exterior of St Michael, Hildesheim

IV. Even the aisles are separate rooms. Interior of the southern aisle of St Michael

construction' but that should not blind us to the fact that no artistic interest is displayed in structure, such as is apparent in Gothic architecture for instance. Shafts or pillars bearing and loads borne are not expressed; the building remains structurally mute, in the artistic sense. The walls are homogeneous; the joint between the wooden roofs and the masonry is a discontinuity.

As a composition St. Michael belongs to the joined type. It consists of a series of spaces—or volumes—strung out along a double cross (main axis and transepts). One conspicuous feature of the scheme is the perfect equality of the two transepts;[15] but for the apses, the building would have two axes of symmetry. Another, and perhaps even more important aspect is the *separation between the elements*. Crossing tower, nave, transept, aisles, staircase towers and apses are all distinctly separate, more or less independent volumes. Even the western apse proper abuts against the higher wall of the chancel. Similarly on the inside, the crossing, the nave, the apses and galleries are all clearly and conspicuously detached from each other. They are unified, true enough, by their function and even more by the system of proportions, but this cannot efface the disjunction; for the impression of simplicity and geometrical clarity depends on that very disjunction. It is particularly visible in the aisles, which open towards the transepts with a double arch instead of a single one. Even they are separate 'rooms'.

2. Analysis

The warp and woof of the design of St. Michael is still the basilical scheme. With The Early Christian basilica, St. Michael has in common: aisles, nave with clerestory, wooden roofing, a longitudinal plan with the main axis of symmetry running east-west, and semicircular vaulted apses.

Different—but not new—are the transepts. The origin of the transept is probably quite practical and down to earth: it allowed more people to stand around the altar.[16] Transepts fell into disuse in the 6th and 7th centuries, after which they were revived in Carolingian times. Charlemagne had re-established the (Western) Roman empire; he also wanted to assimilate Roman culture, in particular the culture of Christian, i.e. Constantinian Rome. Part of that effort was the building of churches

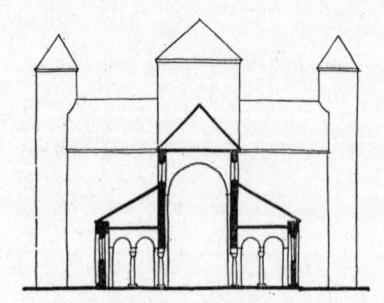

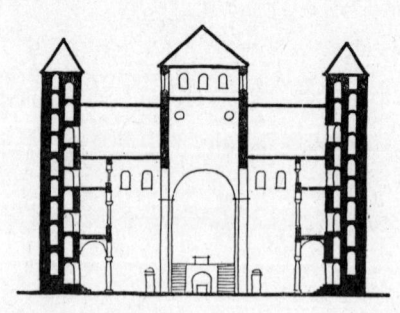

Figure 16. St. Michael; cross-sections (after Beseler-Roggenkamp)

in the Roman manner, as in Fulda and in Hersfeld.[17] The motif had come to stay, for it was just as useful for monastic communities as for the Early Christian clergy. Probably the cruciform plan appealed too as a symbol for the Cross.

Basilical scheme and transept are the residue of tradition in St. Michael, or in more vulgar parlance, the products of habit. Not the double transept of course. Its exact meaning escapes us, but it may perhaps be ascribed to the reversed orientation. The eastern transept then would be the one demanded by tradition, and the other might secure the equivalence of the western chancel with a 'normal' (eastern) liturgical centre. It may also be due to the need to accommodate the eight angelic altars.

The new elements are the significant ones in our quest for meaning. Apart from the second transept, St. Michael differs from an Early Christian basilica on the following points:

1. It has more part-spaces and a greater variety of them: more apses and altars, a western chancel, a crypt with ambulatory and galleries in the transept-arms;
2. It has six towers where the basilica had none (generally) ;
3. Instead of the fragile construction of most Early Christian basilicas, St. Michael has extremely heavy walls and a stronger isolation both towards the outside and between its internal spatial parts; for instance, the crossing is bounded on four sides by arches and the light antique colonnade between aisles and nave is replaced by a rhythmic alternation of pillars and columns;
4. The building is even more smooth in surface and abstract in detailing than the Early Christian basilica, witness the block capitals; figurative art of the Ottonian period is correspondingly further from realism than in the time of Constantine.

The greater differentiation is largely due to the growing complexity of the monastic liturgy: the cult of relics, the growing number of ordained monks, the usages of daily mass and masses for the dead, and the processional form of service on Feast-days. More altars and hence more apses were needed; so the churches together with the liturgy lost their simplicity.[18]

The desire to get into close contact with the relics, led to the construction of crypts below the main altar. There special masses for the dead could be said and the saints would hear them, because their remains, however small, were present. There too, masses could be read for the soul of Bernward, around his sarcophagus. Early crypts consisted of no more than a tunnel. Pilgrims could circulate there past the venerable remains through a corridor inside the apse; but only a small number of them could so be accommodated. When the interest in relics started to grow and masses were held in this restricted space, crypts swelled in size.[19] St. Michael has still the circular corridor, this time on the outside.[20] From the charter of the consecration we know that the crypt was consecrated in 1015, 'by bishop Bernward, the venerable bishop Eggehard of Schleswig and the venerable bishop Thiderich of Munster, to the honour of our Lord and Saviour Jesus Christ, and to his blessed and glorious mother Mary, ever Virgin, and to the Archangel Michael, and the whole heavenly host, and at the same time to the honour of the sixty-six relics, enshrined with due reverence by the aforementioned venerable bishops'.[21]

Ring-crypts consisting of a corridor running along the outside walls of the apse were common in the neighbourhood. They occurred in the cathedral at Halberstadt, in the abbey of Corvey, and in the cathedral at Hildesheim itself (all ninth century work). In particular the corridor at Vreden (ninth–tenth century) has many points in common with that at St. Michael. The idea of a hall supported on pillars inside the crypt—or perhaps even the entire form of the crypt—may have been derived from St. Martin in Tours, which Bernward visited just prior to the building of St. Michael. He occupied the same position in his crypt (with reversed orientation though) as the great French bishop did in his church.[22]

Bernward lies at the foot of the altar of Mary. The Holy Virgin, the human link between man and God was—and still is—called upon to intercede for poor sinners with the Lord.[23]

Other special areas consecrated to special cults are the western chancel and the transept galleries. The chancel has been discussed before. The angels' altars in the transept galleries were probably raised for the same reason which caused St. Michael's altar to stand in an elevated position. This necessitated the construction of staircase towers. Beseler points out that the transepts with their galleries, stair-turrets and central towers have these features in common with the Westwork. It may be added that in particular the Westwork of the archiepiscopal church of Mainz (at the *eastern* end of the church through reversed orientation) closely resembles the transepts of St. Michael—if Kautzsch's reconstruction is correct.[24]

The towers are a prominent feature of the transept and are among the most conspicuous differences between St. Michael and the Early Christian basilicas. Towers on a church appear quite natural to us; in fact we usually identify churches with towered buildings and conversely an edifice with towers as probably a church. If one asks a child to draw a church, he will in all likelihood make its steeple the most salient feature. Towers belong to churches by tradition.

But was it always like that? It does not seem likely, for the Early Christian basilica was towerless, only a few Syrian churches (Thafka, Turmanin) excepted. Should these rare examples be considered the origin of church tower building?[25] It seems rather far-fetched. The tradition of building towers on churches stems from the Early Middle Ages; but there it stops being a tradition and is something really *new*. Churches such as St. Martin in Tours, St. Martin in Angers or St. Riquier in Centula started that tradition; and even the much later Ottonian churches, such as St. Michael, helped to bring it about.

Church towers might be an innovation of sorts, but towers were not. The medieval city was surrounded by a forest of towers, not on churches but on the walls. From fifteenth and sixteenth century engravings we know approximately what the early medieval city looked like from outside: an impregnable fortress with towered gates and strongholds. So much were towers characteristic of the medieval town, that coins struck by the municipalities often show a group of towers as an ideogram for the city: a large one in the middle flanked by two smaller turrets, just like the transepts of St. Michael![26] So it seems plausible to connect St. Michael's towers with these obvious examples, rather than with some distant Syrian forebear. Gate- and wall-towers are the examples after which the early medieval church-towers were modelled.

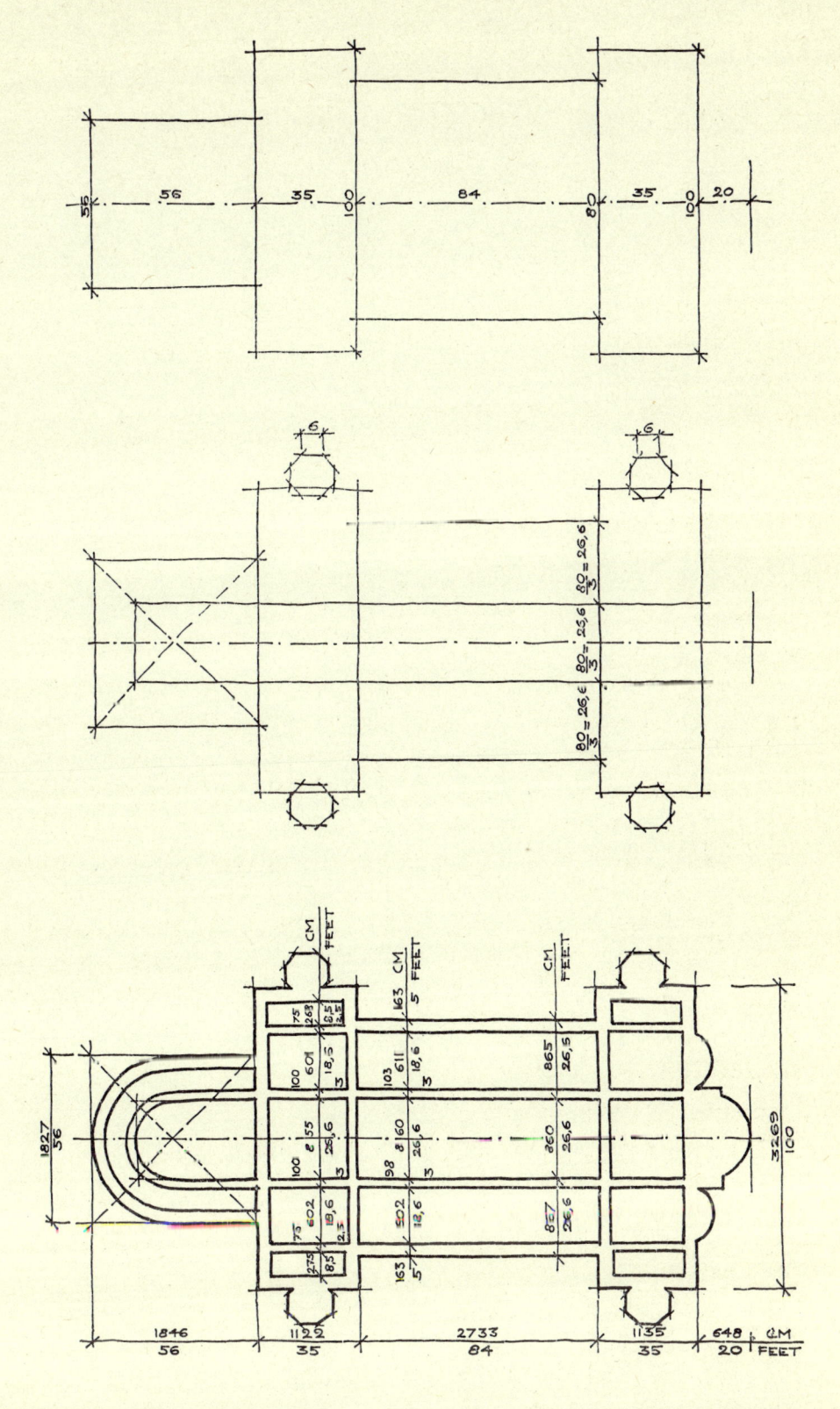

Figure 17. St. Michael; dimensional scheme (after Beseler-Roggenkamp, with modifications)

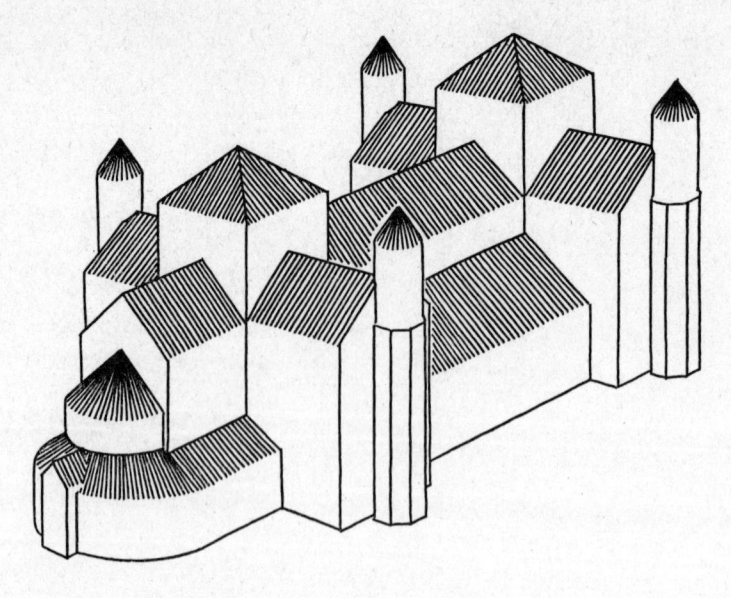

Figure 18. St. Michael; exterior masses

The gate- and wall-towers are purely utilitarian constructions. From them assailants trying to force a breach in the city ramparts could be shot at by archers. The invention of gunpowder rendered them obsolete. But in Ottonian times they were in full use, for Thangmar writes in his biography of bishop Bernward: 'With the greatest diligence he began to surround our sacred town (the cathedral castle or 'Domburg' is meant) with walls, and located the towers on their circumference; he started the work with such competence, that, as all can see, nothing equal in beauty and strength is to be found in the whole of Saxony.'[27] Bernward fortified Hildesheim against Danish raids.

Like the defensive towers, the church towers have a functional root. The ones at the extremities of the transepts gave access to the upper galleries; the towers over the crossings were probably bell-towers.[28] But it seems possible that they had an artistic meaning as well. And if such is the case, then they may furnish us with the clue to the whole building.

For does it not seem likely that medieval man saw the church as a refuge? And if he sought protection inside the House of the Lord, what could be more natural than to fortify it, just as he fortified the city? The city was a fortress with utilitarian walls and towers against real invaders; analogously the church was a bulwark against evil in general. The Hildesheim Annals even state specifically that St. Michael was consecrated 'as a bulwark of the peace of the Church and to the salvation and defense of Christendom.'[29]

Evil was real and tangible enough. Thangmar describes the aftermath of the great migrations in his *Life of St. Bernward:* 'A large part of Saxony was laid waste by the savageness of the pirates and other barbarians and subjected continually to the invasions of these brigands. Endangering himself and his men, he [Bernward] was forever trying to ward off this plague, and attacking them in alliance with others, or sometimes only with his own men, he dealt them heavy blows. But, as these invasions could not be averted, because the barbarians held both banks of the Elbe and all the ships and could displace themselves with the greatest ease over all of Saxony, the vigilant priest, in his care for the community entrusted to him, thought deeply about means to wrest the Lord's people from the barbarian savagery. For they nearly reached Hildesheim in their furious attacks, and already looked upon this holy place as their prize. With divine inspiration he built near the boundary of his bishopric, where the rivers Aller and Oder meet, a strongly fortified castle, garrisoned it, repulsed the attacks of the enemy and liberated the Lord's people from this savagery.'[30] The prevailing lawlessness made architects think naturally in terms of defensive construction.

The idea of the church as a sacred fortress grants us a new perspective of all the other features. With the aid of this tempting supposition all parts of the jig-saw puzzle fall into place. For instance, St. Michael was an abbey church. There is nothing unusual in that, because the Early Middle Ages is the golden era of monasticism. Monasteries sprang up like mushrooms; very many men and women took the vows. May this not also be ascribed—at least in part—to refuge-seeking? Was not the taking of vows and the consecration of one's life to God also a withdrawal from the hostile outside world? Significantly, monasticism decreased soon after the evil days of the great migrations were over. It reaches its zenith in the eleventh and twelfth century; after 1300 monasticism gradually declines. The great Gothic churches are cathedrals and parish churches, built for and endowed by lay people.

Even more than by towers, St. Michael is 'protected' by relics. Like charms and amulets, medieval relics were supposed to heal and work miracles, but foremost to protect one from the devil. And so Bernward packs the building with as many relics as he can get hold of. In an age still pretty close to heathenism, in which salvation may have seemed often far away, relics were a tangible proof of the coming Kingdom. Every relic is one more shield. And when his end has come, Bernward is buried safely amidst the sixty-six relics of his crypt and under the protection of St. Michael and his angels.

The dedication of the church is perhaps the strongest evidence for its protective character. Of all saintly protectors, St. Michael is the protector par excellence, the heaven-sent opponent of the devil. Otto the Great gave battle to the Magyars in his name; under his wings the monastic community might perhaps live in peace. And how beautifully are the 'angelic' altars arranged! They stand in the extremities of the building, at the highest possible points. It is as if the angels are invited to post on the walls as sentries. Such a thought is not so far-fetched, for on the west-front of Corvey abbey we can read to this day the following inscription from the year 885: *Civitatem istam tu circumda, Domine, et angeli tui custodiant muros eius* (Enclose this city, Lord, and let thy angels guard its walls).[31]

The other features of St. Michael have now become more understandable too. The heavy walls and the strong isolation seem to be the natural corollary of defensive symbolism. Of course the walls were not made so massive only to give a strong appearance; then they could just as well have been constructed hollow. The main reason for the heavy walls was probably the same that it would be today; to ensure a strong and enduring building. The architect did not dare to use a lighter construction; and so he put heavy arches below the crossing towers on all four sides, and pillars below the nave clerestory walls. But it points in the same direction. For structural timidity testifies to a mistrust in the forces of nature, and such a mistrust may be closely allied to a withdrawal from nature caused by bad social conditions. The world seemed full of dangers, consequently nature was dangerous too, and construction had to be as solid as possible to withstand all mishaps.

We would therefore expect art to be shy of realism too and this is indeed what we find. The few traces of original ornament found on St. Michael are abstract; so are the capitals. Ottonian bronzes or book-illustrations are even further from reality than Byzantine art. The people depicted on the door presented by Bernward to the Hildesheim cathedral have schematic figures and faces. And the monsters in Ottonian sculpture are large and terrifying, just as Abell's theory has led us to expect.

The same abstraction persists in architecture, in the clear-cut geometrical masses, the severe and smooth walls. The Phileban solids of the parts are simply stuck together, retaining their independence. The resultant building shows but a limited formal coherence, which is entirely in keeping with the perception of the discordant world of the early eleventh century. Formal aesthetics emphasizes contrast over harmony. The disintegration of the simple barn of the basilica is paralleled by the complexity of religion: devotion has spread to hundreds of saints and relics.

To be fair, we have to look at the other side of the medal too. There are unificatory tendencies as well: witness the equal transepts, the careful grading down from centre to sides, the close relationship between function and form as shown in the distribution of the altars and the intricate system of proportions. St. Michael is well designed; compared to the earlier churches at Gernrode or Corvey, it is not far short of being a marvel of unity. These unifying forces gain in momentum in the following centuries, as is evinced in the next chapter.

Notre Dame of Amiens
Amiens Cathedral   1220–1269

1. Description

In comparison with the previous age, the Gothic period was a happy time. The turmoil of the great migrations was over and a well-organized feudal society had sprung up. Long caravans of merchants pushed along the safer roads of Europe; commerce prospered and the population grew rapidly. It is estimated that it went up from 42 to 69 millions between 1000 and 1250, an increase of 65%.[1] Though this seems little enough in modern eyes, it is a tremendous growth compared with the stationary or declining population figures of the Dark Ages. A sharp decline set in in 1350, when the Black Death (plague) and other epidemics ravaged Europe— but that was then still a century off. Food for the teeming millions was provided by an improved agriculture and the reclaiming of waste land.[2]

France was ruled by the pious and ascetic St. Louis (1226–1270) whose just and equitable rule ensured him the loyalty of his subjects. He is known in architectural history as the founder of Aigues Mortes, a town on the Rhône estuary built as a starting point for the first of his two crusades. His truly Christian behaviour and the veneration of his subjects earned him a canonization only twenty seven years after his death.

Amiens was originally a Flemish town. Louis' grandfather Philip August added it to the royal realm (1185). In the tenth century it had suffered severely from the Norse raids, but the later Middle Ages were a time of prosperity for Amiens,[3] mainly because of its strategic location. The trade-route for the wool of Britain from the North, and silk, velvet, brocades and spices from the South ran in the early Middle Ages along the Rhône, the Saône and the Meuse, with trade fairs in Champagne, where the two rivers rise. Better shipping and navigation made coastal transport possible. Therefore the Rhône and Meuse lost in importance; the newer route ran past Narbonne, Toulouse and along the French coast.[4]

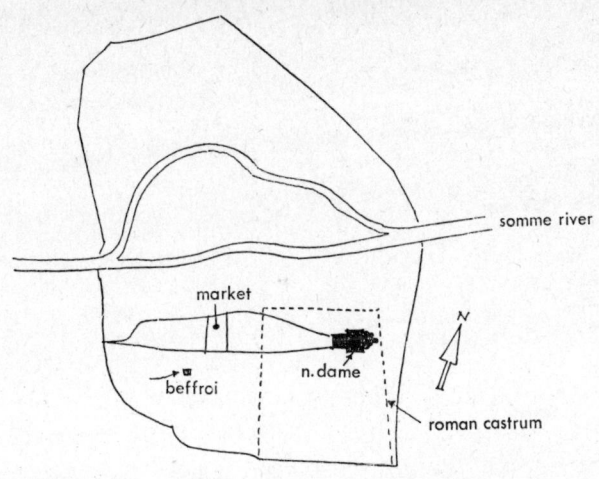

Figure 19. Notre Dame; site (after Ganshof)

The trade of wool and the weaving and dying of cloth became the economic backbone of all Flanders, including Bruges, Damme, Ypres, Ghent and Amiens.

In 1218 Amiens cathedral burned down: it had been consecrated only sixty-six years before. Work on a new cathedral was started at once under the leadership of bishop Evrard de Fouilloy. Two years later sufficient funds had been collected to begin construction; the great work was pushed forward energetically. As a result, Notre Dame of Amiens has been built practically in its entirety in accordance with the design of its original architect, Robert de Luzarches;[5] only the top part of the façade, the lateral chapels and the rose windows deviate considerably from the first design. The speed of construction and the resulting homogeneity in design is rather exceptional in Gothic architecture; many vast undertakings lagged over the centuries or stopped entirely. Rouen cathedral is a patchwork of different periods; the renovation of Le Mans and Beauvais got no further than the chancel and the transept. Economic prosperity in Amiens made the relatively rapid construction of the huge church possible.

Amiens cathedral occupies the site of its predecessor as well as that of St. Firmin, an old church dedicated to the missionary who had christianized the region.[6] It stands at the junction of two important streets, which lead onto a small square in front of the cathedral.[7] The other sides, like the transepts and the chancel with the radiating chapels were originally only visible in part. Narrow alleys ran around Notre Dame on the southern and eastern side; the present squares there are due to the nineteenth century craving for grand vistas. Only the front was intended to be seen in full.

Notre Dame of Amiens has a very deep chancel, surrounded by an ambulatory and radiating chapels, a fairly short transept and a three-aisled nave. The deep chancel was and is reserved for the cathedral chapter; it contains the main altar and is closed at the western end by a gate between the eastern pillars of the crossing.

The central and largest radiating chapel is dedicated to the cult of the Virgin (Notre Dame d'Amiens), the others to St. Augustine, the Apostle James, St. John the Baptist, St. Eloi, St. Nicaise and St. Quentin, of which the latter two are local saints. Nave and transept with the aisles and ambulatory are (and were) public spaces.

Practically the entire interior space is built up of the same spatial unit, varying in dimensions and proportions as need be. That unit is rectangular in plan, and vaulted by a ribbed cross vault. The ribs are carried down to shafts in each of the four corners. By changing the radius of the pointed arches, this unit could be constructed over every rectangle and fitted to each adjoining bay, without lowering the keystones of either transverse or diagonal arches. It is an admirably flexible unit.

The proportions of Notre Dame differ fundamentally from those of the churches previously discussed here. It may be interesting to compare as an example the proportions of the naves of the sixth century church of Sant' Apollinare in Classe, St. Michael and Notre Dame. As the length of the nave we take in Sant' Apollinare the distance from the door to the triumphal arch, in St. Michael the nave proper with the two crossings added and in Notre Dame the distance between the inside of the western front and the rounded bay of the chancel. In each case the same cross-section is carried over the greatest distance:

	width	height	length
Sant' Apollinare	1	1.25	3
St. Michael	1	2	5.4
Notre Dame	1	3	7.3

The proportions show clearly the great increase in height and depth of Amiens cathedral over the earlier churches.

As heavy as is St. Michael, so light and airy is Notre Dame. Though it is a far larger church, and vaulted in addition, only 13.7% of the total area is taken up by solids, and no less than 23% of the total outside surface is glazed! Where St. Michael is isolated, Notre Dame is open, both outside and inside. Not only are its windows larger, but its internal spaces communicate also more easily than in Hildesheim. Nave and transept are separated from the aisles by slender round pillars with four shafts against their sides which correspond to the transverse arches and the nave arcade ('piliers cantonnés' as they are called in French).

NOTRE DAME OF AMIENS 79

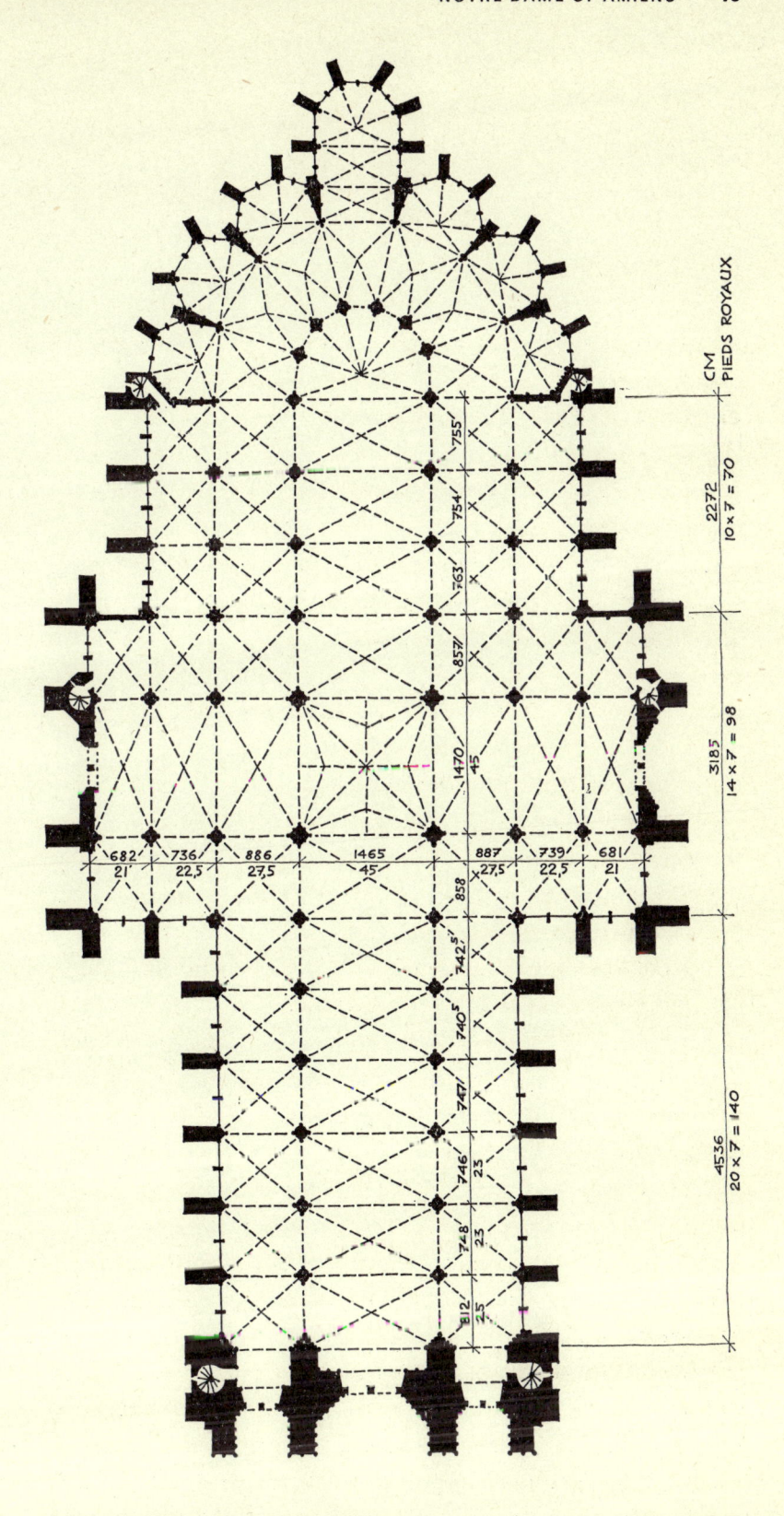

Figure 20. Notre Dame; plan (after Durand)

The shaft of the transverse arch of the nave continues right through the capital of the column. Above that capital two more shafts are added, corresponding to the diagonal arches of the nave vaults. Immediately next to these latter shafts comes the window moulding in the upper part of the clerestory wall. Below that window is a wall area corresponding to the roof over the aisle; it is nearly entirely taken up by a shallow gallery dug into the wall, the triforium. Practically no wall area is left! This contributes greatly to the impression of lightness and plasticity. Again a marked contrast with St. Michael: there we had large unbroken areas of smooth wall; here the wall is reduced to a diaphanous skeleton of shafts, in the characterization of Jantzen.[8] On the outside too there is hardly any wall, only shafts, buttresses and pinnacles. The building is quite plastic, in contrast to the smoothness at Hildesheim.

The plasticity is the natural outcome of the Gothic structural system. A tunnel vault exerts a lateral thrust along its sides. The groin vault, produced by having two tunnel vaults intersect at right angles, gives a lateral thrust only in the four corners. A row of groin vaults in succession lean against each other; the lateral thrust in the longitudinal direction is thus taken up by the vaults themselves. Only at the points of support are we still faced with a lateral thrust, perpendicular to the axis of the row. The vaults of Notre Dame are such rows of cross vaults and the lateral thrust at the supports is taken up by buttresses for the aisles and by flying buttresses for the nave. Raising the crown of the vault above a semicircle has the advantage of diminishing the lateral thrust as well as allowing the vaulting of rectangular bays and the adjustment to neighbouring compartments. The Gothic church can be envisaged as a series of stone canopies supported on slender poles and preserved against tumbling down by flying buttresses.

Such is the basic structure of Gothic. Matters are complicated by the introduction of ribs and shafts; with them we step right into the once famous controversy between Viollet-le-Duc and Pol Abraham.[9] According to Viollet-le-Duc, the webs of the vaults rest on the diagonal ribs and transverse and mural arches; they in turn are supported by their own shafts and finally these bundles of forces are led to the foundations. What Viollet-le-Duc most admired in Gothic architecture was its logic: weights were carried by vertical members, one member for each weight; lateral thrust was taken up by a separate system, i.e. the buttresses. Abraham

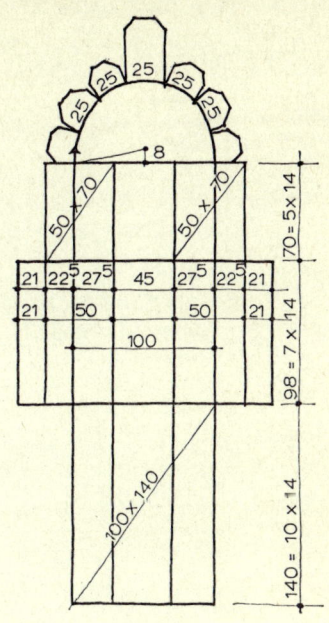

Figure 21. Notre Dame of Amiens; overall dimensions in pieds royaux

attacked this view, which was rank materialism to him. Webs and ribs work in conjunction and it is of course ridiculous to suppose that the slender shafts under the diagonal arches actually carry the weight of the vault. That is done by the total cross-section of the pier, not by one of its components. The ribs and shafts of Gothic architecture are an artistic system, not a form of engineering.

It is here that the separation between physical and symbolic construction can clarify matters. Gothic architecture *is* a system of vaults leaning against each other and resting on slender supports, buttressed from the outside. That much is real, physical construction and unassailable. Whether the ribs really carry the webs, or whether both work in conjunction is often hard to decide, even with the help of modern engineering.

The ribs had however a technical function, if one looks at the *process* of construction rather than the final result. Ribless groin vaults must be constructed over a complete centering, which had to take the full weight of the vaults and hence necessitated a heavy scaffolding as support. With diagonal ribs the construction became much easier. The ribs could be erected over a simple centering and the webs vaulted out of hand. As the ribs weighed only a fraction of the whole vault, the centering supports could be much lighter. But as they are, once constructed, far stronger than a wooden centering, they were able to support the webs, at least during construction. The process of vaulting is greatly simplified by its execution in two stages instead of one.

Also, as pointed out by Foçillon and Frankl,[10] the rib creates an exact line on the groin, which was hard to obtain otherwise. The weight of the ribless groin vault compressed the more or less elastic wooden centering below it, with the result that the groin became a zig-zag line as every second course was bonded in alternately with a different segment of the vault. And finally the ribs are the continuation of the wall shafts, as Gall[11] has pointed out.

Part of the construction is illusory, as Abraham holds. Gothic shafts in Laon stand free of the central pillar; in Canterbury pillar and shafts are made of different stone and not bonded in. Of course such shafts cannot carry much weight. They belong to the symbolic structure; their function is to indicate that the weight of some arch is carried down—'piped down', one might say—to the foundation. In symbolic structure Viollet-le-Duc is no doubt right. The symbolic structure of Amiens is just that model of clarity which he has so eloquently described. The weight of the webs is symbolically carried by the ribs of the diagonal and transverse arches and transmitted to the ground by a strictly logical system of supports, every rib being received on a separate shaft.

Technically the system does not operate with such admirable precision, and even the Gothic architects must have had some inkling of that, as Laon and Canterbury show.

But does that mean that it is exclusively or even primarily a form of art? Admittedly it is so in part, but not necessarily to the extent that we would think today. One cannot apply twentieth century engineering concepts to a thirteenth century building! The calculation of structures practiced today was an art then unknown. Booz and Frankl[12] have shown that Gothic 'science' consisted chiefly of geometry, useful in laying out plans, cutting stone to measure, and transferring drawings into realizable buildings, but hardly sufficient for the calculation of structural stability. For an estimate of the necessary strength of pillars and buttresses the Gothic architects relied on rules of thumb, evolved from actual practice. Arithmetic had not progressed beyond the classical knowledge of Nicomachus of Gerasa, and it seems doubtful whether the architects had mastered even that much. Trial and error determined what could be done and what not; a costly method in modern eyes, but what else could they do? Europe was once littered with Gothic churches which had collapsed soon after their construction. Only the successes still stand today, and they impute Gothic architects with more knowledge than they can take credit for.[13] Even one of the near-faillures has been preserved: Beauvais cathedral. The scaffolding around it is practically permanent.

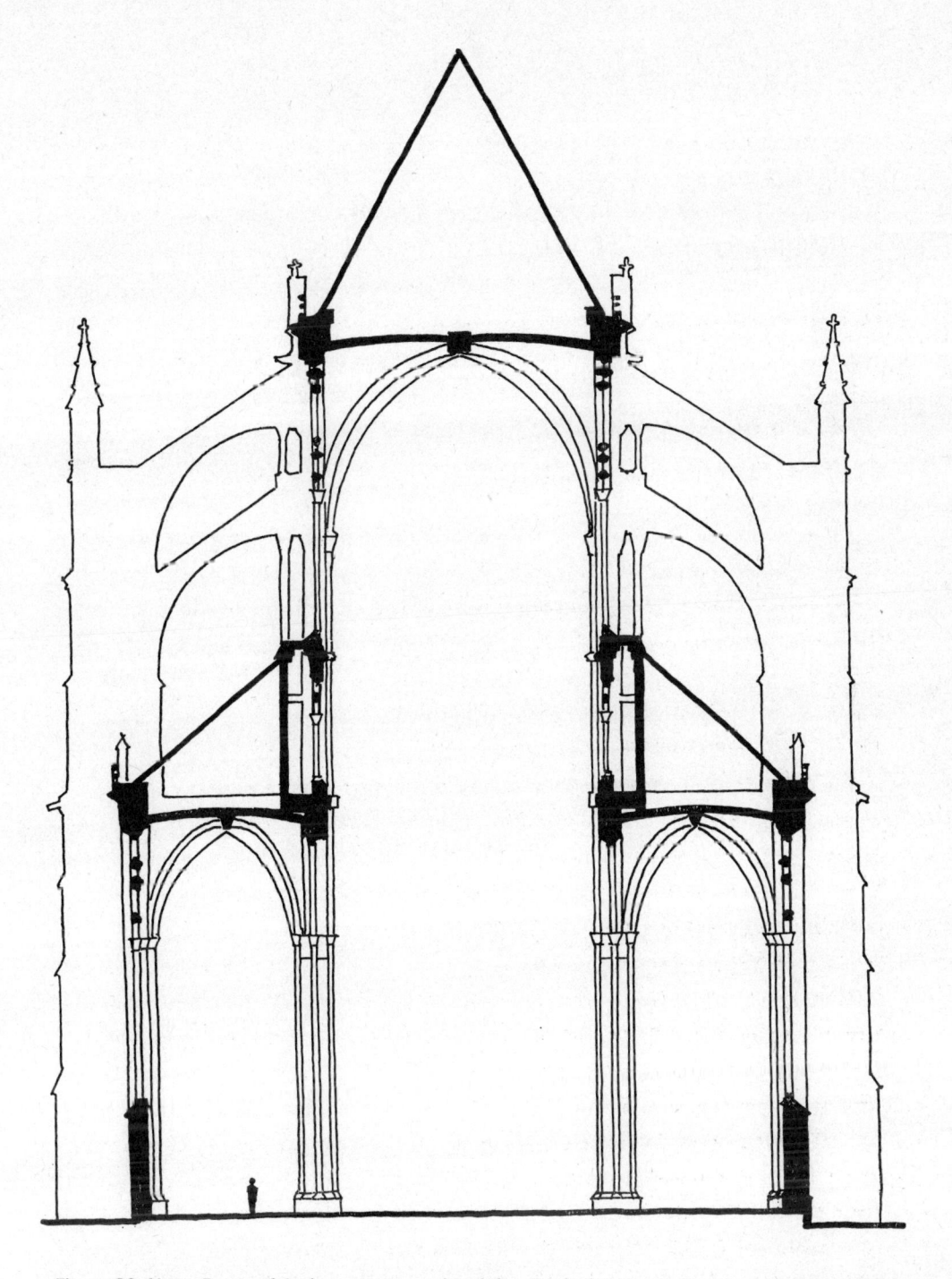

Figure 22. Notre Dame of Amiens; cross-section (after Rapine)

Pol Abraham's view then misses the point. It is not the question whether the ribs actually support the webs of the vaults, but, as Focillon has pointed out, whether the thirteenth century architects *thought* they did; and there is evidence that they indeed believed so.[14] Also, actual and symbolic structure may have been far closer connected in their minds than they are in ours. If even Viollet-le-Duc with far more knowledge of statics could mistake the symbolic structure for the real one, how much easier could this happen to his thirteenth century colleague!

The Gothic architects probably saw symbolic structure as the natural corollary of the actual one—something like two faces of the same coin. They used the system for support, but also for expression, and in all likelihood rarely asked themselves what was what.

The reasons for the ribs—and therewith by and large the *raison d'être* of the Gothic system—cannot be reduced to one single principle. Aesthetically they continue the wall shafts (Gall) and are principal elements of the symbolic structure. Technically they render complete centering superfluous (Kingsley Porter)[15] make a lighter centering possible by construction in two stages (Choisy, Fitchen),[16] facilitate erection (Aubert),[17] reinforce the vault (Masson) and create a precise line on the groin (Focillon, Frankl).

The foregoing discussion and the scanty contemporary records show that Gothic architects displayed a great interest in structure, both actual and symbolic. Once again a profound contrast appears between St. Michael and Notre Dame; the one is structurally timid, where the other is daring; every shaft in Notre Dame has a symbolic structural part to play, St. Michael is structurally mute and indifferent. St. Michael is homogeneous and discontinuous, Notre Dame is of a structure concentrated to the limit (every force seems to be led to some rib or shaft) and largely continuous, as many shafts continue practically without a break to the keystone.

The transverse arches of the nave are received on shafts which here for the first time rise from the pedestal on the ground to the springing of the arch without capitals and bases at intermediary levels. In this respect Amiens represents only a stage in a long-range development, for the ribs and shafts in later Gothic churches have no capitals at all, nor are they interrupted by string courses.

In such late Gothic churches (as for instance St. Maclou in Rouen, begun in 1434) the pillars of the nave and crossing are simply clusters of shafts, without a

Figure 23. Bays of Amiens (left) and Rheims (right)

recognizable cross-section of their own at the core. Here, too, Amiens shows a stage in a continuous process of growth and change. Its *piliers cantonnés* are no longer the perfectly simple cylindrical columns of Hildesheim or St. Benoît-sur-Loire, which were still used in Sens, Paris and Laon. It is a crossbred between that column (ultimately derived from antiquity) and the massive Romanesque compound pier. Its form is an improvement on the experiments in Chartres, Bourges and Soissons and may perhaps have been derived from Rheims. The formal independence of the pillar is safeguarded by arranging four shafts symmetrically around it: two for the transverse arches of the aisle and nave and two for the wall-arches. As the core of the pillar is thicker than the wall above it (Figure 23) the shafts for the diagonal arches could be based on the capital of the main pillar. In Rheims also the shaft below the arch around the clerestory window has its base here. Though this adds to the Gothic relief of the interior, it detracts attention from the simplicity of the structural system, because it treats alike two elements which differ in importance. In this respect Amiens is an advance on Rheims. In Amiens these shafts are based on the heavy string-course below the triforium.

Apart from the almost continuous shaft below the transverse arches, verticality is further enhanced by carrying the central mullion of the clerestory window down, over the central pier in the triforium; by the correspondence in form between the larger triforium arches and the clerestory windows above them, and by the placing of the other window mullions immediately above the apexes of these arches.

Once again, this is an advance on Rheims, where the three parts of the interior elevation (arcade, triforium and clerestory windows) are separated by string courses, stressing horizontality *between* the piers against the verticality of the piers themselves.[18] In Amiens the balance is tipped in the favour of verticality throughout.

An important factor in the excellent preservation of Amiens cathedral are its tremendous foundations, extending no less than twenty-three feet below the floor. The church is constructed of a fine local limestone, giving the widest possible scope to the stone-mason. Capitals and sculpture are renowned for their delicacy and precision in execution.

The capitals of Notre Dame and the large string-course just below the triforium are decorated with vine-leaves and buds, no doubt modelled after the tendrils in the vineyards around Amiens. Naturalism also prevails in the sculpture of the portals. Instead of the stiff hieratical figure of Ottonian times, Christ is represented in the 'beau Dieu' of Amiens as a gentle figure of nearly classical nobility.[19] Mary, in the southern transept portal, shows a faint smile. Other figures like angels, apostles, and saints are smiling too. All are depicted with great naturalness and carefully realistic detail.

The sculpture is distributed in accordance with a strict iconographical programme. The central portal of the western front is dedicated to the Last Judgment, with Christ as the central figure; the two flanking portals are dedicated to the Virgin Mary and to St. Firmin. The transept portals have likewise the Virgin and St. Firmin as main themes. The collation of a mere local saint with the Mother of the Lord may seem strange at first sight, but can perhaps be explained from their function. Both are intermediaries between man and God, somewhat in the same sense as the nobleman in feudal society was a link between commoner and king. Petitions had to pass through the 'proper channels' from commoner through the count to the overlord, and prayer went along a similar line through a saint or through the Virgin. She is of course the most obvious and prominent connection between the purely human world and the divine. The cult of the Virgin, already quite strong in the Early Medieval Church, received a new impetus from the twelfth century change in attitude towards women in aristocratic culture, expressed in the troubadours' love-lyrics and the elaborate ceremonials at tournaments. These factors make the frequent consecration of thirteenth century cathedrals and parish-churches to Mary understandable in part, though they are certainly not the only reasons.[20]

The tympan of the central western portal is divided into three registers. Christ sits enthroned in judgment in the uppermost register, flanked by Mary and the Apostle John who pray—or intercede—for the souls of the dead. Below that the blessed and the damned are represented and the bottom register shows the dead rising from their graves with St. Michael weighing their souls on scales. Figures from the Old and New Testament fill out the rest of the space in the wide archway.

Above the three portals and just below the great rose window stands a row of figures known as the gallery of Kings. According to Mâle[21] they must be interpreted as Kings of Judea. Christ is the last and supreme King; the others have been put there as a demonstration of the continuity of Judean Kingship. Together with the ancestors of Christ from the tree of Jesse, another beloved Gothic motif, they show Christ to be the pre-ordained successor in a line of kings and in a regular family tree, rather than to treat him as a completely isolated phenomenon (as is usual in Protestant theology).

Two features stand out from the sculptural programme. The first is its richness; the cathedral sculpture—as has often been noted—is a sort of Biblical encyclopedia, displaying a large part of the important scriptural scenes from Adam to the Apocalypse. It aims at *universality*.

The second is that of order. As the foregoing shows, and more detailed examination confirms, all persons represented are assigned a particular place in accordance with their relations with the Lord. In other words, the whole scheme is a demonstration of the *hierarchy of heaven*.[22]

Universality, a sense of order and of a hierarchy of values apply also to the building itself.

Gothic churches resemble each other far more than Romanesque ones; their basic scheme remains fixed (at least in France) and their 'modular' unit, the cross-vault on rectangular plan, is always the same. The variety of interior spaces and corresponding exterior masses found in Hildesheim is replaced here by a striking regularity. An endless repetition of perfectly equal bays stretches from west front to chancel. Every part of space, every detail is subordinated to the grand simplicity of the whole; the aisles resemble the nave, the transept has the same cross-section as the nave, and even the apse and ambulatory deviate as little as possible from the set standard. Where St. Michael is 'picturesque' and variegated, Notre Dame is orderly and standardized. St. Michael with its equal transepts and system of proportions shows an attempt at the unification of architectural composition; such efforts are carried to their conclusion in Amiens. Given the functional requirements of a deep chancel and a series of subsidiary altars around it, it is hard to imagine a more regular building around them.

Yet the design does not show the absolute equality of spaces typical of, for instance, a modern apartment or office building. The aisles are definitely subordinate to the nave, and the radiating chapels are similar to, but lower in rank than the apse, or even the central Lady Chapel. Side portals are subordinated to the central portal in size, position and iconographical content; shafts are subordinated to the main piers to which they are attached. Within a regular system parts and details are arranged in a hierarchy,[23] whilst our regular designs are based on absolute equality.

2. Analysis

That the Gothic cathedrals are carriers of a symbolic meaning—in the sense of second level meaning—may seem beyond doubt. The strictly programmatic iconography of the sculpture, similar on all salient points for Chartres, Rheims, Paris and Amiens, is a strong indication for the presence of such a meaning in the buildings; moreover, this meaning is explicitly mentioned in the contemporary or near-contemporary literature. For instance, Abbot Suger of St. Denis writes: 'Thus, when, —out of my delight in the beauty of the house of God—the loveliness of the many-coloured gems (on the reliquaries) has called me away from external cares, and worthy meditation has induced me to reflect, transferring that which is material to that which is immaterial, on the diversity of the sacred virtues; then it seems to me that I see myself dwelling, as it were, in some strange region of the universe, which neither exists entirely in the slime of the earth, nor entirely in the purity of Heaven; and that, by the grace of God, I can be transported from this inferior to that higher world in an anagogical manner.'[24] And as an example of such 'transportation' by means of symbols in the actual church we may quote Suger again: 'The midst of the edifice, however, was suddenly raised aloft by columns representing the number of the Twelve Apostles and, secondarily, by as many columns in the side-aisles signifying the number of the (minor) Prophets, according to the Apostle who buildeth spiritually: *Now therefore ye are no more strangers and foreigners,* says he, *but fellow citizens with the saints and of the household of God; and are built upon the foundation of the apostles and prophets; Jesus Christ Himself being the chief cornerstone* which joins one wall to the other. ...'[25] The italicized passage is from Ephesians, II-19, and the words were evidently taken to be applicable in the figurative sense as well as in a literal one in the building, as the addition of the clause 'which joins one wall to the other' shows. Numerous later books contain lengthy expositions on the symbolic meaning of the church edifice. The most famous of these is the *Rationale Divinorum Officiorum* by Durandus of Mende. He writes: 'The church is also called the House of God, and sometimes the House of the Lord, and at other times basilica (royal house), for the dwellings of the earthly kings are so called, and with so much more reason can this title apply to our prayer houses, the dwelling of the King of Kings!

'Sometimes it is designated by the name of "city", because of the community of saintly inhabitants which, armed with the weapons furnished by the Scriptures, repulse the attacks of the heretics; it is built of stone and a variety of materials, because the merits of the different saints are varied too. ... The disposition of the material church resembles that of the human body; the sanctuary, the place of the altar, represents the head; the transepts represent the arms and hands, and the rest of the building towards the west is the rest of the body.'[26] Such an explanation leaves us in a quandary: is the church to be taken as a heavenly palace, or should it be interpreted as an anthropomorphic symbol? It is typical of the entire Rationale that it heaps meaning upon meaning, without apparent connection. Durandus gives us not one interpretation, but a multitude; and as these meanings are often outright contradictory,[27] we get as little grasp on the building as if he had given us none... For we would like to get down, not to an interpretation which *could* be applied, but rather to the one which *was* applied, in actuality; one which would furnish us with the 'why' and 'how' of its forms. Durandus fails to give us this. His purpose seems to have been to spur his readers on to *find* a theological analogy in every material part; art-historical explanations were as foreign to him as his analogies are to us.

Two explanatory theories of Gothic church architecture have been propounded in recent years. Sedlmayr[28] interprets it as a poetic symbol for the Heavenly Jerusalem. The Gothic cathedral consists of rows and rows of canopies (our modular units) floating on the slenderest of poles. They represent the sky. But the theory itself rests on rather slender supports too: the only evidence which can be adduced is the iconography of the entrance portal (through the last Judgment the faithful enter into the heavenly Jerusalem), the passage in Durandus quoted above, and the rejected theory of Kitschelt.

A second and more elaborate theory is that of Von Simson.[29] His point of departure is the new chancel of St. Denis, the earliest example of Gothic architecture, and fortunately described at length by its builder, Abbot Suger. Suger's books on the building and the consecration of the new parts of the church are strongly influenced by the writings of Denis the pseudo-Areopagite. This Denis was wrongly believed to be the same as the third century French bishop, who was venerated in St. Denis as the patron saint of France. Panofsky in his translation of Suger's books has pointed out the many paraphrases and allusions to the 'Corpus areopagiticum' of the pseudo-Denis. Suger in particular devotes some passages to the increasing amount of light entering his new chancel: ... 'that elegant and praiseworthy extension in (the form of) a circular string of chapels, by virtue of which the whole (church) would shine with the wonderful and uninterrupted light of most sacred windows, pervading the interior beauty.'[30] Light, Suger says elsewhere, is of value in so far as it reminds us of the true Light, the Light of the mind: 'Bright is the noble work; but being nobly bright, the work should brighten the minds, so that they may travel through the true lights to the True Light where Christ is the true door.'[31] Light is indeed an important and novel feature in Gothic churches, and light is *also* one of the main themes of the pseudo-Denis. Hence, Von Simson concludes, Gothic architecture, which started at St. Denis, must be interpreted as a symbolic representation of the metaphysics of light of the pseudo-Denis.

The two theories may have contributed something to our understanding of Gothic, but both must to my opinion be rejected as completely inadequate.[32] Gothic architecture, of which Amiens is such a splendid example, is characterized by a careful equilibrium of parts and an all-pervading unity of design. We do less than justice to Robert de Luzarches and his colleagues if we emphasize one par-

V. Exterior of Amiens cathedral

Overleaf:

VI. Interior of Amiens cathedral

VII. Amiens cathedral: southern aisle with part of radiant chapel on the left

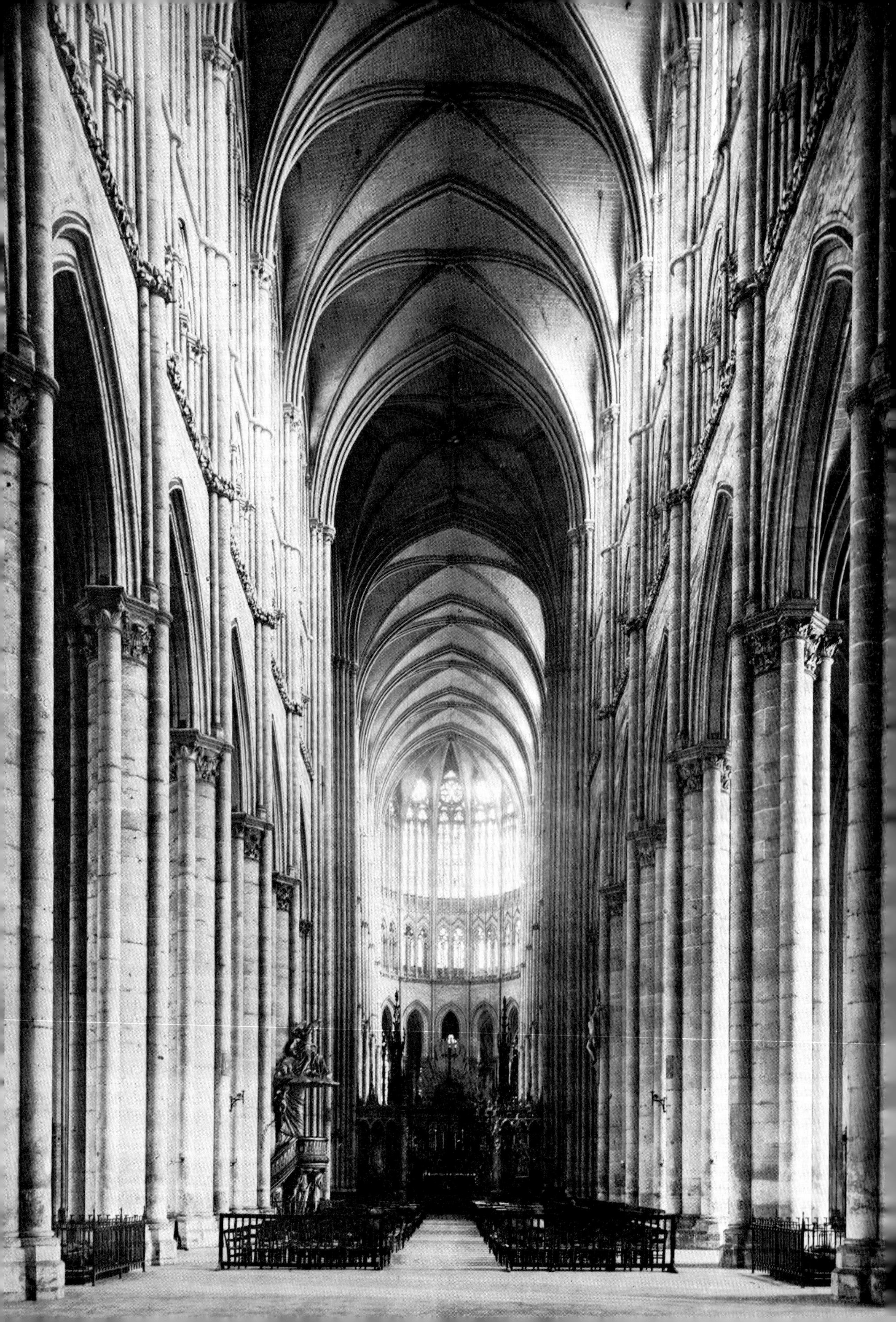

VI   VII

VIII. Amiens cathedral: longitudinal section through the chancel and the Lady Chapel

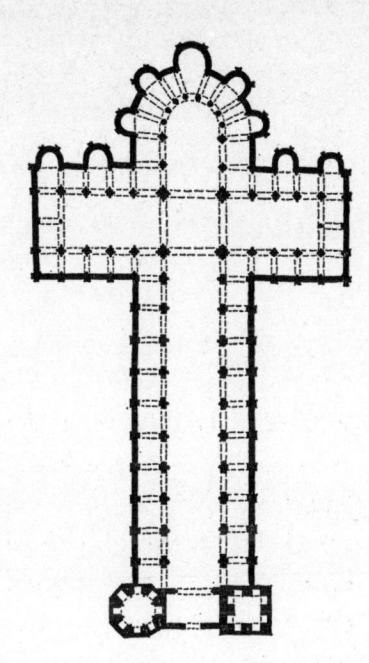

Figure 24. Tours, St. Martin; plan (after Lesueur)

ticular detail, be it the modular unit or the window, as the source from which the design originated.

If Gothic architecture *is* all of one piece, it should also be explained as a whole.

Moreover, the continuity of architectural history does not receive its due by taking *one* building and *one* set of rather accidental circumstances as the main origin of Gothic. St. Denis was a pioneer building, true enough, but it is only one of many. If Von Simson is right, windows would be small before St. Denis and large after; instead they increased gradually. By and large Gothic architecture develops slowly and systematically from Romanesque architecture, *and it is this development, which is significant*,[33] rather than any particular detail. To understand Amiens cathedral, we must compare it with what came before. It is then seen that the (or rather: some) churches of medieval France can be arranged in a chain, in which the differences between each two links are rather small, and in which the transition between early medieval and Gothic architecture is effected gradually and logically. Architects learn from each other and copy from each other and then improve on the schemes they copied. This is done today, and there is no reason to suppose it to be different in the thirteenth century, when no particular importance was attached to originality.

The first link in the chain is again the Early Christian basilica. The elements which persisted through all change are the nave accompanied by two lower aisles, the transept (as a principle, not as a form) and the more or less round apse. As in St. Michael, they are traditional elements.

For a second link I would like to make a large jump in history and take St. Martin in Tours (1003–1014)[34] a building slightly earlier than St. Michael and having perhaps influenced the latter in the design of its crypt. St. Martin, entirely destroyed in the French revolution, is the earliest known example of a church with ambulatory and radiating chapels, a motif created for—perhaps even by—the demands of the liturgy.

As in St. Michael, the cult of relics required a multiplication of altars and hence of chapels. But in contrast to St. Michael there is only an eastern chancel. Monastic reform in France brought about a strict separation of the brethren in the eastern choirstalls and the laity in the western nave.[35]

In form the ambulatory goes probably back to the ring crypt and the circulation of pilgrims around a relic. A crypt was made impossible in Tours by the condition of the ground. And so the ambulatory was put above ground. But for the transept chapels, the larger and deeper 'chevet', and the profound differences in proportions, the plan of St. Martin is that of Notre Dame of Amiens. A link between the two is the plan of Pontigny abbey church (1170).

The elevations of Notre Dame are likewise the happy outcome of much experimentation and fumbling. Roofing in wood was quite as usual in France as it was in Germany around 1000 A.D. But wooden roofs burnt down easily and frequently, especially as the majority of the houses around the churches were still entirely constructed in wood. This stimulated the search for a system of vaulting adequate for the basilical church. The most obvious solution would be to carry barrel vaults over aisles and nave; but such a vault pushes the clerestory walls outward and with their light arcades on the ground they are hardly able to withstand the thrust. One solution was to raise the aisles to the height of the nave so the three barrel vaults would lean against each other; the outer vaults of the aisles were held in place by buttresses (St. Savin sur Gartempe). The basilical cross-section might be preserved by dividing these high aisles into two stories (St. Foy de Conques). But far more promising were the designs which reduced the lateral thrust itself, either by putting barrel vaults with their axis perpendicular to the nave walls over transverse arches (Tournus) or by using groin-vaults (Vézelay).

The latter solution gives a concentrated horizontal thrust at the corners; some thoughtful architects countered this by hidden flying buttresses (Caen, Durham) and the system of Amiens was technically complete.[36]

It only lacked the ribs and shafts. Shafts on the walls—and thus more plastic architecture—occur in the wooden roofed churches of Normandy, for example in

Jumièges and Mont St. Michel. The earliest ribbed crossvaults are found in Durham cathedral (1096–1133), soon followed in France by the chapter house of Jumièges, the ambulatory of Morienval, and the church of Lessay.

The system proved its suitability and strength in practice, and architects gradually became more daring, reducing the walls and increasing the windows. From Centula (799) to Amiens, the churches become ever brighter and more airy. Intermediate links are for instance: St. Foy de Conques, Caen, and Lessay again.

The triforium, due to the wish to dissolve the wall as much as possible, and techically necessary because of the abutting roofs over the aisles, is the outcome of a long series of experiments with galleries. Enumeration becomes tedious; we only mention Mont St. Michel, Cluny, Sens, St.-Germain-des-Prés, Noyon, Cambrai and Paris for the sake of completeness. The two-tower façade of Amiens has again Normandic prototypes in Jumièges and Caen, which were handed down through examples like St. Denis and Senlis. Sculpture becomes more naturalistic with the advance of the Middle Ages: the figures of St. Sernin in Toulouse are quite schematic; Moissac, Vézelay, Chartres West come increasingly closer to realism. And so we can go on and on with long lists of names for every detail. Though entirely in line with the Gothic predilection for hierarchy, it would bore the reader as much as the author; let it suffice that it can be done, and the curious may be referred to other literature.[37]

What does it all mean? It shows that Notre Dame of Amiens is the outcome of centuries of experiments, and in a way, a summing up of all knowledge hitherto acquired. Amiens cathedral itself is but a link in a chain; later churches become even lighter, more 'steely' in their slender supports, and have still larger glass areas.

This precludes any form from being the intentional carrier of a particular literary meaning. All forms are links in a morphological chain; every one of them belongs to church architecture by habit rather than by conscious choice. *Not the forms in themselves are important, but the development.*

Disregarding for the moment minor points of detail, this development is consistent throughout.[38] All through the two centuries between St. Michael and Notre Dame, the churches become loftier, more airy, less isolated. The interest in symbolic construction grows as the problems of vaulting are mastered. Smooth wall surfaces are gradually covered with a panoply of shafts; architecture becomes ever more three-dimensional. Composition evolves from the disjointed masses of Hildesheim to the perfect unity of Amiens. Sculpture changes from schematism to naturalism and sculptural detail from the abstract to the naturalistic. And in a perfect parallel to this development, society turns from the chaos of the migrations to the relative order of the thirteenth century; hard times are followed by increasing prosperity. It seems obvious to connect the two.

After this lengthy analysis, we are now perhaps in a position to disentangle—however tentatively—the various levels of meaning. The first is the parallel between the dazzling brightness and exalted height of Amiens cathedral and the relatively bright and happy times; only too obvious as a parallel, yet perhaps useful for pointing the way to deeper layers of meaning.

On the second level, that of conscious symbolism, we are faced at once with abundance and paucity. Durandus and Suger provide us with a wealth of material; but its very richness shows it to be of little use. If the church is a symbol for such a diversity of things, and for all at the same time, how are we to pick on the symbolism which influenced the form of the building? The theories of Sedlmayr and Von Simson tackle the question from the wrong end, I believe.

Certainly the daylight in the church was seen as a symbol for the Light of Heaven, but this need not have been the creative force behind the larger windows. Undoubtedly the church was called a symbolical image for the heavenly Jerusalem; the Apocalyptic central portal shows as much. But this interpretation followed rather than preceded the church actually built. Nowhere did it influence the Gothic architects, whose humble origin and practical training precluded such philosophical speculations. The intentions of Suger and Durandus were quite different from imposing a symbolical image beforehand. They did not try to explain the design of the church in terms of modern art-history, but to provide their readers with food for spiritual thought. The faithful should use the church and its decorations as a lever to elevate themselves into a spiritual realm. In the humblest stone, the tiniest base they should seek an analogy to the Scriptures. This way of thinking is not quite as outmoded as it may seem, for many a modern parson commends his flock to look for the hand of God in the tiny flowers in the field. In Amiens cathedral—as in these flowers—one looks in vain for a direct connection. It is an allegorical symbolism, *using* the forms rather than creating them.

Even the two-tower façade has lost its original meaning in the mist of history. Its origin is hazy, as it is of most early medieval forms. But *if* it was a symbol, it was probably connected with the (symbolic) defense of the church against demons from the west, like the western chancel of St. Michael and the towers around that church.[39] By the thirteenth century towers have become part and parcel of the architectural appearance of churches, much as they are today. They are traditional elements.

A tradition developed for over two centuries determined the main outlines of Notre Dame. To it we owe the basilical plan and cross-section, the transept, and the chancel, ambulatory and radiating chapels. The deep chancel was also a functional element, for an important cathedral like Amiens had a long list of canons and prebendaries.

There remain as *new* elements, new in comparison with St. Martin de Tours: the immense size and exalted proportions in depth and height; the openness both towards the outside and within Notre Dame itself; the plasticity of the surfaces, accompanying and partly resulting from the explicit symbolic structure; the confidence and apparent ease of construction as compared to the timidity of St. Michael; the unity of the overall composition; the naturalism in the sculpture and finally, the hierarchies in iconography and composition. All are products of a development, and all can—I believe—be explained from the social conditions.

We start with the last, the preference for hierarchies. Panofsky has shown that the hierarchy in Gothic architecture is closely paralleled by the hierarchies of Scholastic philosophy.[40] The very same system of subordination of parts to the whole, and parts of parts below them pervades the *Summa* of St. Thomas. Should we consider Scholastic philosophy then as the originator of this form of architectural composition? It seems more reasonable to suppose a common source for both. Scheler has suggested that the hierarchical way of thinking, which is typical of Scholastic philosophy, reflects the structure of feudal society.[41] It, too, is characterized by relations of subordination and superposition: the king at the top, below him his vassals, below that more vassals and the tenants and serfs at the bottom of the pyramid, exactly like the theological pyramid of Thomas with God at the top and the people at the base. To think of the organization of heaven in terms of the earth seems the most natural thing to do. Hugh of St. Victor writes in the twelfth century that from the visible hierarchy of men the invisible hierarchy of heaven may be learned.[42] Today we would only reverse cause and effect. Schelers remark can be extended, I think, to Gothic architecture.

Order and prosperity made the thirteenth century a happy time, though not perhaps to a modern observer, had he been transposed to Gothic France. He would have found, as Abelard did, 'princes violent, prelates drunken, judges mercenary'. But it was a good time to live in *in comparison to the preceding age*. We would sorely miss our railroads, hospitals, policemen and plumbing; but not thirteenth century man, who was ignorant of such blessings. To him feudal order, a relative reduction in warfare, an abundance of food, and an increase in material conditions in general represented the march of civilization. He had good reason to be optimistic: all went better and better all the time.

Perhaps the most remarkable feature of Gothic society in comparison to the periods before and after it, was its feeling of unity. Relations between serf and master were on the whole still felt as a blessing ensuring protection, not as a yoke hard to bear. Unity and high-mindedness made the crusades possible; who would be able to conceive, let alone carry through, such idealism today? Several passages from thirteenth century writings testify to this happy sense of 'all belonging to one family'. We quote Suger on the building of St. Denis: 'Whenever the columns were hauled from the bottom of the slope with knotted ropes, both our own people and the pious neighbours, nobles and commonfolk alike, would tie their arms, chests and shoulders to the ropes and, acting as draft animals, drew the columns up; and on the declivity in the middle of the town the diverse craftsmen laid aside the tools of their trade and came out to meet them, offering their own strength against the difficulty of the road, doing homage as much as they could to God and the Holy Martyrs.'[43]

Another story in the same vein, but less sermonizing, is the following anecdote from de Joinville's *Memoirs of Louis IX, King of France*. The ship on board of which the king returned from his first crusade has struck on a sandbank and been damaged. The mariners advise the king to change to another ship. 'The king summoned his council on what was to be done, and they unanimously agreed to what the mariners had proposed; but the king called the captains again to him, and asked them, on the faith and loyalty which they owed him, whether, if the ship were their own, and full of merchandise, they would quit it. They all said they would not; for that they would prefer risking their lives to the loss of such a vessel, which would cost them from forty to fifty thousand livres. "Why then," said the king, "do you advise me to quit her?" They replied, "Sire, you and we are two different sorts of things; for there is no sum, however great, that can be had in compensation for the loss of yourself, the queen, and your three children; and we will never advise that you should put yourself in such risk."

' "Now," said the king, "I will tell you what I think of the matter. Suppose I quit this ship, there are five or six hundred persons on board, who will remain in the island of Cyprus for fear of the danger that may happen to them should they stay on board; and there is not," added the king, "one among them who is more attached to his own person, than I am myself, and if we land they will lose all hopes of returning to their own country. I therefore declare, I will rather put myself, the queen, and my children, in this danger, under the good providence of God, than make such numbers of people suffer as are now with me." '[44]

This sense of unity is reflected in Amiens cathedral, on the third and unconscious level of symbolism. The same modular unit is used throughout; perfect regularity reigns everywhere. The regularity grew in architecture as order increased in society. As people felt unified, architects strove for unity in design too, doubtless without being conscious of any causal relation.

And unity characterizes not only an individual church like Notre Dame, but the Gothic style as a whole. Gothic churches, notwithstanding their variety, resemble each other to a far greater extent than either Romanesque or Renaissance ones. That universality is, to my opinion, due to that same sense of unity. Finally, the comprehensiveness of the iconographical programme—the church as an encyclopedia of Biblical history—is yet another testimony to the effort at unification.

As conditions improved, medieval man slowly emerged from his battlemented fortress, like a turtle from his shell. His attitude to the outside world changed; it was not so bad after all. Feeling gradually more at ease, he began to trust his fellow creatures and discover the beauties of nature. Figurative art shows the results of this change of mind. Villard de Honnecourt, a Gothic architect, draws animals and plants in his sketchbook from real life, and no longer copies them from books. The vineleaves on the string-course and capitals in Amiens and the naturalistic sculpture on the portals may tell us that Gothic man is on a good footing with nature, because he trusts the outside world in general.

This confidence carries over into the realm of construction. Again, the gradual lightening of supports, the increase in window sizes, and the development of the Gothic vaulting system go hand in hand with the improvements in social life. Of course the accumulation of technical experience plays a large part, perhaps the largest. But Gothic architects stretch their daring to the limits of the possible, and sometimes beyond them. For that I can think of no better reason than their confidence in the forces of nature and their belief in their own skill. The whole apparatus of ribs, shafts, responds and pillars demonstrates that they *knew* what they did and were proud to show it. And in structure too they worked for unification. St. Michael had a discontinuous and homogeneous structure; Amiens cathedral is continuous and concentrated.

Continuity increases still after Amiens; in fourteenth and fifteenth centuries the capitals disappear, one single rib runs from floor to keystone.[45] Two different members have merged into one.

Notre Dame is far more plastic than St. Michael. Partly this is caused by the welter of ribs and shafts, but the plasticity continues even there where it is not needed by the symbolic structure, as in the deeply recessed portals. This heightened plasticity can perhaps be interpreted in part as an expression of naturalism, and its opposite in Hildesheim as a form of 'abstraction'. For is not the world of nature three-dimensional too? And, more telling to a modern architect, is not our modern abstract art accompanied by the same smoothness we find in Hildesheim?

As confidence increased the church lost its defensive appearance. No heavy wall separates inside from outside in Amiens. Aisles, nave, transept and chancel are open towards each other and daylight pours in through enormous windows; isolation has gone. As the need for protection decreased, the symbols of defense went out. People opened their hearts and churches their walls.

And finally, the immense size and the exalted proportions may be also ascribed to optimism, I think. None but a man confident in his skill and believing that God's blessing rested on the work of his hands, would dare to raise huge vaults to such dazzling heights on such slender supports. And from that, may be, we can understand why proportionately so many Gothic churches took centuries to finish, if they were ever finished. The confidence of the age induced the patrons to start on the grandest schemes, without questioning themselves whether they could ever be completed. The cathedrals of Cologne, Ulm and Regensburg were only finished in the nineteenth century; Beauvais was never finished at all. Countless churches in Western Europe have a Gothic chancel and ambulatory; a silent testimony to an age of optimism in which kings could be canonized and crusades believed in.

Pazzi Chapel
Florence   1443–1478

1. Description

Every year, thousands of tourists circulate through the huge church of Santa Croce to enjoy its art-treasures. Only a small proportion of them pays a visit to the Cappella Pazzi, and most of these hastily withdraw from its austere gray and white interior to the sunny cloisters outside, wondering why this little building is marked with three stars in their guide-books.[1] Its serenity and simplicity are deceptive; it is an architecture for the architect.

The chapel was commissioned by the Pazzi, who were rival bankers of the Medici and therefore at enmity with them. At a time when the Medici were embroiled with the pope, the Pazzi financed the papal acquisition of Imola, which threatened the trade routes of the Florentine republic. Lorenzo de Medici countered by depriving the Pazzi of an inheritance. The Pazzi then attempted to finish off their rivals. They succeeded in killing Giuliano de Medici, but Lorenzo escaped. Popular feeling ran high against the murderers and Lorenzo had all participants hanged, including an archbishop from Pisa (1478). The surviving Pazzi were banished with loss of property. They returned in 1494 when Piero de Medici had been exiled in turn.

In 1429 Andrea dei Pazzi committed himself by contract to the Franciscan convent of Santa Croce to build a new chapter house.[2] His aims were the same as those of bishop Bernward of Hildesheim: a votive offering to God, a dignified family grave in the neighbourhood of the altar and relics of the church, and the obligation to the monks of Santa Croce to pray for his soul. As Bandmann has shown, chapter houses were quite often used for such purposes, particularly because the daily prayers for the dead were a standard part of the transactions of a monastery when it convened in chapter.

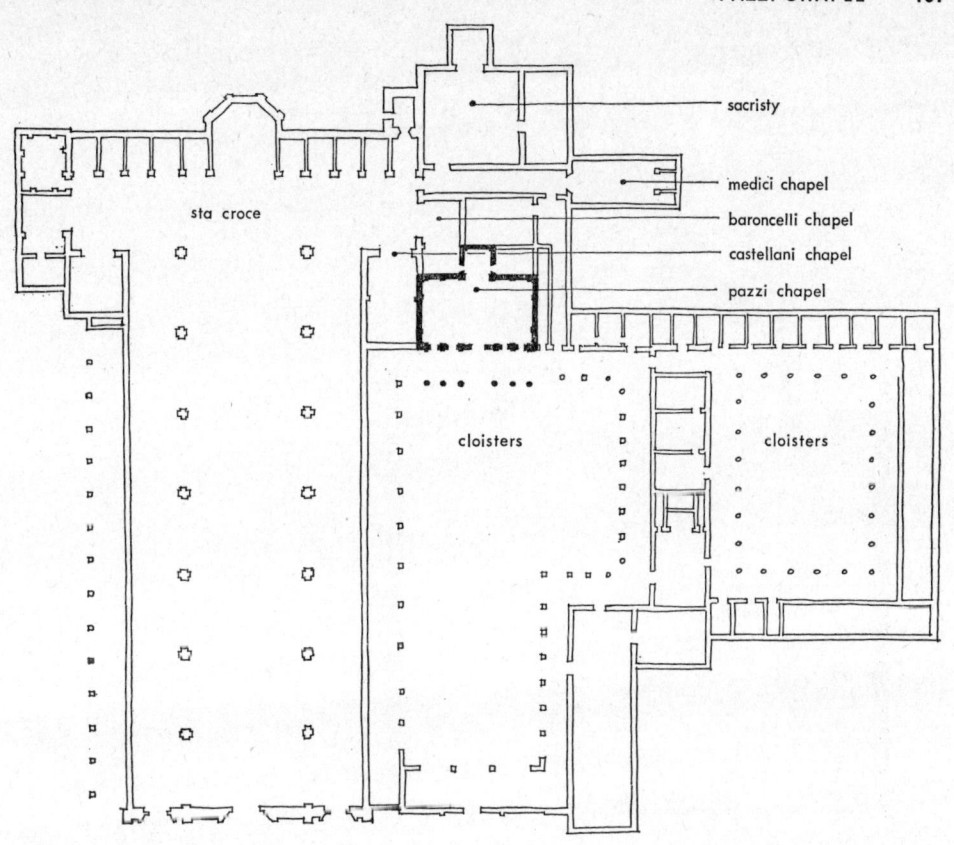

Figure 25. Pazzi Chapel; site (after Paatz)

Other Florentine families built chapels in the S. Croce complex: the Niccolini, Salviati, Bardi, Castellani, Baroncelli and also the arch-enemies of the Pazzi, the Medici. All these chapels cluster around the transept and chancel of the church and all were intended as mausolea. The Pazzi Chapel adjoins the earlier Castellani and Baroncelli chapels.

A plan or a model for the Pazzi Chapel was made by Filippo Brunelleschi, perhaps already in 1430. Work on the building was probably not started before 1443,[3] three years before the death of the architect. The completion of the building trailed over the years; Sanpaolesi has found recently that the main dome was completed in 1459 and the dome over the entrance only in 1461.[4] It is still not finished entirely: the top part of the portico is clearly a provisional arrangement. The abortive conspiracy of 1478 put a stop to all further construction. As work continued for a long time after the death of the architect, it is far from certain whether the chapel follows Brunelleschi's design in all respects, particularly as Brunelleschi is described in the biography of Manetti as relying often only on a ground-plan, indicating what he wanted as elevation 'by word of mouth'.

The interior of the chapel though has never been called in question. It corresponds in style and details closely to other works by the same architect, such as San

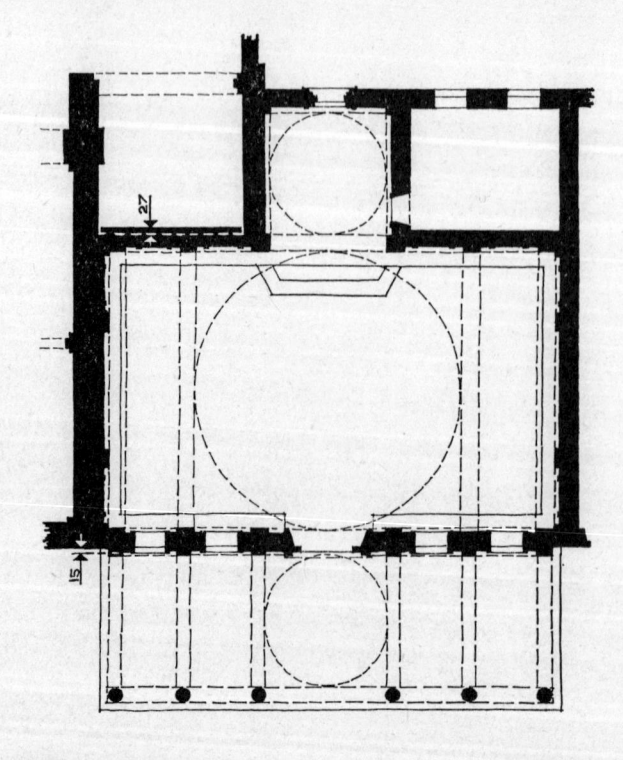

Figure 26. Pazzi Chapel; section and plan (after Stegmann-Gegmüller)

Lorenzo with its Old Sacristy, Santo Spirito and the Palazzo di Parte Guelfa. The portico though is different in style; the vault, completely covered with small-scale ornamentation, would seem foreign to his preference for large, simple forms.

Sanpaolesi has suggested that this entire portico is a later addition,[5] which deviates from the original plan; Brunelleschi intended to finish the chapel with a façade in relief. In support of this theory he points to the recessed layers of brickwork and the walled-up window above the vault of the portico.

I believe this theory to be untenable for three reasons. First, traditionally, chapter houses give onto the cloisters of the convent, which run past their entrance. In Sanpaolesi's hypothesis, the Pazzi Chapel would be an exception to this rule and the only building on the S. Croce cloisters without a portico, which could not be entered dry during rain. The second reason is even more decisive. Without a portico, the daylight falling through the large windows in the front of the chapel would dominate completely. The small bull's-eyes in the cupola would not make any sense, as their contribution to the lighting would be negligible. Such a method of lighting, from the side rather than from above, seems aesthetically objectionable to me, and stands in sharp contrast to the lighting of San Lorenzo, the Old Sacristy and S. Spirito. Finally, the proportions of the Pazzi Chapel may also contain an argument in favour of a portico, as will be shown later on.

But Sanpaolesi is right in his doubts about the portico in its present form. It seems possible that the architect who continued the work after Brunelleschi's death in 1446 had only a plan to work from, and finished the superstructure to the best of his abilities. Brunelleschi may have intended to put a flat ceiling and a simple lean-to roof above the portico (Figure 29).

The interior of the chapel consists of a square central compartment, covered by a melon-dome on pendentives, and on each side a very short adjacent compartment with a tunnel-vault over it. The elevation of the central compartment below the dome, with its two concentric arches, corresponds with the two lateral elevations, and shows the same system as the interior elevation towards the chancel of the Old Sacristy. The two large blank walls in the centres of the lateral elevations were undoubtedly intended, as Van Regteren Altena has said,[6] to be used for the funeral monuments of the Pazzi family. The correspondence between lateral and frontal elevations suggests a central plan.

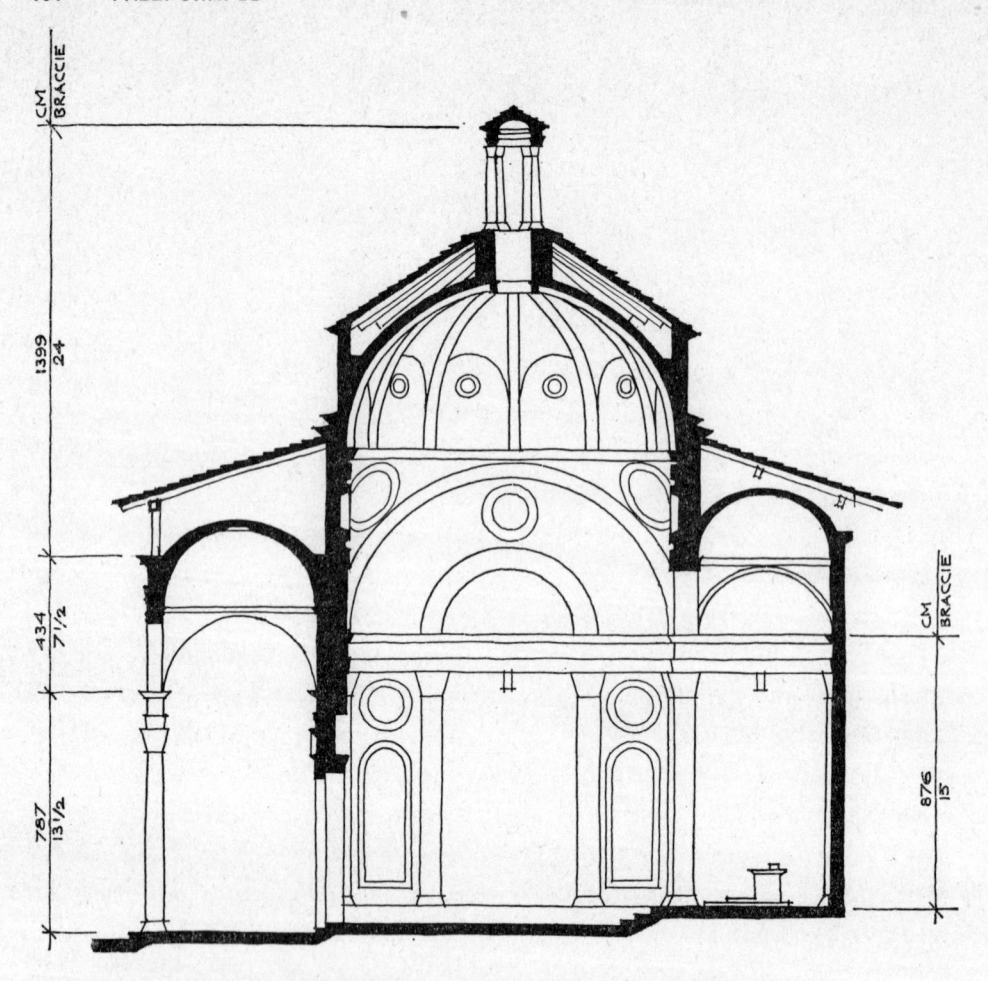

Figure 27. Pazzi Chapel; longitudinal section (after Stegmann-Gegmüller)

The transverse arches which border the tunnel-vaulted compartments rest on pilasters, with which they correspond nearly in width.[7] The smaller arches framing the apse are received in the same way on pilasters. Above the pilasters runs an architrave around the entire interior perimeter of the chapel.

Pilasters, columns and architraves are for Brunelleschi primarily means of subdividing space, not elements of physical or symbolic construction. With the help of the classical apparatus he divides his interiors into clear-cut geometrical volumes, i.e. Phileban solids. The pilasters are placed at regular intervals and the wall runs as a screen at a small distance behind them. On projecting corners he gets two adjoining pilasters, but on the re-entrant angles only a very small slice of the pilaster remains visible (Figure 32). Brunelleschi accepts this for subsidiary spaces such as altar niches or side-chapels, perhaps because the small scale of such cubicles would hardly allow a full-sized pilaster. For the corners of a larger room this is not enough. In the Old Sacristy, in the Pazzi Chapel and on the exterior of San Lorenzo he folds the pilaster around the re-entrant angle; in the salon of the

Palazzo di Parte Guelfa (it it *is* his work) and in the S. Maria degli Angeli he uses two pilasters at a short distance from one another, one on each side of the corner (Figure 32). The architrave connects all pilasters or parts of pilasters and demonstrates the system of spatial division.

The Pazzi Chapel was probably built on the same site as the previous chapter house. The size of the latter may have played a role in the dimensions of the Pazzi Chapel.[8] Certainly the dimensions of the adjacent fourteenth century Baroncelli and Castellani chapels put a strict limit to Brunelleschi's freedom of design. Did the adjacent buildings determine the dimensions of the Pazzi Chapel in its entirety? I believe that I can show that Brunelleschi, notwithstanding the severe limitations of his site, used a system of proportions (Figure 30).[9]

The choice of a proportionate system of 5–5–9.5–5–5 (all in *braccie* or Florentine ells) may seem strange at first sight, and more likely to be dictated by the available room than by any so-called system. Vitruvius describes in Book IV, Chapter III, that the Doric hexastyle temple demands 29.5 modules in width, and the tetrastyle 19.5 modules. Hence the intercolumnar intervals are (29.5–19.5):2 = 5 modules, and the central opening becomes 29.5–4×5 = 9.5 modules. The distances from centre to centre between the pilasters of the Pazzi Chapel correspond exactly to this scheme.

That the dimension of 29.5 braccie is not a dictate of necessity but a deliberate choice can be demonstrated with the Old Sacristy. That building shows four pilasters in its main interior elevation; and the distance between the centres of the exterior pilasters is again 19.5 braccie (Figure 31).

Did Brunelleschi really use the Vitruvian prescriptions in his grid?[10] The width of the pilasters is not two braccie, as Vitruvius requires, but one and a quarter. Also, the numbers for tetrastyle and hexastyle temples are given for the Doric order, whereas Brunelleschi used the Corinthian and composite throughout. Both must be admitted as flaws in the analysis.

The second point might perhaps be answered with a quotation from Vitruvius himself: 'The other members which are placed above the columns are, for Corinthian columns, composed either of the Doric proportions, or according to Ionic usages; for the Corinthian order never had any scheme peculiar to itself for its cornices or other ornaments.'[11] Therefore, there is no typical Corinthian spacing either.

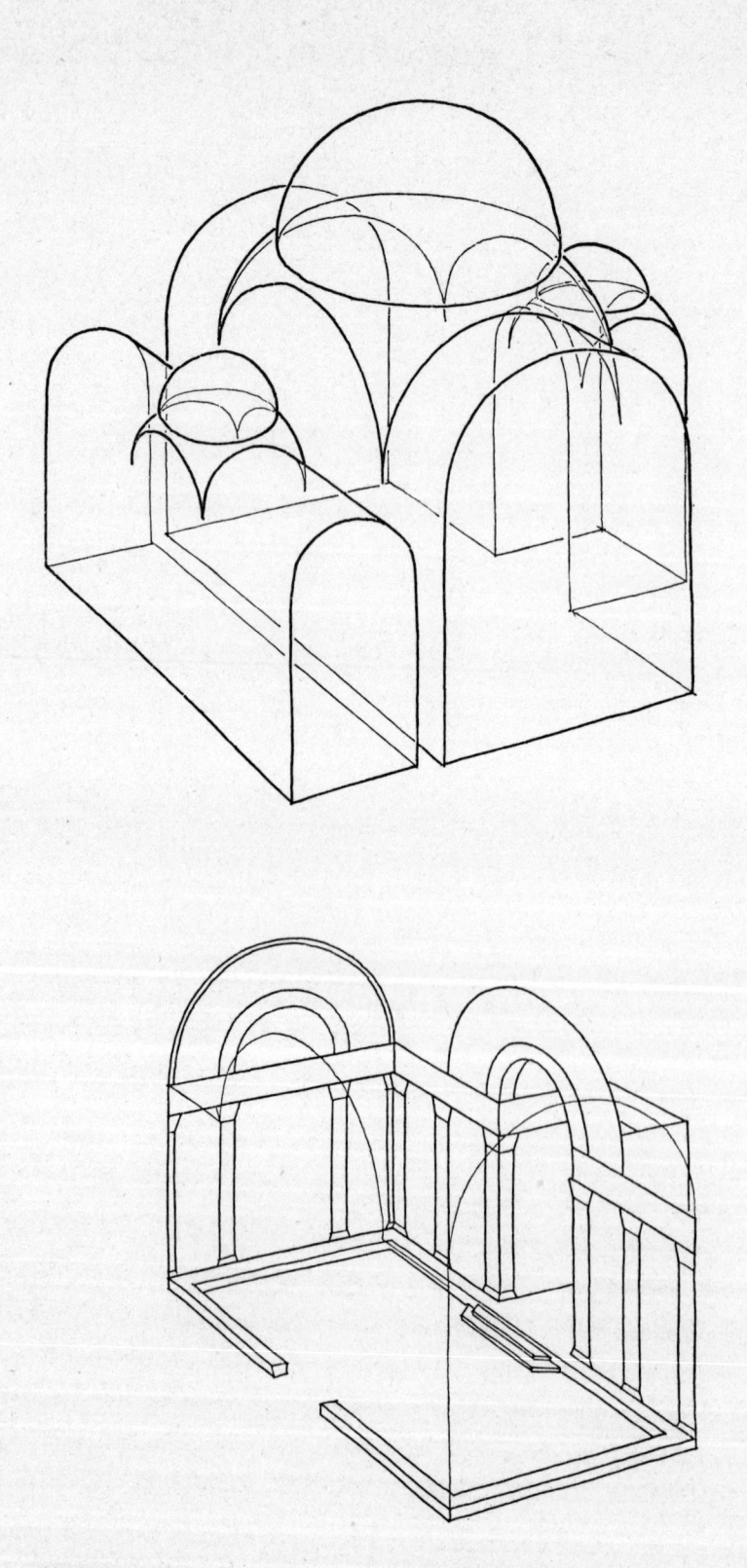

Figure 28. Pazzi Chapel; spatial scheme of decorations

Figure 29. Pazzi Chapel; tentative reconstruction of exterior

Brunelleschi did not space his pilasters in accordance with the module; neither did he use Vitruvian proportions for the heights of his members, as the following table shows:

	module (m) width of pilaster	full height (h) incl. base and entablature	$\frac{h}{m}$	entabl. (e)	$\frac{e}{m}$	capital (c)	$\frac{c}{m}$
Pazzi Ch. interior	73 = $1\frac{1}{4}$ B	876	12	123	$1\frac{2}{3}$	84	$1\frac{1}{7}$
Pazzi Ch. exterior	63 = $1\frac{1}{12}$ B	787	12.5	119	1.9	83.7	$1\frac{1}{3}$
Old Sacristy	63 = $1\frac{1}{12}$ B	694	11	98	$1\frac{1}{3}$	69	1.1

Apart from the numerical simplicity of the proportions, there seems but little consistency. Perhaps the buildings which Brunelleschi is said to have measured in Rome convinced him that the Ancients also took liberties with these relations.[12]

If the source of the horizontal proportions of the Pazzi Chapel is indeed Vitruvius, the case for a portico in front of the chapel would be strengthened. It would indeed show the entrance façade to be something in the nature of a temple-front. It would be a demonstration of the correct method of using columns, 'all 'antica', in contrast to the barbarous, decadent Gothic columns of the cloisters and the arcade along S. Croce.

It is however also possible that Brunelleschi, noting the close correspondence between the available width for the Capella Pazzi and the interior dimensions of the Old Sacristy, decided to use the same dome and the same details again, and therefore once more used 19.5 braccie as his basic dimension.

The existing walls of the adjacent chapels allowed the use of this proportionate scheme, but of course it did not fit perfectly. The available width was too much and the available depth too little. Brunelleschi overcame the first difficulty by putting a full pilaster of $1\frac{1}{4}$ braccia on the longitudinal wall in the corner. Had he followed the system of the Old Sacristy, he would have put only a $\frac{3}{4}$ pilaster, so that the two parts on each side added up to one full pilaster, rather than to $1\frac{1}{4}$ as they do now. This was still not quite sufficient, and the lateral wall had to be thickened 10 cm *more* than the side wall of the apse. The quarter pilaster on the

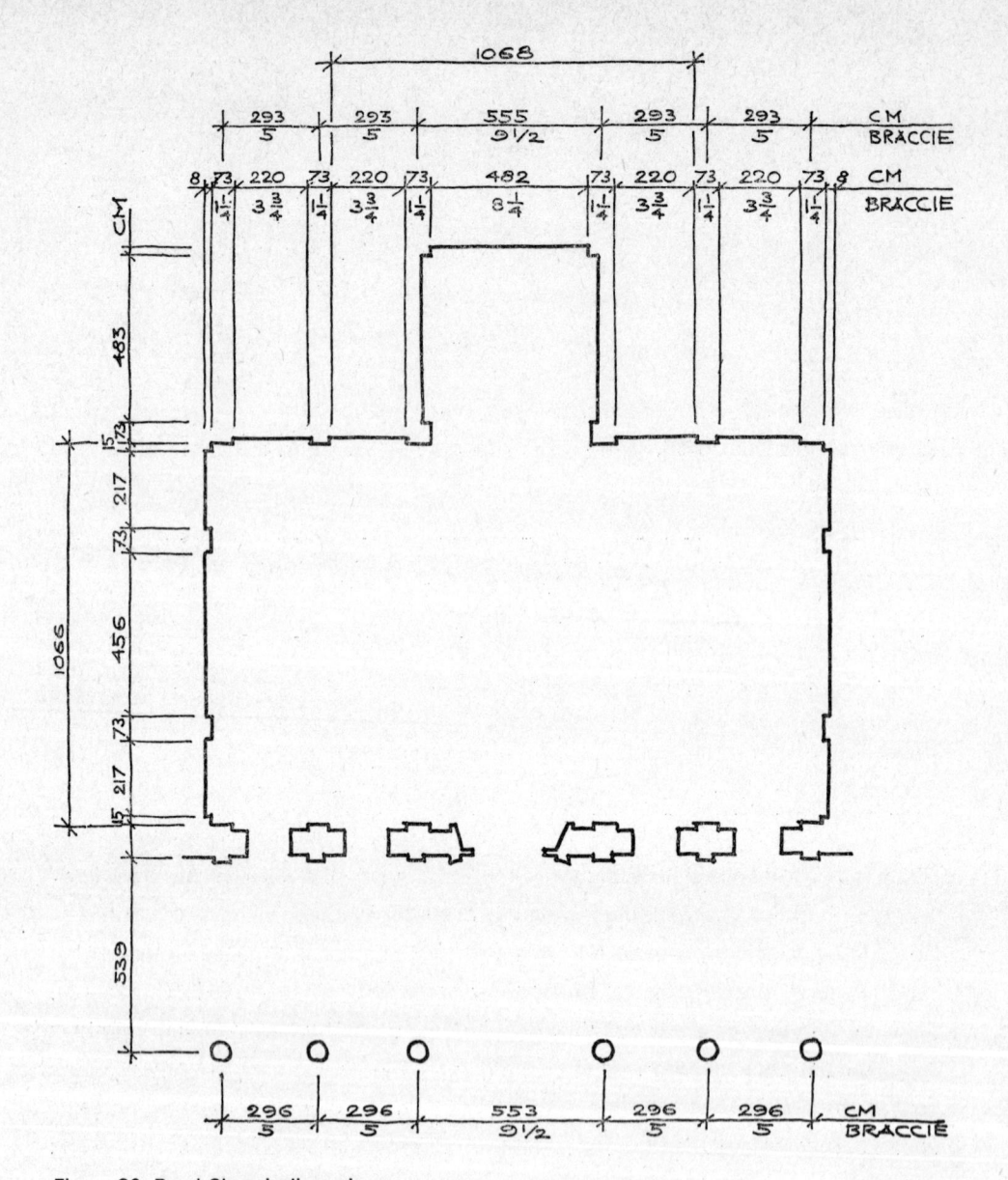

Figure 30. Pazzi Chapel; dimensions

lateral wall is formally necessary, for otherwise the overhang of the capital on the full pilaster disappears into the plaster. A wall-arch similar to the wall arches below the pendentives is received on this quarter pilaster, enhancing the correspondence between lateral and frontal elevations. As this wall arch fits entirely within the arch around the tunnel-vault, and this arch has obviously to correspond to the wall arch above the sanctuary, absolute correspondence was impossible.

The depth was increased by letting the façade of the chapel proper project 15 cm beyond the building line of the adjacent parts of the convent (Figure 26) and by digging into the end wall of the Baroncelli Chapel. This made it necessary to strengthen that end wall on the other side; it now stands 27 cm further inward than originally.

The larger intervals between the interior pilasters are taken up by the entrance, the opening towards the chancel, and leave room supposedly for the funeral monuments. The smaller intercolumniations are used for windows in the façade; blind windows between all the other pilasters carry the motif around, thereby adding once more to the symmetry and concordance of parts. In the words of Alberti: 'I shall define Beauty to be a Harmony of all the Parts, in whatsoever Subject it appears, fitted together with such Proportion and Connection that nothing could be added, diminished or altered, but for the Worse.'[13] or '...the very first Thing we are to take Care of must be that every part, even the most Inconsiderable, lie duly to the Level and Plum-line, and be disposed with an exact Correspondence as to the Number, Form and Appearance; so that the Right may answer to the Left, the High to the Low, the Similar to the Similar, so as to form a correspondent in that Body whereof they are Parts.'[14] The Pazzi Chapel exemplifies these precepts to perfection: in its correspondence between exterior and interior, between lateral and frontal interior elevations, and between pilasters and the arches above them.

Above the blind and the real windows are twelve roundels filled with coloured terracotta reliefs of the twelve Apostles, from the workshop of Luca della Robbia. Meiss has suggested that the partition of the melon dome in twelve sections, with twelve lights, may perhaps be connected with these twelve Apostles below.[15]

Larger roundels with the four Evangelists appear in the four pendentives below the cupola. They differ in style from the della Robbia roundels, and some scholars[16] have suggested that they might have been made by Brunelleschi himself. Most of the chapel, and certainly the higher parts, were built after Brunelleschi's death; the attribution seems therefore doubtful. It depends on how far construction had advanced at the death of Brunelleschi in 1446.

These decorations and the little cherubs on the friezes inside and outside display the idealism characteristic of Quattrocento Art, and so well known from the pictures and sculpture of Botticelli, Fra Angelico and Donatello. Apostles and Evangelists look down upon us with serene faces. The sweetness of della Robbia's work makes it still a beloved model for the souvenir shops, in which thousands of small copies of his 'tondi' (roundels) of the Florentine Foundling Hospital are yearly sold to kind-hearted lady tourists.

The dome of heaven is also there. The little cupola over the apse shows a fresco with an astrological theme against a blue sky, perhaps related to the hour of birth of Andrea dei Pazzi. The altar is consecrated to St. Andrew (because of Andrea dei Pazzi).

2. Analysis

The function had only an insignificant influence on the design. The Pazzi Chapel corresponds in plan to other chapter houses of the Trecento, such as those of S. Maria Novella and S. Annunziata.[17] When the monks convened, they could sit on the projecting plinth.

Equally insignificant is the influence of construction on the design. Brunelleschi, the architect of the dome on the cathedral of Florence, is renowned for his engineering skill,[18] but none of it appears in any of his later works. The two barrel-vaults of the main interior space are connected by tie-rods, to counteract the lateral thrust; surely a rather make-shift solution for an architect so finicky about his details. Perhaps the melon dome was adopted for constructive reasons; its webs could be vaulted out of hand over the supporting ribs, reducing the amount of centering necessary. Everywhere else construction seems to have been sacrificed deliberately to artistic ends.

What can these ends have been? Thanks to Wittkower's famous study[19] we are fairly well informed about the principles of Humanist architecture. The major source is Alberti's *De re aedificatoria*, which appeared in 1485, but was written mainly in the 1450's. Can Alberti's theory be applied to Brunelleschi's work, even though it was written later? Brunelleschi's churches come very close to the 'serene and almost puritanical architecture'[20] of the Temple in *De re aedificatoria*. According to Alberti, the 'Temple ought to be somewhat raised above the level of the Town',[21] as San Lorenzo and Santo Spirito are; it should 'be surrounded on every side with great streets, or rather with noble squares',[22] as were intended around S. Spirito; 'the Windows in the Temple ought to be small and high',[23] such as for instance the windows in S. Lorenzo, S. Spirito and the Old Sacristy; mouldings around apertures ought to look as if they are 'all of one Piece',[24] and Brunelleschi runs his mouldings around niches or windows without a break; the columns in the

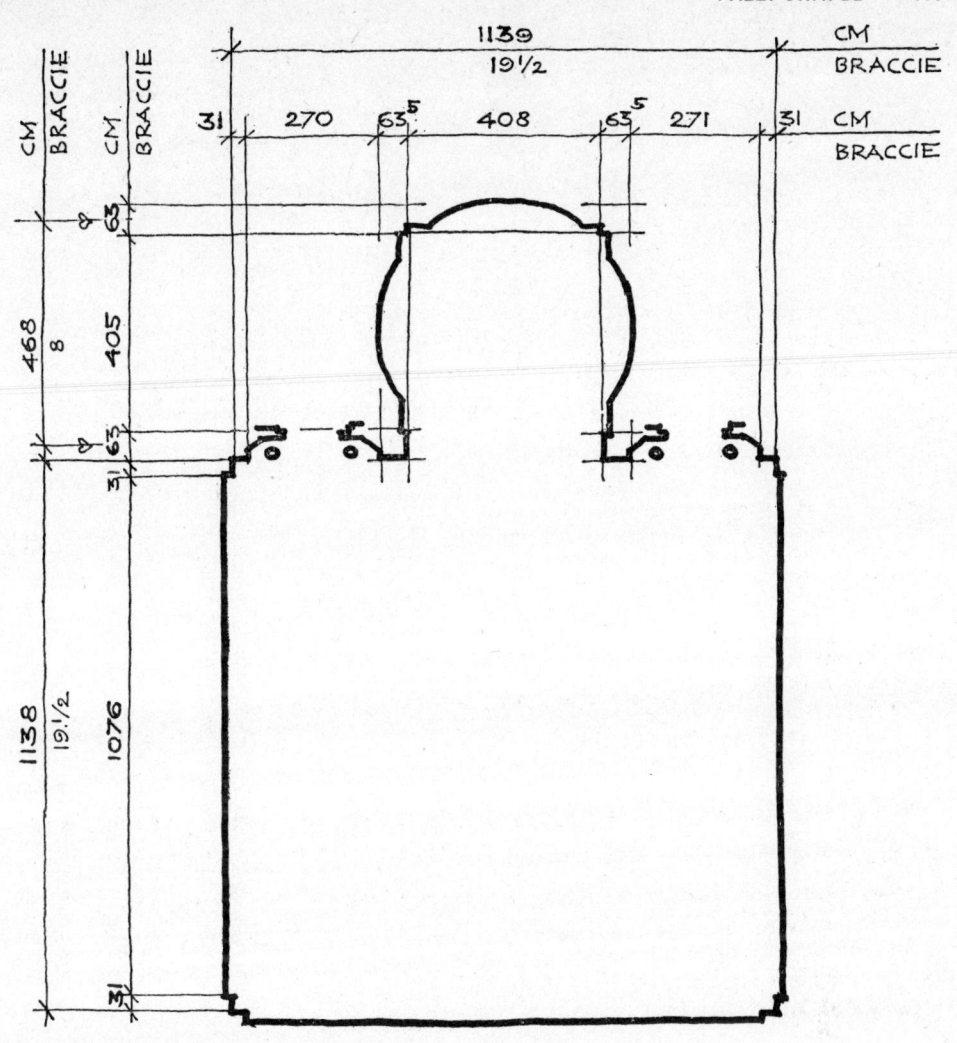

Figure 31. Old Sacristy of S. Lorenzo; dimensions of plan

interior have to be pure and simple, white for instance,[25] and again all Brunelleschi's interiors conform to this precept. Alberti criticized old St. Peter's: 'it was ill advised to draw a very long and thick wall over so many frequent and continued Apertures without strengthening it with any curve Lines';[26] he advocates the use of arches, such as those of S. Lorenzo and S. Spirito again. On the other hand, Alberti requires that the proportions conform to the Neo-Platonic musical scale; but only in the scheme of Santo Spirito do we find a simple proportionate relationship of 1:2:4, and that based on a module of eleven braccie, not a Neo-Platonic 'perfect number'. The proportions of Brunelleschi's columns, pilasters and entablatures vary and do not fit Alberti's prescriptions.

Alberti knew and admired Brunelleschi, as he says in the preface to his book *On Painting*. The connection between *De re aedificatoria* and Brunelleschi's buildings is tenuous, undoubtedly. However, Alberti's architectural theory provides by far the best explanation of what Brunelleschi may have aimed at. Brunelleschi shared the Renaissance preference for religious buildings with a central plan, a preference which is apparent already in the Old Sacristy, becomes more pronounced in the Pazzi Chapel and S. Spirito and culminates in S. Maria degli Angeli. This predilection cannot be entirely attributed to imitation of centrally planned monuments, considered to be genuinely Roman by the Renaissance architects. Those included the Pantheon, S. Costanza, S. Stefano Rotondo and the baptistery at Florence. This group is far outweighed in numbers by the other antique structures including temples and Early Christian churches, whose design was marked only by a simple symmetry. Nor is the theory of perspective, invented by Brunelleschi, of any help;[27] perspective vistas are characteristic of basilicas like S. Lorenzo or S. Spirito, but not of the Pazzi Chapel or S. Maria degli Angeli. Only Alberti's theory gives a satisfactory rationale for Brunelleschi's 'hantise de la circularité'.[28] The key to this rationale is the belief in the harmony of the world, the 'Harmonia Mundi'. God has built the universe on a strictly mathematical plan, which shines through all his creations, from the smallest plants to the stars in the sky.

Harmony and order reign throughout the cosmos. Simple figures govern the growth of trees and the movements of the planets; thus, to please God and to be in harmony with the universe, our designs should be based on simple figures too. In particular the circle and the sphere, which have only one dimension, are among the most harmonious and therefore most beautiful forms.[29] The Pazzi Chapel abounds in such round forms: in the cupolas, the barrel-vaults, the window heads, the roundels above the windows and in the pendentives. The similarity between the long and short interior elevations creates a semblance of the multi-axial symmetry of a central plan. The astrological picture of the sky in the dome over the apse lends some support to a cosmic interpretation of the larger dome over the chapter house; however, this fresco need not have been planned by Brunelleschi. Harmony is the keynote of Alberti's treatise and Brunelleschi's design. And harmony pervades the figurative arts as well: the paintings of Fra Angelico and the gentle cherubs of Della Robbia. The very sweetness of Raphael's madonnas endeared them to our grandmothers and is the reason why they appear sometimes too sugary to us. But now a curious contrast emerges: harmony is certainly *not* the chief characteristic of Renaissance social life. The age of Raphael is also the age

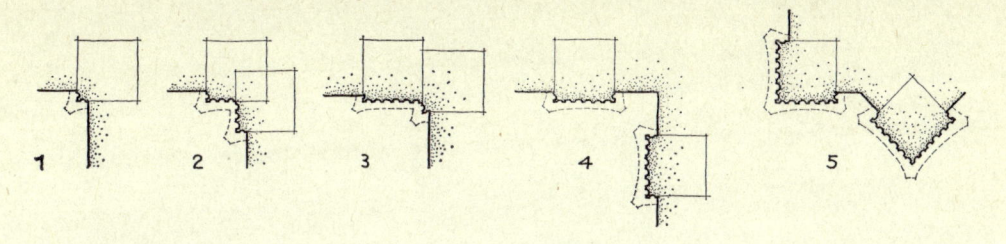

Figure 32. Brunelleschi's re-entrant angles. 1. Chancel of Old Sacristy; 2. Old Sacristy; 3. Pazzi Chapel; 4. Palazzo di Parte Guelfa; 5. Sta Maria degli Angeli

of the condottieri and of the Borgias. Renaissance history reads like a fascinating cloak and dagger story: it is one endless series of murders, exiles and intrigues. City fought with city and family plotted against family. The misfortunes of the Pazzi were no exception, but rather the rule. How could such a fiercely combative society produce such gentle and harmonious art?

The answer lies, I think, in the very opposition between the two. Renaissance society presents a picture of discord, and just for that reason harmony and gentleness were ideals worthy to be striven after. As a weakling of a boy dreams to be one day captain of the rugby team, and a simple clerk pictures himself as the next company director, so Renaissance man could aspire to a world full of harmony, just *because* his world was so far from harmonious. Dreams often present us with an ideal world in contrast to the one we live in; travellers in the Sahara dream of great expanses of water; hungry explorers on the Antarctic ice dream of an abundance of food. Dreams are a form of wish fulfilment; of private desires in the case of the boy or the clerk, of collective needs in the case of the Renaissance.

Medieval architecture can be interpreted as a reaction *to* the outside world: people sought refuge in the sacred fortress of the Romanesque church, or, later, expressed their trust in the world they lived in by the openness and daring construction of Gothic cathedrals. Renaissance architecture on the contrary symbolized a cosmos *in contrast* to the world they lived in. It seems obvious to look for a reason for the contrasts between medieval and Renaissance society. They have been admirably described by Enea Silvio, the later pope Pius II. This is how he characterizes Genoa in a letter of 1432:

'It would have been a flourishing city, if only its inhabitants could have lived in peace. But their discord has been so great, that the one has tried to assassinate the other, and also to remove his followers. All have been bent on injuring their neighbours, killing them, plundering them or exiling them. That is the reason that most nobles of this city ... have to stay abroad.'[30] And with a tinge of jealousy he notes of Basle in 1434: 'The walls and the bastions of the city would scarcely be able to withstand the fierce sieges and fighting of Italian wars, for they are neither high nor strong enough. Probably you will agree that the strength of the city lies in the concord of its citizens. For a united citizenry is invincible to any enemy; but it is easy to conquer them when they are not united. There is a great delicacy of feeling in the attitude of the citizens towards each other, and in that lies their strength. They know of no feuds in government. Nobody complains about the quartered soldiers, and they would rather die for their liberty than surrender.'[31]

Dangers came to the citizens of Basle, still living in feudal harmony with each other, from *outside*. They were met by practical measures, and also by their belief in the magic of architecture to protect them. Genoa on the contrary suffered from *internal insecurity*, which could not be countered by a protective architectural shell. The attitude to the outside world was still optimistic, as in the earlier Gothic period. In comparison to the social instability that world looked more friendly and dependable than ever. Architecture became a projection of the harmonious cosmos.

Renaissance architecture is the first of the dreamlands. It is characterized by the conscious symbolization of the Neo-Platonic philosophy of the 'Harmonia Mundi' and the deliberate adoption of Antique forms as carriers of meaning. The latter is also the result of an idealization.

The feuds between families within a city, such as Genoa or Florence, were mirrored in the constant battles between the small city-states. The German invasions in the Middle Ages had arrested the growth of a united Italy; later on, the popes too did their utmost to prevent it. But national unity *had* once been achieved, in the great days of Rome. For an Italian, Classical antiquity was above all an Italian affair.[32] 'I say', wrote Alberti, 'this Art (of architecture) having had her ancient Seat in Italy, and knowing with how much Fervour she was courted there, she seems to have resolved that this Empire of the World which was already adorned with all other Virtues, should be made still more admirable by her Embellishments.'[33] Ancient Rome was therefore turned into another dreamland. Its authors were looked upon as nearly infallible. Ciceronian Latin became the hallmark of literary elegance and Roman architecture the standard of taste.

Moreover, this dream had once been true: witness the ruins of Rome and the extant literature and art. Its reality 'proved' that the unity of dreamland was not unattainable, for it had been attained in the past. And with the superposition of this verifiable piece of make-believe on the Phileban solids of Neo-Platonism, the latter gained in reality too. A state of perfection grounded on historical fact is much more convincing than an invisible harmonious cosmos.

The rude disruption of the paradise of Rome was blamed on the foreign invaders,

IX. Exterior of the Pazzi Chapel, Florence

X. Interior of the Pazzi Chapel, showing the correspondence between the main and the lateral interior elevations

Goths and Germans. And consequently, it were they, too, who had debased the 'good old style' of the Ancients, and introduced the barbaric forms of Gothic.[34]

Symbolic aesthetics determined the use of the classical orders and the subdivision of space into the pristine forms of the Phileban solids. The Pazzi Chapel has these latter in common with St. Michael in Hildesheim. But their formal coherence is far greater than in the Ottonian church. The formal aesthetics of the Renaissance architecture demands a greater unity, in keeping with the more positive evaluation of their world and correlated with naturalism in the representative arts.

The parts of the Pazzi Chapel are tied together by repetition, continuity and symmetry. Repetition of the long elevations in the short ones, of pilasters, windows or niches and roundels; continuity of pilasters and arches and symmetry in the whole space as well as in its parts. The cornice running along the entire interior perimeter strings all parts together including the apse.

We may now try to summarize the several levels of meaning in the architecture of the Pazzi Chapel. On the first level we have the opinion of Ruskin, that a worldly community of pleasure-seekers recreated pagan architecture. In other words, the secularization of society is paralleled by the revival of a pagan style.

The symbolic background of Renaissance architecture, admirably described by Wittkower, is the second level of meaning. The Pazzi Chapel may owe its centralizing plan, its use of domes, and its preference for circles and squares to the theory of the 'Harmonia Mundi'. The subdivision of space into the Phileban solids, required by this doctrine, is effected by the classical pilasters and entablatures. The use of the classical apparatus itself, and perhaps also the proportions, may be interpreted as a symbol for ancient Rome. Neither the 'Harmonia Mundi' nor the revival of antiquity are satisfactory as ultimate 'causes' of Renaissance architecture, on the third level of meaning. As in the previous examples, I am inclined to look for such final causes (if ever they exist) in social history. Three aspects of social history can be taken, I believe, as characteristic of the fifteenth and sixteenth centuries in Italy, in comparison to the preceding epoch. They are: social mobility, individualism and the rise of capitalism. All three are inextricably interwoven; they present themselves as three sides of the same die. Wealth quickly acquired made people move on the social scale, but could be amassed only by entrepreneurs who took personal, i.e. individualistic risks. If this is indeed the prime difference between

Renaissance and late medieval society, it may perhaps furnish us with the missing links in the causal chain.

Social mobility meant a lively, albeit unstable society. It prevented (in part) the union of cities into a national Italian state, and even the unity of the people of the city itself. Platonic philosophy fled from this perpetual battlefield. Ficino in his philosophy of love exalted the very thing his compatriates lacked so conspicuously. Perhaps it was his irenic character which led him to praise contemplation above action, rest above motion: 'I believe, however, that the mind, because it knows rest and judges rest itself to be more excellent than change, and because it naturally desires rest beyond motion, desires and finally attains its end and good in a certain condition of rest rather than of motion.'[35] But may the *un*rest of his age not have contributed to this view? The concord which was so fervently desired, found expression in philosophy and in the arts: on one hand in the idealization of ancient Rome, on the other in the 'Harmonia Mundi'. To that the Pazzi Chapel may owe its classical architecture and quasi multi-axial symmetry, and to that the architecture and decoration together their expression of serene repose.

Imperial Library
Vienna   1681–1726

1. Historical setting

Since the end of the middle ages, Vienna had been the capital of the Holy Roman Empire. It was the residence of the Habsburg House, from which by tradition the emperors were elected by the German prince-electors. In theory, the Habsburgs succeeded to the heritage of the Hohenstaufens, the Salians and the Ottonians, that is to the original empire of Charlemagne. In practice of course their rule stretched no further than their own resources and their opposing neighbours permitted. Depending on whom they could array as allies, their territory was now large, then small. It had reached its maximum extension through the marriage of Philip of Habsburg with the mad Joanna of Aragon, whose son Charles V came closest to establishing an empire comparable to that of Charlemagne. After Charles's retirement in 1555, his son succeeded to the throne of Spain and the rule of the Spanish Netherlands and colonies, and his brother Ferdinand to the Holy Roman Empire. Tedious as the genealogical account may be, it is indispensable to our story.

At the end of the seventeenth century, the Empire consisted of Austria, Czechoslovakia and Hungary, and in Italy of Milan, Naples and Sicily. The rule over Germany was one in name only; the German princes went their own way, as they had done ever since the Ottonian period. The Reformation had driven another wedge between the Catholic emperor and many of his Protestant subjects in Germany and Hungary. The attempt of Cardinal Richelieu to establish a French hegemony in Europe did much to further the cause of Luther.

The French threatened the Empire from the West, and the Turks attacked it from the East. In 1683 the Turks besieged Vienna unsuccessfully. It proved to be their swan song. Prince Eugene of Savoy, known to English readers principally as a comrade-in-arms of Marlborough, beat the Turks back in a series of brilliant campaigns. As spoils of the battle the whole of Hungary was brought under

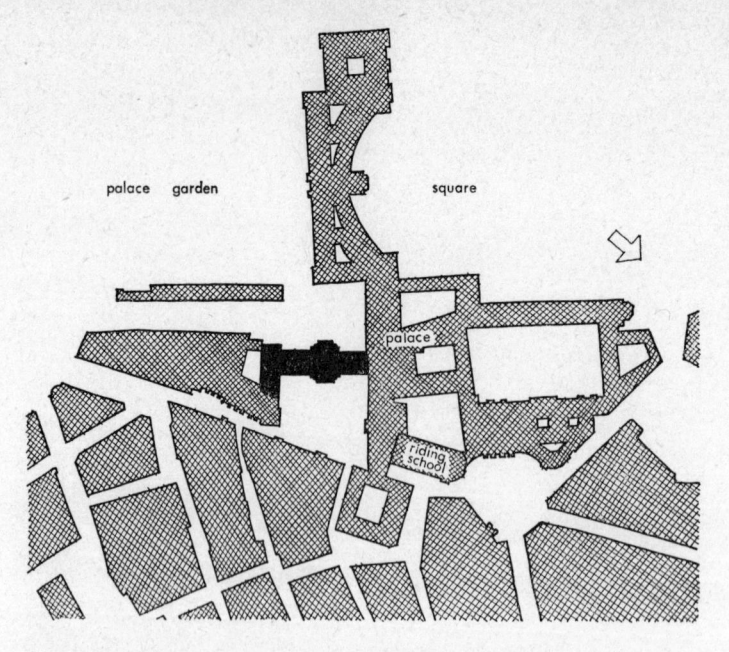

Figure 33. Imperial Library; site at the end of the 18th century

Austrian domination, adding one more independent ethnic group to an empire already embracing Czechs, Italians and Tyrolese. The fierce Magyars were none too keen to exchange a Turkish sultan for an Austrian emperor as overlord. Differing in language, customs, race and partly in religion from their Austrian masters, they soon rebelled and were only brought back to the fold with difficulty (1703–1711).

Internal difficulties never seem to be an obstacle to the ambition of rulers. On the contrary, dreams of glory feed as easily on defeat as on victory. Only tight police control could keep Bohemia (Czechoslovakia) from straying and Hungary from rebellion; the imperial rule was scarcely recognized in Germany and not at all in Italy, but all the same the Habsburgs aimed at further extension of their domain. A chance of an undreamed of aggrandizement came in 1700 when the Spanish throne fell vacant. The two pretenders to the throne, the Austrian Charles and the French Philip could lay equal claims, for they shared Philip III of Spain as a great-grandfather. Both claimants went to Spain, to contest the prize, the Austrian with the help of the English and the Dutch. Though the Spaniards were on the French side, the first victory in the Spanish war of succession went to the Austrian party: Gibraltar fell to British attacks in 1704. It proved to be the only durable success; in 1713 Philip was king of Spain.

Charles, the other pretender, never officially recognized his defeat. In 1711 he had travelled back to Austria, to succeed to the Imperial throne, as the Emperor, his elder brother had died. For years and years he continued to protest his rights; only in 1725 did he renounce them by a secret treaty. Even the consolation prize of Gibraltar, won in his name, remained in English hands. The only token of the short lived Spanish glory was Charles' escutcheon. On it were depicted two columns with below them the motto 'Constantia et Fortitudine'. The columns represent the

Pillars of Hercules, as Gibraltar was called in antique mythology, and refer also to the temple of Solomon, in front of which stood two columns called 'Jachin' = 'he established', and 'Boaz' = 'in him is strength,' which Charles' motto paraphrases. Charles, as all his good Catholic forefathers, saw himself as the foremost protector of the Church, i.e. as another Solomon; this task was implied in his election as Holy Roman Emperor.[1]

Studying the figure of Charles VI, one is amazed by the number of his pretensions. He was a pretender to the Spanish throne; he pretended to be the successor of Charles V and Charlemagne, and through them of the Roman emperors; and he believed himself to be the elected champion of the church. Not one of these claims could he substantiate, although he might adduce legal grounds for each of them. Exalted aspirations were not however restricted to Charles VI of Austria; all kings and princes of eighteenth century Europe were, in modern eyes, immeasurably conceited. The best known example is that of Louis XIV, 'le Roi Soleil', whose smallest act was surrounded by pomp and circumstance, starting with the famous 'Levée'. Like Louis, Charles was the centre of a sycophantic court ceremonial. On holidays, the Emperor supped with his Empress in the presence of a crowd of generals, ambassadors and government officials, who were not invited to the table, but were only allowed as a favour to look on, standing of course along the walls. Four times a year a dinner was held called 'the Great Table'; then the Emperor dined alone surrounded by all his court dignitaries. His plate passed through twenty-four hands before it reached him—no doubt stone-cold by then.[2] Charles was his own prime minister; he wanted to sign all important papers personally. When later in his reign, his interest in the affairs of the state waned, the machinery of government slowed down to a near stand-still. ...

2. Description

This paragraph and the next describe the functional and technical components of the design, and the symbolic meaning on the second (iconographical) level. We will follow the exhaustive analysis of W. Buchowiecki's monograph on the building.[3]

A new library had been needed for a long time. The growing collection had been

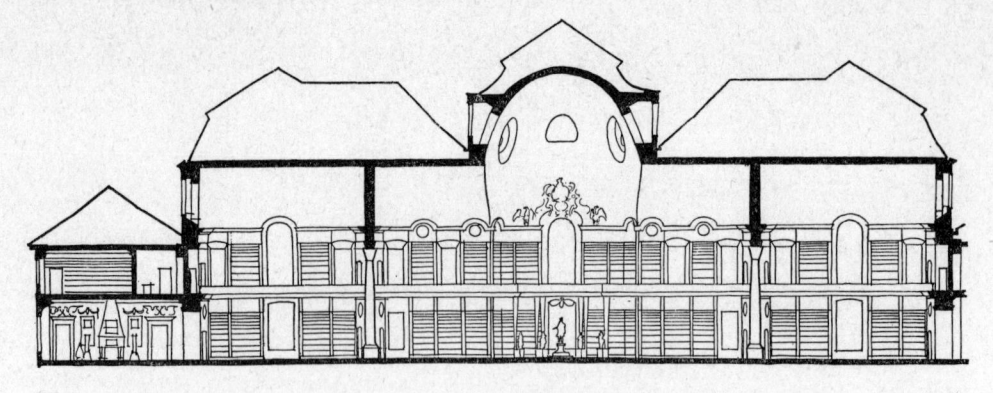

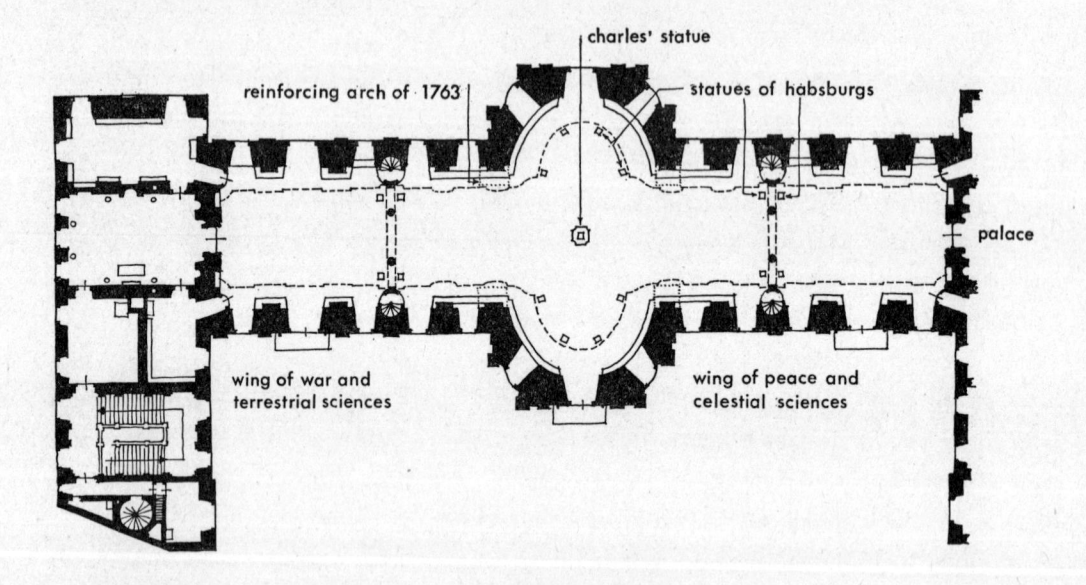

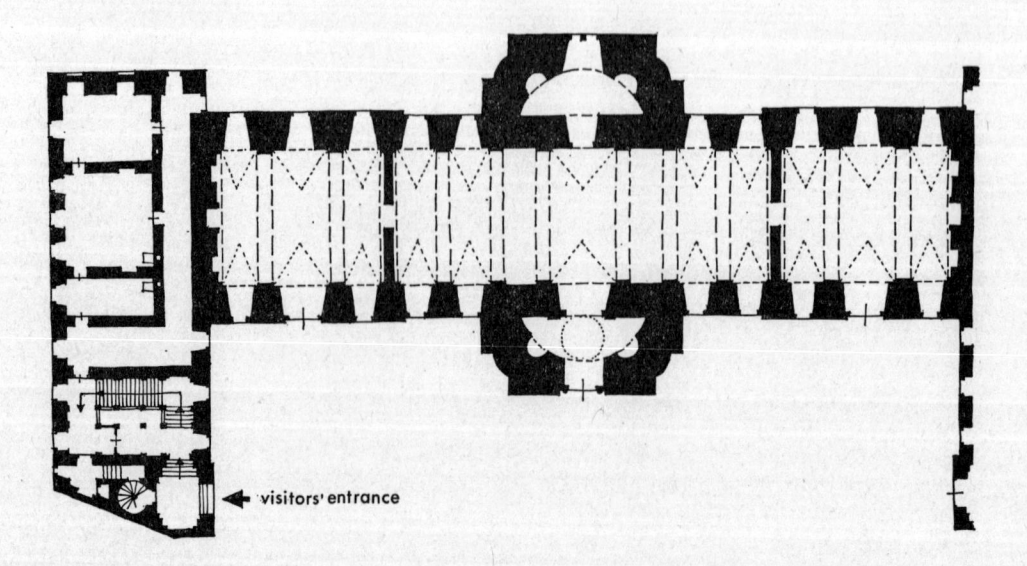

Figure 34. Imperial Library; section, plan (after Kleiner)

housed in a Franciscan monastery from 1558 to 1623 and from then onwards in a wing of the imperial offices. Its size in 1669 is estimated at 80,000 volumes. This mass of books represented centuries of collecting by the Habsburgs and their relatives; a sheaf of precious medieval manuscripts forms the core of the library to this day. Clearly, some more permanent and worthy accommodation was indicated.

Charles' father, the emperor Leopold I, commanded a new building to be erected. It was to have two storeys, the ground floor intended for the riding academy, and the first storey for the imperial collection of books. Construction was started in 1681 and the roof of the new library had just been completed when the Turkish siege of Vienna put a stop to all further work (1683).

The building of Leopold I is the core of the present library. It was a plain rectangular block, practically devoid of decoration. When construction was resumed in 1722 the edifice was clearly outmoded and far too dull for the sybaritic taste of the age. The original core was preserved, but it was remodelled practically beyond recognition. Buchowiecki offers good reasons for ascribing the remodelling to the architect Johann Bernhardt Fischer von Erlach.

The original combination of a library and a riding school may seem peculiar. And so it is, considering their functions; but there was a sound architectural reason behind it. Both needed long rectangular halls of considerable size; the riding school needed space to allow the horses to gallop up to the jumps, the library to accommodate a great number of books in one supervisable room. The combination was dropped during the remodelling and a separate riding school was built between 1729 and 1735.

The Imperial Library stands adjacent to the palace, and lay originally on the periphery of early eighteenth century Vienna, with its back windows overlooking the fortifications. The small square in front of the library was originally the tiltyard, perhaps used in the seventeenth century for outdoor riding exercises in connection with the old riding academy. The latter was replaced by the plain building of Leopold I on the same site, and the first floor was allocated to the library, as mentioned before.

Modern libraries usually consist of a series of public spaces: lending desk, reading room, periodical reading room etc., and offices and a stock building inaccessible to the reading public. The present Austrian national library, the successor to the

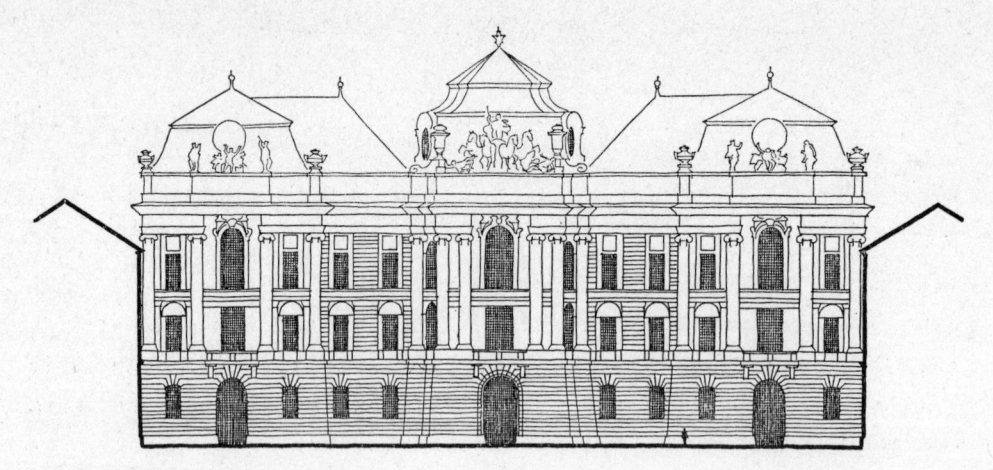

Figure 35. Imperial Library; façade

Imperial Library, operates on the same principle; but the original scheme was far simpler than that. Except for the entrances, vestibule, librarians room and a few tiny cabinets, the entire library consisted of the large hall on the first floor. Problems of cataloguing, and extension of the stock area were not considered in those days; for who could have then foreseen the accelerated growth of book collections and the concomitant problem of finding the particular book one is looking for? It had taken the Habsburgers centuries to amass their collection; the library was viewed as a static and permanent monument of learning, and not as an ever-changing, ever-growing organism as it is today. Consequently no extension of the collection was envisaged and the ingenuity of more recent librarians has been severely taxed in their search around the building for more storage space.

In putting all the books in one large hall, the Viennese library conforms to type. The Laurentian library of Michelangelo in Florence, the famous library on St. Marks Square in Venice by Sansovino, the libraries in the Escorial in Madrid or in the Vatican, all consist of a single large hall full of books, and all go back (at least) to late medieval examples. Bookcases along the walls had gradually replaced the storage below the reading desks; but even in that detail the earliest known example (in Avignon) dates from 1407. With the growth in area of the halls the height increased too, and narrow galleries subdivided the walls of books in easy-to-reach tiers. The Viennese imperial library is—in principle—such a long rectangular hall, with the books along the outside walls and a gallery dividing them. A survival of this type of library can be seen in the main reading rooms of a score of famous libraries, in New York, London, Paris and The Hague for instance.

But the Viennese library deviates also from the standard in some important respects. The rectangular library is interrupted in the middle by a huge domed oval hall, and the remaining areas are each subdivided by a screen wall, supported on

XI. Exterior of the Imperial Library in Vienna in 1780, after a watercolour by Carl Schütz. The wings on the right and the left of the main block have been raised, resulting in a loss in articulation in the principal masses

XII. *Overleaf*: Interior of the Imperial Library. The two columns supporting the screen wall are, according to Buchowiecki, probably an emblem for the escutcheon of Charles VI

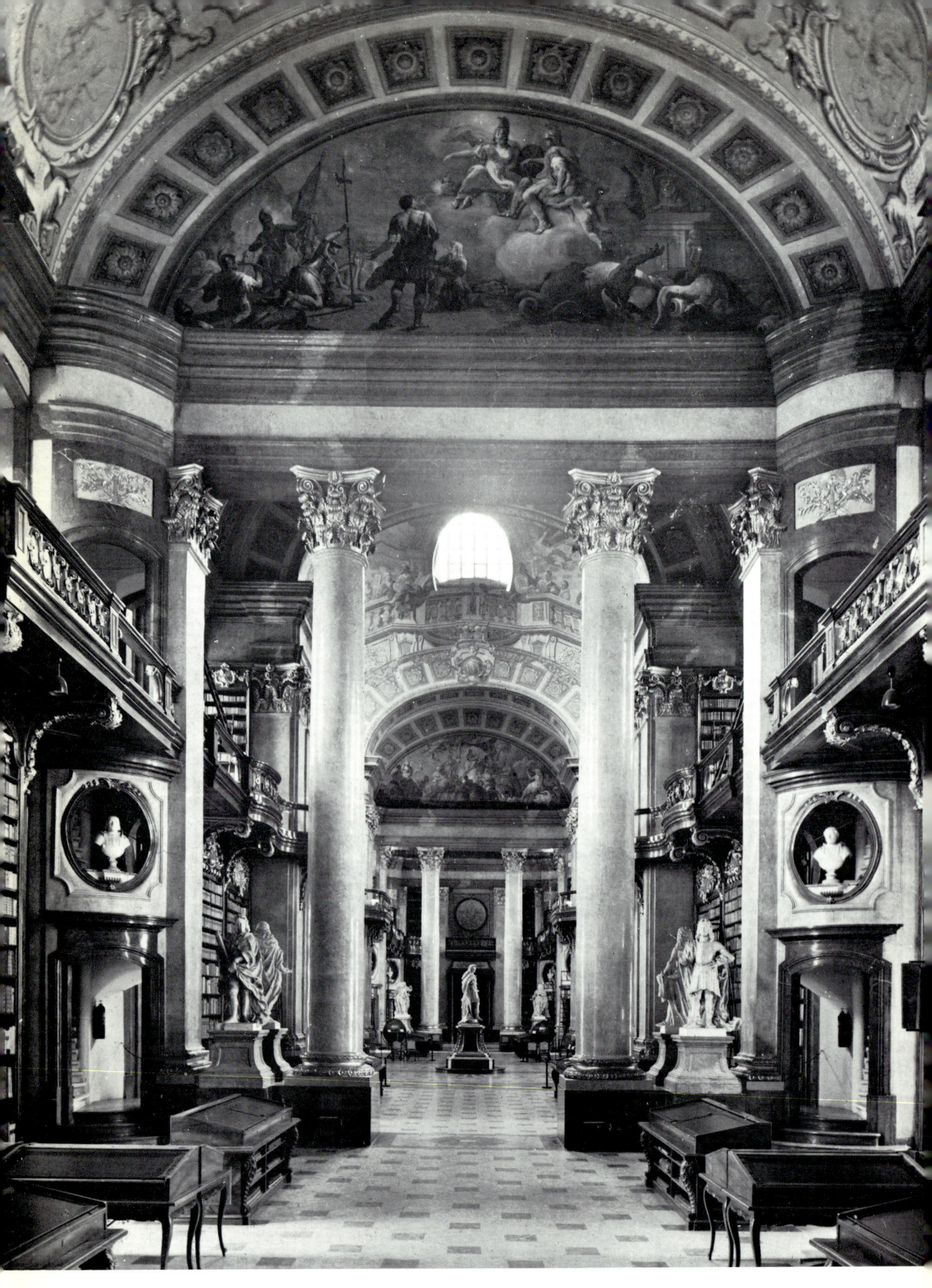

two columns. The central oval, the focal point of the entire spatial composition, is a hall of fame for the Emperor Charles VI.

It is easy to show that the interior alteration of the original building of Leopold I consisted primarily of the addition of this oval room, the screen walls, and probably the vaulting of the library. The rectangular core of the Leopoldian library and riding school is still visible in the ground-floor plan. A continuous joint between the projecting parts of the oval and the straight wall behind them was visible during the restoration of 1955. In 1760, less than forty years after its completion, the new library is reported to have shown dangerous cracks and a radical restoration was deemed necessary. The openings between the central hall and the two adjoining wings were reinforced by heavy pilasters and strong arches below the original ones; the walls in the cellar were reinforced and unnecessary apertures there were bricked up. The restoration proposal has fortunately been preserved, together with some drawings. From them it becomes evident that the cracks were probably due to the weight of the large vaults and walls on the light seventeenth century foundations, not designed to bear them, and above all to the oval extensions added to the rectangular structure. Not bonded in with that structure, constructed forty years after the foundations of the latter had been laid, the building could not but crack at that point.

The alteration of the rectangular block of Leopold I is of the greatest interest to our study, because here, for once, we can clearly distinguish between functional and 'other' influences on a building. The original plain hall sufficed for the storage of books; the oval hall and the screen walls must have been added for non-utilitarian reasons.

The original space may easily have seemed rather dull; nor is a room five times as long as it is wide generally considered to be of elegant classical proportions. By introducing the central hall and by subdividing the remainder with screens into compartments, the architect has adroitly transformed the monotony and disguised the proportions. The longitudinal section shows clearly that the library is divided lengthwise into three sections: two compartments at the ends and a long section with the dome in the centre. The two short bays 2 and 4 adjacent to the cupola opened originally (in 1726) with their full cross-section onto the central hall. They were 'fused' with that hall and isolated by the screens from the outer com-

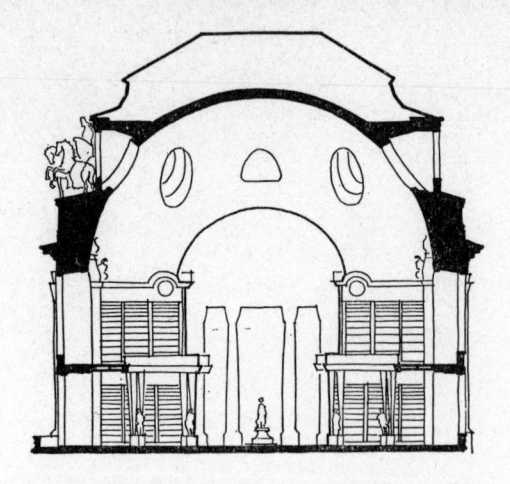

Figure 36. Imperial Library; cross-sections (after Kleiner)

partments 1 and 5.[4] Thus, walking from the ends towards the middle, one experiences a spatial climax: first come the rectangular compartments before the screens, then the cruciform space beyond the screens, and it ends in the huge domed hall. The reinforcing arches of the restoration of 1763 have unfortunately diminished the openings between the short bays and the central hall, and thereby materially altered the spatial effect.

This progression towards the centre is exactly the one that was intended. The library has two entrances: one from the palace, by a simple door in the middle of compartment 5, and the other on the opposite side, for the public. Readers passed from the square in front of the library, through a narrow entrance, a staircase and a series of small cabinets to the library proper; the sequence can be easily followed on the plans. There too, a climax is built up: from the entrance to the vestibule in front of the main hall, the rooms become gradually larger in ascending scale until they culminate in the huge library itself. The library was in fact the largest of its time, measuring 255 feet in length, 46'5" in width and 50'6" in height: a true cathedral of books!

The spatial sequence is underlined by the contrast in plasticity between exterior and interior. Outside pilasters and architraves project barely beyond the stringcourses and rustications. Staircase and vestibule show the same restraint, but the library hall abounds in plastic forms jutting out from the walls.

The colour-scheme contributes also to the climactic effect. The exterior is all white and grey, enlivened with small bits of gold on the sculpture and inscriptions. Stairway and corridor are predominantly white. Then, on entering the library hall itself one is struck by the exuberant colouring: red marble, brown walnut bookcases, and animated ceiling frescoes.

Along the entire inside perimeter of the hall runs a narrow gallery on tapering wooden pilasters, giving access to the upper tiers of books. It is reached by four spiral staircases at the outer edges of the screen walls. To correspond to their convex projections into the library the other corners have been rounded off.

The main hall is quite isolated: 20% of its floor area is taken up by solid masonry, and only 7% of its total outside surface is glazed. Partly this may be due to the Baroque predilection for heavy, massive buildings, but the main reasons are probably practical. Heavy walls were needed to support the vaults and as every available inch of wall space was needed for bookcases, there was little area for windows left. Some windows were walled up immediately after completion, to make room for more books; others are screened by movable cases.

Though all large-scale forms show the heavy plasticity typical of Baroque architecture, the surfaces are quite smooth. The outside is rusticated in the French manner, and the pilasters of the giant order below the main cornice scarcely project beyond the wall. This is no doubt due—at least in part—to the preservation of the plain Leopoldian core. Any architect would shrink from building fifty foot high pilasters without being able to bond them in. But inside the smoothness cannot be due to such secondary influences. Vaults and walls show large unbroken areas; they remind us of eighteenth century brickwork which also aimed at smoothness and unity in contrast to the intrinsic nature of masonry. In my opinion *unity* is one of the keys to the Baroque attitude to surface. This unity is similar to that which was aimed at in the fusion of the domed hall and the two adjacent compartments. The bookcases are built into the wall: another instance of unification, namely of wall and furniture.

The building is constructed of brick, with details such as capitals, window-mouldings and the like in stone. All brickwork is covered by stucco. Heavy walls support the equally heavy vaults. The fire hazard would rule out a plaster vault above a precious book-collection.

The phenomenal structure of the exterior looks somewhat like a skeleton: pilasters on a rusticated basement supporting cornices and roofs, with fill-in walls between them. It is of course entirely a homogeneous load-bearing wall. Baroque architects cared even less than their Renaissance predecessors about a correspondence between physical and phenomenal structure. They thought nothing of phenomenally load-bearing columns of lath and plaster or stucco vaults suspended from roof-trusses. The practical problems of building and the make-believe world of architecture belonged to completely different and separate realms.

The giant orders were used for the same purpose as in the Pazzi Chapel: to subdivide space. The long and monotonous Leopoldian hall has been broken down into a set of pavilions connected by intermediating volumes. The central pavilion projects strongly; its independent roof detaches it still further from the wings (Figure 35). The rectangular core of the earlier building made it impossible to let the corner pavilions project slightly: their façades would certainly have cracked, had they been built in front of the original masonry. Their conceptual volumes were therefore indicated by all other means which were available: giant pilasters, strongly emphasized symmetry, projections in the roofs and sculptural groups on the Attic. They correspond with the interior compartments 1 and 5.

The three pavilions are formally tied together by their similarities. Each has four pilasters arranged symmetrically around a large vertical set of openings which starts with a door and ends with an arched window cutting through the architrave.

The scheme of the three pavilions, the rustications and the general flatness of the wall treatment were derived by Fischer from seventeenth-century French architecture, as Sedlmayr has shown.[5] Fischer used the three-pavilion-scheme in the Schönbrunn, Klesheim and Gallas palaces. The giant orders were probably inspired by Bernini, to whom Fischer had been apprenticed in his youth.

3. Iconographical programme

The Italian Renaissance architects used antique decoration as a symbol of their own national past. Do the classical motifs on the Viennese library also bear a historical meaning? Or are they, as seems far more natural to suppose, the joint result of imitation and habit? After the Italians had given the example, all Europe had gradually adopted the classical fashion in architecture, albeit in sometimes very unclassical form. Seventeenth century order books had provided the architects of England, France and Germany with models to copy, in the absence of real Roman remains. The Italian style had dazzled visitors from the backward Northern countries by its novelty and splendour, and the spread of classical literature through the printing press had reinforced the taste for antiquity. Renaissance architecture had been adopted probably in the main because of the glamour of Italian culture in general, rather than for any profound reason. The Italians were rich and seemed advanced, and consequently their manners and customs in dress, literature and architecture were copied. Today modern architecture spreads over the globe to Brazil, Mexico and Japan for similar reasons. It is the style used by the 'best people' and so one can do no better than follow suit.

But by 1720 the Renaissance was an old story. The novelty of classical detailing had already long worn off; from a mark of progressiveness it had turned into a habit. Is this then the background of the antique details on the library? In part it certainly is; but there is strong evidence that classical forms had as profound and historical a meaning for Fischer von Erlach as they had for Brunelleschi. The bulk of this evidence is to be found in the figurative decoration.

The Imperial Library is a storehouse of art treasures, being nearly as full of them as a modern museum. Sometimes its architecture serves merely as a convenient foil for the opulence of its sculpture and paintings. With seventeen lifesize statues of members of the Habsburg house, twelve busts, and nearly all the available wall area not taken up by books, as well as the entire ceiling covered with frescoes, the building was literally stuffed with art. Did a simple enjoyment of things beautiful, combined with pride in such a splendid building, cause this rich display? Not at all; every statue and each painted scene has been designed and placed in accordance with a strict iconographical programme, whose prime function was to do homage to the Emperor. This programme is understandable only in connection with Charles' fortunes, which were for that reason described at some length in the first section of this chapter.

The focal point of both architecture and decoration is the oval hall, in the centre of which stands the statue of Charles VI. He wears the costume of a Roman emperor, and the Latin inscription on the pedestal reds 'IMP.CAES/CAROLO. AVSTRIO/D.LEOP.AVG.F.AVG/HERCVLI.MVSARVM/P.P.' or, freely translated: 'The Emperor Charles of Austria, son of the late Emperor Leopold, as Hercules Musarum.' The last epithet, which can only be clumsily translated as 'Hercules of the Muses', requires some elucidation.

Charles' brother Joseph II, had at his coronation been glorified as 'Sun-king', like Louis XIV. Such a blatant plagiarism of the French court was however too much for his successor, especially as the political relations with France were none too cordial. Therefore a new title of glory had to be devised, and the name of

'Hercules Musarum' seemed to offer a worthy solution. As 'Hercules', Charles posed as a strong man in war and politics; his patronage of the arts and sciences, referred to above and shown in particular in the new library, was honoured by the addition 'Musarum', 'of the Muses'. 'Hercules' was of course the obvious title for the one-time conqueror (in name) of the pillars of Hercules, i.e. of Gibraltar.[6]

The pillars are to be found in the building too, for in all likelihood the pairs of columns below the screen-walls may be interpreted as a material representation of Charles's escutcheon, in which the two columns referred to the victory at Gibraltar.

The sixteen life-size statues of Habsburg ancestors of Charles stood originally in a palace garden. When the garden was needed for further extensions of the palace, another place for the statues had to be found. At that time the decoration of the library had not yet been completed and so they were put there, according to Buchowiecki. But there may have been something more behind the decision than mere expediency: The extension of the palace may have provided a material reason, but there can easily have been a symbolic one too. Ancestors' galleries are common in seventeenth and eighteenth century palaces, but they are unusual in a library. The books in the library had been collected by generations of Habsburgs, and the Emperor was evidently proud of the fact, for the dedicatory inscription on the front specifically mentions the 'avitam bibliothecam', the ancestral library. Secondly, the library is a sort of temple for Charles VI, whose claim to fame was largely founded on his descent. Amongst the ancestral statues we find represented: Leopold I, Charles's father; Philip II of Spain and, Charles V as one of the first statues to be seen on entering. It was on Philip and on the fifth Charles, that the sixth Charles founded his unrealizable claims to the Spanish throne. Heraeus, the imperial medallist, epigraphist and inspector of antiquities has left us a description of Charles's escutcheon, in which the connection between the two namesakes is made explicit: 'The pillars of Hercules and of Charles, justly regained, not only because of the identity in name, family and imperium [of the two Charles's], but especially because of the similarity of the expeditions to Cadiz of the sixth and the fifth Charles, are here the symbolic elements. Their meaning accords well with the motto [Constantia et Fortitudine], as 'Strength' is usually depicted carrying a column, and 'Constancy' leaning on a column. ... Therefore [we see that], after this explanation, Charles's columns express the Emperor's Strength and Constancy even without any motto. But to express better the character of the Hero (which is the principal task of Symbols), the laurel assigns one column to War, the palm the other to Peace; that peace which in the conclusion of Hercules' tasks at home, demands a no less praiseworthy constancy.'[7]

This division into 'War' and 'Peace', in both of which Charles was supposed to be a Hercules, can be found again in the iconography of the frescoes. Fortunately, their meaning is entirely clear, because their programme has been preserved.[8] What Daniel Gran, the painter of the frescoes, had to depict, was meticulously prescribed by a courtier well-versed in mythology, Adolph von Albrecht. Practically every figure and each attribute goes back to the directions of Von Albrecht, and it is to Gran's great credit that he could turn this dull and pedantic programme into such lively scenes.

Just as the building, the programme is divided into three parts, one for the oval hall and one for each of the two wings.

The wing with the public entrance is devoted to war and the terrestrial sciences. Its main scenes show Cadmus sowing the dragon's teeth, Vulcan forging arms, and allegories on the science of war and political wisdom.

The opposite wing adjoining the palace and containing the imperial entrance is suitably dedicated to peace and the heavenly sciences. The latter are glorified in the form of allegorical figures, shown by their attributes to represent theology, astronomy and orography (the geography of mountains). The 9 muses are depicted on Parnassus and Aurora (dawn) is shown riding her heavenly chariot, 'so as to indicate that by raising this wonderful book-collection an entirely new Sun has risen, which owes its shining Rays of Generosity to the illustrious Imperial Apollo, as the Ancients used to call him.'[9] The 'Imperial Apollo', prince of the Muses, is again the Hercules Musarum, or Charles VI.

On the lower zone of the central cupola is painted the School of Athens, the classical example of a university. Above that we find the now familiar picture inside domes, i.e. a representation of the sky, with an apotheosis of the Emperor. We quote again from the programme: 'As both the Roman and the Greek peoples believed that Kingdoms could be held by the Arts as much as by Gallantry—consequently their valiant Hercules was also called Musageta—therefore Hercules

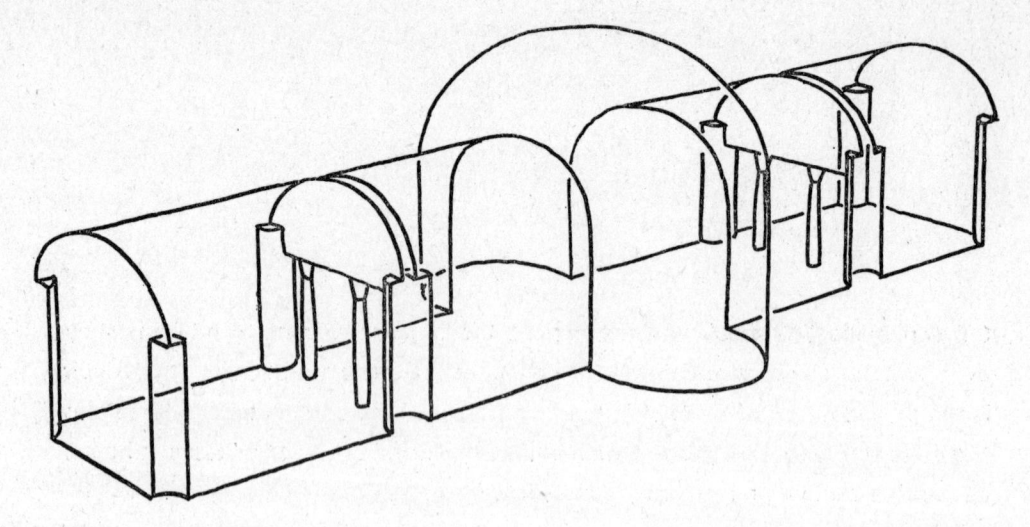

Figure 37. Imperial Library; spatial scheme

appears in the middle of the painted Vault, clad in the Nemean lion-skin, holding a large medallion with the Portrait of the Almighty Emperor Charles VI, and stretching his right arm for the reception of Gifts. At his feet kneels a Genius, who threatens to kill the three-headed Cerberus with an iron Bludgeon. The Acts of the most Gracious Monarch in Spain, and the Columns left there by Hercules Gaditani; the astonishing oratorical Gifts of the Emperor and Alcides' power to captivate the Human Heart; they all show such Similitude that in any case the God of Strength had to be chosen to support the Portrait of the Emperor. But the figure of Cerberus represents the triple Spanish, French and Turkish war, each fought to the Conclusion of Peace.'[10]

The Imperial Likeness is surrounded by allegorical females representing: Wisdom in Government, Experience in Wars, Happiness of Wise Government, Eternal Memory of Posterity, Glory of the Habsburg House, Mildness, Constancy, and, perhaps the funniest of all, the Gratitude of the Scientists. All of them pay homage to Charles, the gentlest, mightiest and proudest, the most learned, illustrious and glorious Emperor that ever had been...

The division into two wings, devoted to the terrestrial and the heavenly sciences, is shown also on the outside. On the Attic of the terrestrial wing stands Tellus, supporting the earthly globe, and on the opposite wing Atlas bears the globe of heaven. In imagery too, the inside and the outside of the building were made to correspond.

The Attic of the central hall is crowned by a Minerva in a quadriga, representing the triumph of the sciences. As the symbolism is everywhere quite involved we may perhaps surmise that this group alluded also to the original functions of the building: Minerva rising above her horses as the library above the riding school.

XIII. 'As both the Roman and the Greek peoples believed that Kingdoms could be held by the Arts as much as by Gallantry — consequently their valiant Hercules was also called Musageta — therefore Hercules appears in the middle of the painted Vault, clad in the Nemean lion-skin, holding a large medallion with the portrait of the Almighty Emperor Charles VI, and stretching his right arm for the reception of Gifts. At his feet kneels a Genius, who threatens to kill the three-headed Cerberus with an iron bludgeon. The Acts of the most Gracious Monarch in Spain, and the Columns left there by Hercules Gaditani; the astonishing oratorical Gifts of the Emperor and Alcides' power to captivate the Human Heart; they all show such Similitudo that in any case the God of Strength had to be chosen to support the Portrait of the Emperor. But the figure of Cerberus represents the triple Spanish, French and Turkish war, each fought to the Conclusion of Peace'

XIV. Perspective drawing by S Kleiner of the central hall of the Imperial Library

The other interior decoration of the library proper consisted of busts, some of which were presumably antique, and of medallions of antique authors on the bookcases. This brings us back to the question touched upon in the beginning of this section: the meaning of classical motifs. Not only the architectural details are classical, all the other decoration is dressed up in a classical garb too. All inscriptions are in Latin, the mythological figures are classical and so are the authors mentioned by name on the bookcases. The public stairway and the vestibule were decorated with real Roman remains commemorative tablets, tombstones, altar fronts and sarcophagi excavated in Austria in the period during which the library was built.

The use of classical mythology to convey an allegorical meaning and the respect paid to the famous authors of antiquity are traditions which stem from the Renaissance; but the insistence on antiquity is too strong to be due to habit alone. As Sedlmayr has pointed out,[11] it can only be understood in the context of the political mission of the Habsburgs. Charles, like his forefathers, was the Holy Roman Emperor, i.e. the legitimate successor to the Empire of Constantine and Honorius, and more recently of Charles V. Regardless of the size of his domain in reality, he was the theoretical ruler of all Italy and Germany, by virtue of his election as Emperor; with the same rights as the Ottonians and Salians—and with the same inability to enforce his rule. His immediate predecessors could lay the same claims of course; yet they were (at least in art and pomp) more modest. The beginning of the eighteenth century witnesses a great increase in the exaltation of princes, kings and emperors, with France and Louis XIV as the leading example. With the growing consciousness of the Imperial dignity, more stress was laid on his Roman heritage. A habit was reinforced by a political intention.

Two themes dominate the iconography of the library: classicism and the Emperor. The first theme is an ancillary to the second. The extensive use of ancient mythology in the decorations, the Latin of the inscriptions, the display of real Roman stones in the anterooms and the classical details of the architecture are intended to strengthen the Emperor's claims as the only true and legal ruler of the Roman empire.

And thus the entire library is a monument to the greater glory of Charles VI. The columns below the screens allude to his escutcheon; the two wings of peace and war refer to his supposedly glorious achievements in both, as well as to his armorial symbol. The books in the library point to his function of protector of the arts and sciences; ancestral statues reinforce his claims to the Spanish and the Imperial throne. The entire composition culminates in the huge central hall, with Charles's statue in the middle and his apotheosis above. The library is indeed a temple of the Muses, but Charles is its major deity.

4. Analysis

A fairly clear pattern begins to emerge in the realm of meaning. The functional core is the traditional seventeenth and eighteenth century library: a rectangular room with its walls covered with books. Probably in part to protect the books from fire, and in part to give the library a greater splendour, it was covered with vaults. The original scheme of Leopold I caused it to be put on the first floor of the building. All the rest: the oval, domed hall, the screen walls, and the entire decorative apparatus, were added for artistic reasons.

On the first level of artistic meaning we find the obvious parallels between the pomposity of baroque art and the glitter of the baroque court, between the dominance of the emperor over the court and of one motif—the oval hall—over the whole architectural composition.

The second level has been fully discussed in the preceding section. The library should be interpreted as a temple for the greater glory of the Emperor. His statue stands in the middle; his escutcheon is symbolized in the iconography; all decorations emphasize his perfect taste, his supreme power and his infinite wisdom.

The adulation for the person of Charles VI is entirely foreign to our minds. The cold analysis of modern history reveals him as an unbending formalist, with rather less insight in the politics of his time than most of his contemporary colleagues; or, to put it more harshly, a vain and superficial monarch not possessing to any remarkable degree the gifts so lavishly praised in the library. And so one is inclined to ask: why? Why the sycophancy? the pomp and display? What need is there to exalt one already so elevated by birth and election? Is he really the great man he is said to be, or does it have to be repeated over and over again because he is not quite up to the mark? In truth Charles was far from almighty or invincible, and even the fruits of his one-time victory in Gibraltar remained beyond his reach. All the adulation breathes the *wish* to believe in his might. His effective power was very small in Italy and nearly negligible in Germany; his subjects in Hungary were chafing under the imperial yoke; during his reign the Empire shrank still further.

To explain the library as the outcome of Charles's personal circumstances however would oversimplify the issue. Austrian Baroque[12] is part and parcel of European Baroque, and not all European monarchs were as helpless as Charles VI. But his predicament is partly the outcome of a far more widespread social phenomenon: the gradual disintegration of society. The bonds of feudal society had been broken in the Renaissance and the Reformation. Feudal society was static, and people were linked to each other by mutual relations; it mattered little if this was often no more than theory, as long as it was *experienced* as a bond. In contrast, the main characteristic of sixteenth century society was its mobility: everyone fended for himself and success was a token of the Lord's blessing. As people started to move in the social field, they naturally tried to improve themselves. Those who succeeded in bettering themselves believed this mobility to be temporary and relative, and therefore suppressed their inferiors as much as possible. Thus the cleft between rich and poor, between ruler and ruled gradually became wider and wider.

For this reason, Baroque architects strove for unity in design, to counterbalance the social disunity, just as the Renaissance architects aimed at a non-existent stability. One of the greatest social cleavages was that between Catholics and Protestants, which was particularly troublesome to the Habsburg Emperors as they had subjects of both denominations. Leopold, Charles's father, went out of his way to reduce friction and bring the parties together. He nominated an Inspector General of the Union (of creeds) and in the Imperial decree of appointment we read: 'that Divine and human law impose as a duty, and that several addresses and Protestant letters to the Bishop, point out the necessity to strive for a perfect Unity in worldy and spiritual matters in the Christian States, both within and without Germany, and especially in the present distress; and [that we have] to remove the existent differences and mutual suspicion, if not on all (though the Scriptures and common sense make us hope for that too), then at least on the essential points of Faith; for it may seem, and has been found indeed [on investigation] that the discord in the minds and meanings on the principal points arose only from a lack of mutual and affectionate patience, of clear understanding and correct explanation of the thoughts according to their true contents, and finally from the diversity of words and the different uses made thereof.'[13]

Leopold may still have believed that a little heart-to-heart talk would heal the rupture; but this naïve view faded soon before the facts. And with the growth of the differences between Protestants and Catholics, between powerful and powerless, the need for unity became ever more apparent. Baroque society (or rather its leading faction) saw this unity as a form of enlightened despotism. The Austrian emperor ruled over all dissident factions; he alone could join all the forces, pacify the enmities; in his person all the different strands came together. And indeed he was the only hope, for the greater part of his domain clung together because of imperial family ties and not because of any natural geographic or ethnic boundaries. The ideal of an autocratic ruler, who could rally his discordant subjects around the throne was common to all Baroque courts, from Louis XIV to the tiniest German principality. In France, nothing much came of this rallying round as the Revolution was soon to show, for an ever widening gulf separated the monarch from his subjects. And this was only one of the rifts in the delicate social fabric. As medieval society converged, Baroque society diverged.

The problem was still the same as it had been in the Renaissance, but it had been aggravated. The dream of a harmonious cosmos, which had 'truly existed' in Antiquity, had failed to come off; on the contrary, it seemed further from reality than ever. The old symbolism had grown a bit stale; already in the Age of Mannerism it seemed no longer adequate. Baroque architecture tried to overpower disbelief in dreamland with the strongest means it could think of.

It used imposing size. Baroque was the Age of the 'grand manner'. All its building programmes were on a vast scale: Versailles, Blenheim Palace, the Würzburg Residence, and also Fischer's completely irrealistic first designs for Schönbrunn. The Imperial Library is colossal too, in its width and height and particularly in its huge domed hall of fame. Colossality is enhanced on the exterior by the vertical grouping of openings in the centres of the pavilions, the giant pilasters and the vertical projecting mass of the central hall.

Massiveness is another device. The crisp elegance of the Early Renaissance seemed too much 'out of this world'. It had been gradually replaced by a heavier treatment of masses. The projecting central part of the façade of the Library punches you in the nose. The plastic treatment of the interior, with its rounded-off corners, strong columns, deep window recesses and heavy mouldings emphasizes the material existence of the architectural symbol.

The way in which the outside world is experienced and evaluated affects formal aesthetics, according to our tenets. Baroque architecture is less coherent than Renaissance: it uses bolder contrasts in form and proportion. The great hall is angular on the outside and oval within; it is sharply separated from the wings in the roof area, whereas it is united to them on the interior. The disjunctions may have added to the impression of realism.

But unity, in opposition to social divergence, remained the ideal. In Versailles, Kassel, Bruchsal, Karlsruhe and in Fischer's projects for Schönbrunn, landscape and palace were bound together by an axis of symmetry which stretched as far as the eye could see. In principle it should embrace the cosmos. In the Library, the compartments 2 and 4 were 'fused' with the central hall, with the help of the undulating contour of the balconies. Renaissance architects created conceptual spaces in the form of Phileban solids; Fischer treated it more like a dough-like mass, with somewhat indeterminate boundaries.

The desire for unity pervaded the details, witness the bookcases absorbed in the wall surfaces, and the smooth exterior skin of the stucco and paint. Part of the Baroque preference for plaster is due to the unity of surface which can be obtained with it.

This symbolic unity is however not that of the modern office block with its dreary monotony. The composition of the library culminates in the central hall of fame. The visitor to the Library is led to this climax with infinite care; every part-space is a link in the chain. Like the statuary, with its waving arms and *contrapposto*, it has *movement* as a central theme. Hence the preference for oval above circular plans: they combine the uniqueness and enclosure of the circular space with a directional emphasis. Movement was supposed to create an illusion of life in painting and sculpture, enhancing their reality. It served a similar purpose in architecture. Renaissance buildings are independent of the spectator; they do not present 'special views' and it usually matters but little where you enter them. The Baroque aims at *involvement:* the visitor's progression through space is carefully planned and he is to be visually shocked as often as possible. He should be submerged, drowned in the spatial experience; because then he will believe in the reality of the symbol too.

To us it seems all rather theatrical. The Baroque is the great age of the spectacle, replete with optical tricks. Charles VI employed Galli-Bibiena as an imperial stage-engineer. Daniel Gran's allegorical figures reach out of their painted architectural framing. The view from each entrance, down the gallery, towards Charles' statue is obviously a staged perspective (Plate XII).

The building, the decoration and the texts quoted honour Charles as the great, wise, benevolent and well-loved Emperor; they fail to convince us, and perhaps we may read from their exaggerations that they failed to convince their authors too. All the art of the truly great masters of the Imperial Library is put at the service of the Emperor, and at the idea of a unified society, behind that one man.

But their hearts do not seem to be in it and it remains the unity of make-believe

Westminster New Palace
London   1835–1865

1. Description

Approximately in 1052 Edward the Confessor founded Westminster Abbey and close to it Westminster Palace. In 1066 William the Conqueror earned his nickname at Hastings. His son, William Rufus, started to extend the palace and though he got no further than Westminster Hall (1097–1099), the complex was henceforth called Westminster New Palace.[1] The present hall is Norman only in its substructure; it was covered with a hammer-beam roof by Hugh Herland and extensively restored by Henry Yevele in the fourteenth century. It was used for state ceremonies, like coronation feasts or important trials.

Various kings added to the Palace, which gradually grew to be an irregular conglomerate of halls, rooms and corridors. Worthy of note from the historic viewpoint is only the addition of St. Stephen's chapel,[2] founded by the obscure King Stephen (1135–1154), pulled down and rebuilt by Edward I and completed by Edward III, who turned it over to a religious college. St. Stephen's was a typical palace chapel with two stories, like the Sainte Chapelle in Paris. The lower story, dedicated to Mary, is still preserved, albeit heavily restored, below the oblique passage between Westminster Hall and the octagonal hall in the middle of the Palace.

The deacons of the religious college gathered for services on the first floor. A palace chapel is by its very nature rather small, so they were pressed for room; therefore they altered the traditional arrangement of the choir stalls into rising tiers of benches, one on each side. With the secession of the English Church under Henry VIII the college was disbanded, and from 1547 to 1834 it was used for the meetings of Parliament. The House had the chapel modernized several times, but it retained the seating arrangement of the college.[3]

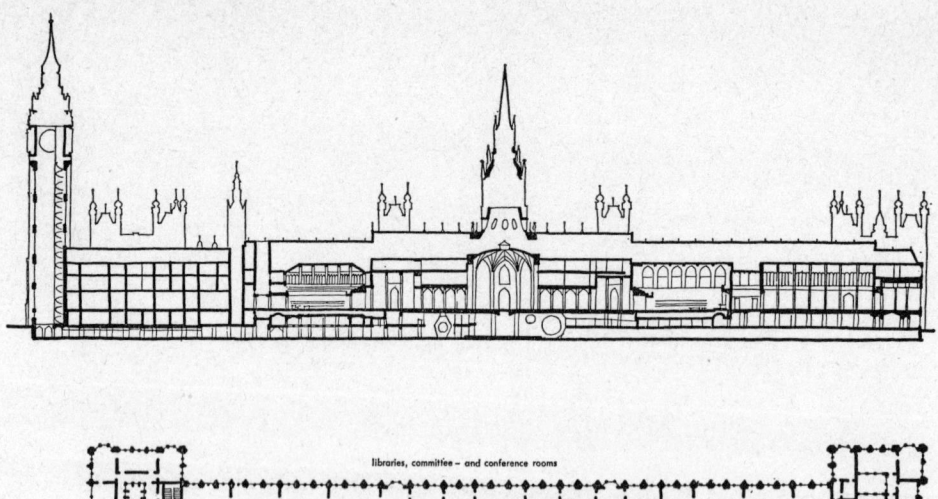

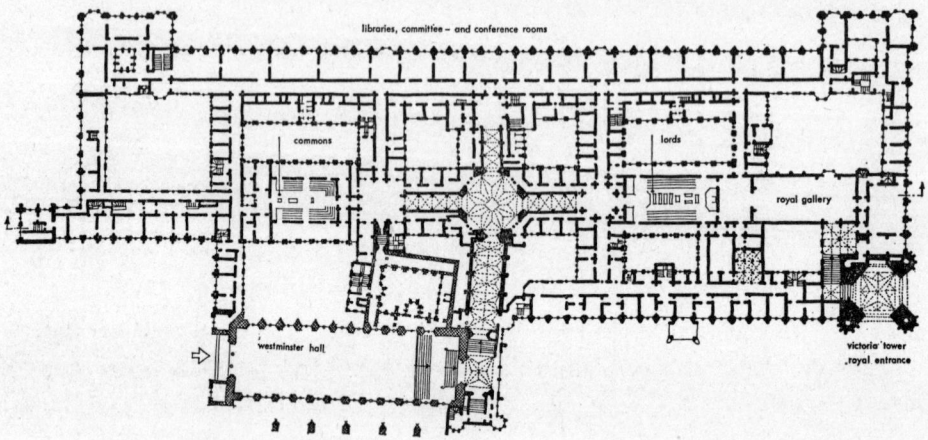

Figure 38. Westminster New Palace; section and plan

In 1834 a truly magnificent fire destroyed the whole historic complex, with the exception of Westminster Hall, St. Stephen's cloister and the ground floor of St. Stephen's chapel. The government held an open competition for a new and more spacious Parliament building. It had to accommodate the House of Lords, the House of Commons, a royal entrance for Queen Victoria to open the Parliamentary sessions, and further a string of committee rooms, libraries, and offices. The extant portions of the old Palace were to be incorporated in the new building, and to preserve some unity between the old and the new work, it was specified that the design should be either Gothic or Elizabethan.

The competition was won by Charles Barry. His plan was as simple as it was convenient. The two Houses of Parliament, central to the function of the building, were laid out also in the centre of the complex, one on either side of an octagonal hall. Members had to enter the House through Westminster Hall, climb a staircase at the end and turning left, walk through a high, and vaulted corridor towards the octagonal hall.

Behind the House of Lords lies the Royal Gallery. Queen Victoria entered through the porch below Victoria Tower, ascended a staircase, and could prepare herself for the opening ceremony in the Queen's Robing Room and the Gallery.

The rising tiers of benches of St. Stephen's College, which had proved so convenient in Parliamentary practice, were, on the express wish of the House, retained in the new building. Thus a chance solution created by a college cramped for space, was perpetuated in the greatest of English institutions.

All other rooms required by the programme were laid out around a series of quadrangles, the main committee rooms and libraries along the river front. As is evident from the plans, Barry had a clear eye for essentials, and he succeeded in incorporating the extant remains in the most natural manner possible. One can only applaud the decision of the jury.

What about the style required? Barry's son has left us an extensive biography of his father,[4] and a large portion of the book is devoted to the Houses of Parliament, in which the important questions of style, decoration, plan etc. are treated at length. Barry's own opinion would have been even more worthwhile, but he had neither time nor inclination for writing. So I quote the Rev. Alfred Barry: 'Between the prescribed styles of Elizabethan and Gothic there was no long hesitation. The former appeared a bastard style, unfit for a building of such magnitude. Gothic was at once chosen. Of all its styles Mr. Barry admired most the Early English; but he then thought it hardly fit for other than ecclesiastical purposes. Finally he chose Perpendicular, thinking it would lend itself most easily to the requirements of the building, and to the principle of regularity, which he intended to introduce in his design.'[5]

The correct execution of a building in a style of the past is not to be thought of lightly, not today but not in 1835 either. One had to study its characteristics and to get thoroughly acquainted with its manner of detailing. Such work requires years of study, and is clearly the job of specialists. Barry's own specialization was the 'Italianate manner', by which was meant High Italian Renaissance. This style he had studied in detail during a tour of Italy, and continued to use all through his professional life. 'But he felt that, under all circumstances, Gothic was the best style fitted for the New Palace, and if Westminster Hall was to be made a feature in the design, the only style possible; and he was consoled for the loss of Italian mainly by the thought of the facility given by Gothic for the erection of towers, the one method by which he thought it possible to redeem from insignificance a great building, and for which a low and unfavourable site had been provided.'[6] Therefore he called in a renowned specialist in the Gothic style, August Welby Pugin. Under Barry's supervision, Pugin clothed a building Italianate—if anything—in plan, in a Gothic attire.[7] Of course Pugin protested that it was archeologically indefensible to put Gothic façades and Gothic details on such an un-Gothic building. 'It's all Greek' he is reputed to have said to a friend, meaning the plan and the masses. Yet, to our eyes and after a century has passed, the union of the incompatibles seems a happy one. It has certainly produced a building far more interesting than any of Pugin's own 'true' Gothic churches. The Perpendicular proved indeed easily adaptable to the great variety of rooms, towers and pavillions. Nowhere are we struck by jarring inconsistencies, either in plan or in detail. Barry's choice of an expert could not have been improved upon; we have reason to be grateful once more.

The analysis of the building is comparatively simple. Practically all spaces and masses are rectangular in form. With such a vast programme no other shape is possible. Exceptions are the octagonal hall in the centre, the vaulted corridors and the trapezoïdal ceiling over the House of Commons, which was considerably altered shortly after the opening, for it was originally rectangular too.

The surfaces of the elevations visible to the public and of the more important interiors are covered with a fine mesh of Gothic details. Alfred Barry gives his fathers opinion on the decoration: 'His notion was that a general spread of minute ornament, a kind of "diapering" of the whole, was rich, but more simple, because less likely to interfere with the main outline, than ornaments on a large scale more sparingly employed. In the particular case before him he thought that smallness of scale in details would help to give an appearance of size to the building. But his feeling always was that ornamentation, if right in kind, could not be overdone; he did not recognize the value of plainer portions to act as a "setting" of the decoration; to him they appeared as "neglected spots" and partiality of ornament he considered as tawdriness.'[8] Barry shared this last opinion probably with the majority of his contemporary colleagues, for all nineteenth century architecture is notorious for a surfeit of decoration. Only the interior courtyards and the subsidiary rooms were left plain.

The construction shows some interesting details. The building is of the traditional type with floorbeams supported by bearing walls. As the previous palace had gone up in flames, great attention was paid to adequate fireproofing. The floors consist of brick jack-arches between cast-iron joists, the latter resting on the limestone outside walls or the brick interior walls; the floors were then levelled with cement. Most unusual are the roofs: galvanized cast-iron plates are screwed onto iron rafters. The Second World War has proved that these roofs are fully as fireproof as Barry expected them to be.

The symbolic structure is mainly a 'sham'. As appears from the description above, the walls are continuous and homogeneous. But the Gothic decoration is concentrated, as Gothic should be. In contrast to the eighteenth century, the nineteenth century architects were dimly aware of the discrepancy between real and symbolic structure. Barry junior writes: 'At the same time a change was made as to the buttresses of the whole front. They had no thrust to sustain, they interrupted the cornice and string-courses, and interfered with the panelling. For these reasons Mr. Barry himself disliked them, and, external criticism coinciding with his own feeling, he resolved to change them into turrets, which were free from all these objections, and which would tend at once to elevate and break the sky-line, and, by their greater projection to relieve the flatness of the front.'[9] A structural fake was exchanged for a functional one, for where do the turrets lead to? They contain no stairs, but serve art only.

Even more outspoken is Pugin. On the first page of his *True Principles of Pointed or Christian Architecture* he states: 'The two great rules for design are these: 1st, that there should be no features about a building which are not necessary for convenience, construction or propriety; 2nd, that all ornament should consist of enrichment of the essential construction of the building. ... In pure architecture the smallest detail should have a meaning or serve a purpose; and even the construction itself should vary with the material employed, and the designs should be adapted to the material in which they are executed.'[10] And further on we read: 'All plaster, cast-iron and composition ornaments, painted like stone or oak, are mere impositions, and although very suitable to a tea-garden, are utterly unworthy of a sacred edifice. Let every man build to God according to his means, but not practise showy deceptions; better it is to do a little substantially and consistently with truth, than to produce a great but fictitious effect.'[11] A modern architect may well rub his eyes: here is the principle of 'form follows function', which made Louis Sullivan famous, and to which many modern architects paid their homage. Poor Pugin is blamed with the sins of the Gothic Revival, for (in our eyes) he did not practise as he preached. Yet his views and his work are consistent in the main. He fought against the stucco vaults and the plaster columns; against *structural* deceptions. But he was an advocate of stylistic shamming, of using Gothic forms on nineteenth century buildings, and for that he is reproached today.

If Pugin contributed the bulk of the detailing, Barry must be held responsible for the composition, and it is a truly remarkable achievement. The difficult requirements of the programme are met with ease; the extant remains of the previous building have been incorporated in the New Palace without a hitch. The main features of the composition are three: the regularity of the overall scheme, the predilection for spatial dramatization and the lively skyline.

As an Italianate architect Barry was naturally wont to think in orderly, symmetrical layouts, regardless of the decoration. His son writes: 'The plan and style being thus fixed, the composition of the design next suggested the question, whether there was anything in the Gothic style which ought to interfere with the principles of symmetry, regularity and unity, so dear to his artistic taste. Many (and his friend Pugin especially) contended for irregularity, picturesqueness and variety. They would have had a group of buildings rather than a single one, or at any rate a building, in which there should be a general unity of style, rather than an actual symmetry of design, which they stigmatized as "clothing a classical design with Gothic details". But Mr. Barry's notions were widely different. He conceived that, if certain first principles were true, they could not vary in different styles.'[12] And indeed, if I assess Gothic architecture correctly, he was more nearly right than he knew, for regularity and order seem to be prime characteristics of the Gothic we encountered.

Formal, regular plans of the type of Westminster New Palace go back however to the seventeenth and eighteenth century palaces and country-houses, and ultimately to the Renaissance with its preference for symmetry and order. Barry's creation can be linked with the work of Soane, Wren, Inigo Jones and finally Palladio.[13] Formal planning continued to exercise its spell over many nineteenth century architects; in particular the pupils of the Ecole des Beaux Arts were once renowned for their formal plans. An ill-reputed example in our own time is the Palace of the League of Nations in Geneva, which has many points in common with Barry's creation. Easier on the modern eye, but as formal as any of them, is the work of Mies van der Rohe.

Irregularity versus regularity, after having been a whimsical sideline in the eighteenth century,[14] became an issue in the nineteenth. Early irregular examples are the cottages by Gandy and the gardens of Capability Brown, famous for their 'natural' informality. Then Sir Uvedale Price defended irregularity as an artistic principle in its own right (1794),[15] and the debate was on. All through the nineteenth century the 'irregulars' grew in strength and numbers. Among the better known architectural examples are the London Law Courts, St. Pancras Hotel, Balmoral Castle and the Red House of William Morris. Famous modern 'irregulars' are Wright and Aalto. Both types of composition will be encountered in the next three chapters, the Amsterdam Exchange and the Ronchamp Chapel belonging to the irregular school, and Johnson's house to the opposite party.

The object of irregular planning is the same as the axial composition of Versailles: a unification of building and landscape. But whereas the Baroque scheme subordinates the park land to the rigorous symmetry of man-made design, irregular planning adapts the building to the landscape. The idea arose through the cult of nature in the eighteenth century. A composition embracing landscape and building can be interpreted as a symbol for social unity.

Irregular picturesque massing appears in the Houses of Parliament in the disposition of the towers. However, the backbone of the scheme is still the regular plan of the preceding tradition.

Likewise traditional (at least in part) is the love of spatial drama, already encountered in the Viennese Library. The unsuspecting visitor to the Houses of Parliament enters through Westminster Hall, ascends a grand staircase and follows a majestic corridor to the central octagon. How can he help but feel deeply impressed by the majesty of the building, and, by inference, by the august dignity of Parliament? Barry only regretted that he could not finish this progression in a grand climax (as in Vienna): 'He disliked, as an error of principle, the necessary duality of the design, and the need of carrying on the great line of approach to inferior rooms, while the Houses of Lords and Commons lay on the right and left. He would have preferred some one feature incontestably the chief, so as to give the unity which he craved. But the plan adopted was recommended by grandeur, simplicity and convenience, and these considerations kept him firm and unhesitating in his adherence to it.'[16]

Westminster Hall, so difficult to provide with an adequate function within the complex, was used as a gigantic entrance porch. 'For the embellishment of the hall he (Barry) had... grand dreams; frescoes, trophies and statues were to have met the eye, "set" in profuse enrichment of colour and mosaic, and the whole was to have formed a British Walhalla.'[17] The progression of the Queen from the porch below the Victoria Tower to the House of Lords goes through a sequence of rooms, similar to that from Westminster Hall to the octagonal hall and nearly as impressive. As in the Viennese Library (only to a lesser degree) it seems a theatrical effect in our more sober eyes.

The lively skyline of the Palace, which makes it such a grateful subject for amateur photographers, is not the logical outcome of the distribution of rooms, but a feature intentionally grafted onto the design, to counteract the supposed monotony and lowness of the masses. Alfred Barry writes; '... two general tendencies must be noticed. The first was the desire to increase as much as possible the upward tendency of the lines of the design, to elevate and vary the sky-line throughout. Every ventilating shaft was taken advantage of; every turret was heightened, till the central lantern, itself an insertion, was surrounded by a forest of louvres and spires. The whole character of the design was changed and the change arose, partly from the original predilection for the spire form, partly from an advancing knowledge of Gothic architecture, but principally from practical experience of the great architectural disadvantages entailed by the site, and the comparative lowness of the building itself. The other tendency was to profuse ornamentation.'[18] The location once innocently chosen by Edward the Confessor had for historic and practical reasons to be used again. But Barry would have infinitely preferred to raise his palace on a spur or a bluff, and to see it towering over the entire city of London. When the nineteenth century architect was given a free hand, as in numerous country-houses for instance, he put them invariably on the highest point of the landscape, where today their splendour still offends our eyes. Nineteenth century architectural perspectives are always taken from an extremely low point of vision; once again to dramatize the buildings depicted.[19]

2. Analysis

The requirements of the programme determined to a large extent the disposition of the rooms around the courtyards. Today we would have a slightly different view of functional planning, and build more compactly. A modern architect would probably collect all public areas like the two Houses, the committee rooms and lobbies into one large low building and the office space (which, due to Parkinson's Law, would be probably much larger) into a skyscraper. The result would be something like the U.N. building in New York. But Barry did not dispose over an advanced technique in steel or concrete, and the lengthy corridors were no obstacle to his more leisured contemporaries. He was also a functionalist, in *his* time and *his* style.

In part however, the gridiron plan and the symmetry are also due to artistic intentions, as was explained above. The other artistic points of interest are: the symmetry of the river front, corresponding to the symmetry of the gridiron plan; the 'grand entrances' of the Queen and of members and visitors through Westminster Hall; the lively silhouette; and the elaborate Gothic details.

The symmetry and regularity can, in my opinion, be largely ascribed to tradition. Formal compositions had been in vogue for two centuries. The dignity of the government and the unique historic site recommended a formal layout in the grand manner. As in Vienna, there was the (reasonable) wish to impress.

The spatial sequences of the royal and public entrances are also a heritage of the past. As in the Imperial Library, great attention was given to a variety of spatial impressions: witness for instance the Queen's ascent in the Victoria Tower, followed by the vestibule (Robing Room), the Royal Gallery and finally the House of Lords. Theatrical lighting effects, such as the huge window at the end of Westminster Hall, or the oriel in the Royal Gallery, heighten the effect. The entire layout has been designed around these stately progressions from Westminster Hall to the two Houses and from Victoria Tower to the House of Lords. Summerson has remarked the similarity between the central octagon with its four abutting corridors and the plan of Wyatt's Fonthill Abbey.[20] The probability that Barry was inspired by Fonthill is greatly increased if we note that the main entrances correspond too: each consists of a large hall with a hammer-beam roof and has a majestic staircase opposite the entrance. The object of such spatial sequences was of course the same as in the Baroque. Barry wanted to *involve* the spectator in his building. It is a means to emphasize the reality of the architectural dreamland.

New in comparison with the Baroque is the rich Gothic decoration. From this richness we can draw our parallel of first level meaning, trite though it may seem. The wealth in forms and details corresponds with the rich and rapid development of nineteenth century England. New branches of knowledge arose: Darwin discovered evolution, Maxwell and Faraday penetrated into the secrets of electricity. Cooperative societies and trade unions came into being; literature and philosophy flourished, with Dickens, Carlyle, Thackeray, Spencer and Mill. English explorers like Livingstone, Burke and Stuart travelled through areas still white on the maps. Industries sprang up like mushrooms and in 1851 England showed the world with pride the extent of its production in the Great Exhibition. It was certainly an interesting period, and the variety in all sections of culture was parallelled by a variety of styles in building, often practised by one and the same architect. Barry used Gothic on the Palace, Italian High Renaissance on the Reform Club and Jacobean on Highclere Castle. Westminster New Palace is a romantic building in a romantic age, full of inventions and adventure, rich in wealth and variety of production.

But Gothic was not chosen only for its richness, or even only because of it having been specified by the competition programme. The Palace is one of the great monuments of the Gothic Revival, which had such a profound Christian significance to Pugin. He stresses also its national character: '...the erection of the Parliament Houses in the national style is by far the greatest advance that has yet been gained in the right direction. The long lines of fronts and excessive repetition are certainly not in accordance with the ancient spirit of civil architecture, but the detail is most consoling. We have the arms and badges of a long succession of our kings; images of ecclesiastical, military and royal personages; appropriate legends in beautiful text run on every scroll: each emblem is characteristic of our country. The internal decoration is to be of a purely national character—the ab-

XV. 'Every ventilating shaft has been taken advantage of, every turret was heightened, till the central lantern, itself an insertion, was surrounded by a forest of louvres and spires. The whole character of the design was changed and the change arose, partly from the original predilection for the spire form, partly from an advancing knowledge of Gothic architecture, but principally from practical experience of the great architectural disadvantages entailed by the site and the comparative lowness of the building itself' (A. Barry)

XVI. 'For the embellishment of the hall he had grand dreams: frescoes, trophies and statues were to have met the eye, "set" in profuse enrichment of colour and mosaic, and the whole was to have formed a British Walhalla' (A Barry). St. Stephens Porch at the end of Westminster Hall

XVII. ...'but the detail is most consoling' (A. W. Pugin). The lower part of Victoria Tower, Westminster New Palace

XVIII. ...'his feeling always was that ornamentation, if right in kind, could not be overdone; he did not recognize the value of plainer portions to act as a "setting" of the decoration; to him they appeared as "neglected spots" and partiality of ornament he considered as tawdriness' (A. Barry). The interior of the Peer's Lobby in Westminster New Palace

surdities of mythology utterly rejected—and, if the architect's design for the great tower be carried out, we shall have a monument of English art which was not been surpassed even in antiquity. This building is the morning star of the great revival of national architecture and art; it is a complete and practical refutation of those men who venture to assert that pointed architecture is not suitable for public edifices; for the plan embodies every possible convenience of access, light and distribution of the various halls and chambers, without the aid of false doors, blank windows, mock pediments, adapted temple fronts and show domes to make up an elevation.'[21] Yet, though there may be as little mock construction as Pugin says, there is plenty of mock Gothic.

Why such admiration for the past in a truly modern and progressive age? Architects were not alone in professing an ardent love of history; the Victorians enjoyed reading the praises of medieval art sung by Ruskin and the historical novels of Sir Walter Scott. Antiquarian too was the church revival. In part the ardent cultivation of the English past may have been founded on the same motives as the Renaissance revival of antiquity. The economic and industrial expansion, the conquest of distant colonies and the Napoleonic wars created an upsurge of national feeling. The rapid changes in society (compared with the eighteenth century) may have brought about an attitude similar to that of tumultuous fifteenth century Italy. And so the picture of Gothic England, stable and thoroughly English, could appear as a true expression of the early Victorian ideal.

But there is more. We saw in the preceding chapter how cracks had appeared in the social fabric between people of different creeds, or of different social station. The full extent of the disintegration of society became evident in the French Revolution. England had been spared such bloody trials, but did that mean that the English were united? or rather: *felt* united? Carlyle writes: 'We call it a Society; and go about professing openly the totalest separation, isolation. Our life is not a mutual helpfulness; but, rather, cloaked under due laws-of-war, named "fair competition", and so forth, it is a mutual hostility.'[22] True, democracy progressed with the enfranchisement of the Reform Bills, and Shaftesbury's efforts at social improvements were not without avail. But the rapid development of society through the Industrial Revolution produced something like an earthquake: where one gap was closed, another appeared just next to it. The growing division of labour chopped up the process of manufacture into a series of meaningless routine tasks: man got estranged from the product of his own hands. Architect and engineer became different professions, whereas they had been one in the eighteenth century. The artist turned from a recognized member of society into the bohemian he has to be today. The political differences slowly disappeared, but the social ones increased. Particularly the *awareness* of poverty of the poor increased, when they met their fellows in the slum; mass destitution replaced the unobtrusive poverty of the individual in the village. The results were the well known tales of horror of Dickens, Mrs. Gaskell and others.

Here is a description of a visit to the London slums by Taine: 'I recall the alleys which run into Oxford Street, stifling lanes encrusted with human exhalations; the seats on London Bridge where families, huddled together with drooping heads, shiver through the night. Every hundred steps one jostles twenty harlots; some of them ask for a glass of gin; others say: "Sir, it is to pay my lodging." This is not debauchery which flaunts itself, but destitution—and such destitution! The deplorable procession in the shade of the monumental streets is sickening; it seems to me a march of the dead. That is the plague-spot, the real plague-spot of English society.'[23]

Carlyle could complain and Dickens could expose, but the majority of the Victorians did what most of us would do at a very unpleasant sight: they closed their eyes. They drew their heavy curtains and lost themselves in a contemplation of the past; of things distant, foreign and whimsical sometimes, but in any case far from the madding crowd. The Victorian age is that of the fairy tales of Edward Lear and Lewis Carroll, of the fantastic journeys on paper by Jules Verne, and in reality by explorers like Livingstone. Evasion is the keynote of much Romantic and Victorian literature; the evasion of the individual, like Thoreau in Walden, or of a small perfect society in some secluded place, like the Phalanstères of Fourier. Coleridge has left us a vivid description of this monastic ideal: 'What I dared not expect from constitutions of government and whole nations, I hoped from religion and a small company of chosen individuals. I formed a plan, as harmless as it was extravagant, of trying the experiment of human perfectibility on the banks of the Susquehanna; where our little society, in its second generation, was to have combined the innocence of the patriarchal age with the knowledge and genuine refinements

of European culture; and where I dreamed that in the sober evening of my life, I should behold the cottages of independence in the undivided dale of industry,—
    And oft, soothed sadly by some dirgeful wind,
    Muse on the sore ills I had left behind!
Strange fancies, and as vain as strange!'[24] Coleridge reacted to the 'sore ills' of around 1800, but though the villains changed, the ills remained, and with it the desire to get away from it all.

This is to my mind the fundamental cause of the eclectic architecture of the last century. Victorian hotels and railway stations are castellated; town halls, office buildings and even simple schools are decked out in Venetian Gothic, Pisan Romanesque, Hindoo, Moorish, Byzantine or French Renaissance. To some of us they look like nightmares, and to none probably do they look like real, solid architecture. The impression, I believe, is in a way correct; they are 'castles in the air', dreams come true in stone. Hence their fantastic aspect, but hence, too the eclectic preoccupation with 'correct' design; for the dream should be made as real as possible. Also, to strengthen the realism of the fantastic, detail was heaped upon detail, till the incredible profusion of—for instance—Westminster Palace was reached.

The past was a natural refuge from reality. With yet scanty knowledge of its contents, it could be idealized beyond all limits. Here Pugin draws an enthusiastic picture of the merry England of his beloved Gothic period: '...and the almost constant residence of the ancient gentry on their estates rendered it indispensable for them to have mansions where they might exercise the rights of hospitality to their fullest extent. They did not confine their guests, as at present, to a few fashionables who condescend to pass away a few days occasionally in a country house; but under the oaken rafters of their capacious halls, the lords of the manor used to asemble all their friends and tenants at those successive periods when the church bids all her children rejoice, while humbler guests partook of their share of the bounty dealt to them by the hand of the almoner beneath the groined entrance of the gate-house. Catholic England was merry England, at least for the humbler classes; and the architecture was in keeping with the faith and manners of the times—at once strong and hospitable.'[25]

This charming fantasy shows the aims of the Gothic Revival clearly. It contrasts a unified society of the past with the divergent society of its day. Social divergence had increased since the Renaissance; it now embraced all classes. The classical dreamland had gone stale and had clearly failed to work. Hence, a different symbolism was tried. But even the belief in dreamlands as such was undermined. Several possibilities offered themselves: Moorish (Nash), Chinese (Chambers), or Greek (Adam, Soane); none could command universal belief. Therefore Pugin pleads so eloquently for the Gothic Revival; he wants to convince himself as much as his readers.

As in Baroque, the reality of dreamland was stressed with as much emphasis as possible. The spatial sequences and the preference for elevated sites stemmed from the same principle: the spectator should be overpowered, his doubts silenced. Barry regretted his lowly site and used a forest of towers to impress us with the reality of his creation.

But the make-believe shone through, ever more clearly now that eclecticism offered a variety of dreams. That is what makes Pugin inveigh against shams and formulate the doctrines of functionalism.

But some will protest: not all nineteenth century architecture was a sham. For instance the Crystal Palace, or the great sheds of the railway stations, or Britannia Bridge over Menai Straits, are marvellous pieces of honest architecture, without any 'castellated' nonsense. Those are works we can admire, and how pallid does eclecticism appear by its side!

None of these examples can however be counted as a work of art, in the sense that the word has been used here. What emotional appeal they may have is accidental and meaningless. Paxton, the architect of the Crystal Palace, was a gardener; the other examples were designed by engineers. All set about to solve some technical problem, and artistic intentions were far from their minds. 'That is why they produced such good work!' modern critics will say. I can agree when it is differently phrased: 'That is why they produced work which still appeals to *us* so strongly.' The clean simplicity of the engineering designs is not appreciated for any positive artistic feature, but negatively, rather for the lack of it.

Amidst the welter of eclectic forms they are conspicuous for being bare. If we consider them to be more truly works of art than the eclectic architecture, and try to be consistent and just, we have also to raise medieval ships to the level of Gothic cathedrals, or windmills to that of Renaissance architecture, for ships and mills too are nearly pure engineering constructions. To my mind such speculations do not get us any further. We may admire a sunset, but we will not mistake it for a work of art; and I hold our admiration for the great Victorian feats of engineering to be on the same level. For the architecture of the period we should take and study what was intended as such and not any sideline, however interesting it may appear. Another matter is the reason why *we* evaluate Victorian architecture so differently from the Victorians themselves. The next chapters may partly answer that question.

The Amsterdam Exchange
Amsterdam   1898–1903

1. Description

Holland had become a dependency of France in the French revolution. The British blockade of the continent during the Napoleonic wars cut off all its maritime commerce, traditionally one of the mainstays of this seafaring nation.

The Dutch economy recovered but slowly from these setbacks. Only in 1870 did Holland begin to industrialize: then a unified Germany became an eager client for Dutch transit trade, steamship companies were founded and trade with the Dutch East Indies increased steadily.

As trade began to recover, the existing Amsterdam Exchange (built 1841–1845) soon became too small. After endless discusions a two-stage competition was held between 1883 and 1885. It did not lead to any results. The winner, the French architect L. Cordonnier, was shown to have copied the façade of his main elevation; this was too much even for nineteenth century taste. The later architect, Hendrik P. Berlage, got a fourth prize with a Neo-Renaissance project. Neo-Renaissance was popular in Holland, because it was the first truly 'national' style, and because it was associated with the Golden Age of the Dutch Republic, an age which was to be emulated now. In 1896 Berlage was asked to give expert advice on the technical and financial aspects of a new Exchange. Later in the same year he was commissioned to design the building.

Berlage, at that time 40 years old, had completely changed his ideas. He had abandoned eclectic architecture and now strove for an ever greater simplicity. Signs of his new attitude can be seen in two office buildings for insurance companies, the 'Algemene Maatschappij van Levensverzekering' on the Damrak of 1893 and the 'Nederlanden van 1845' on the Muntplein of 1895. His radicalism in design and his leftist leanings may have made him an attractive choice for the radical alderman of the Amsterdam municipal council, Treub, who headed the

THE AMSTERDAM EXCHANGE 153

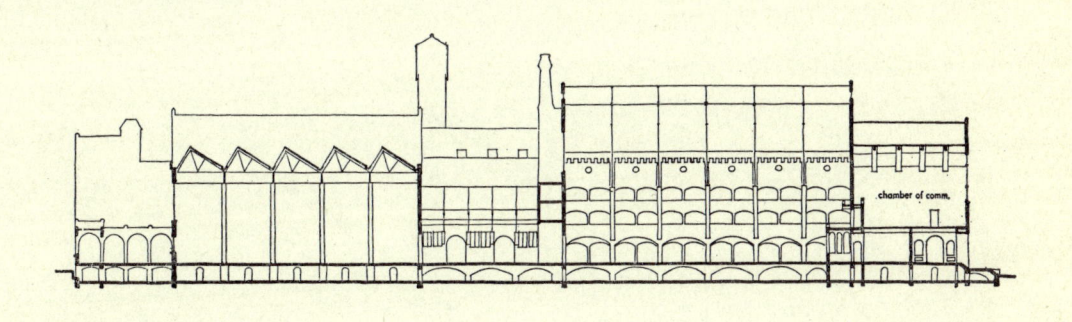

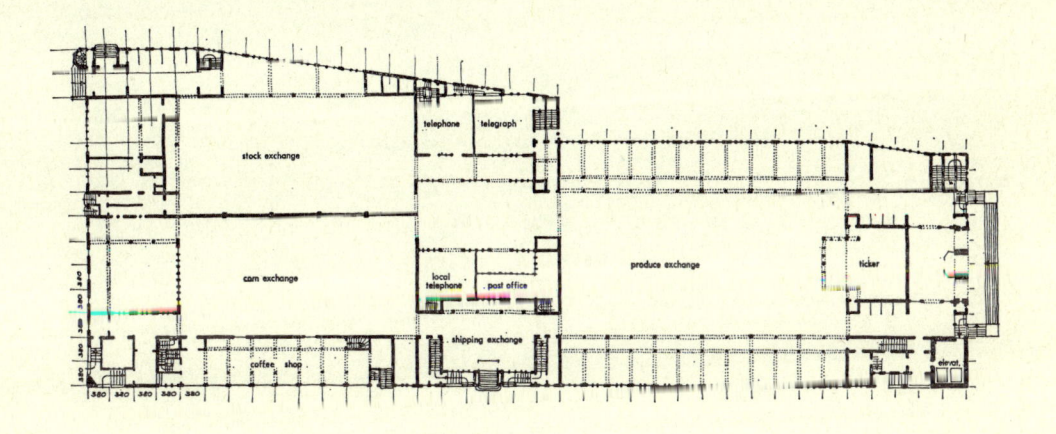

Figure 39. The Amsterdam Exchange; elevation, section, plan

committee in charge of the Exchange question. The Amsterdam Exchange marks the beginning of modern architecture in Holland.

Late medieval and Renaissance exchange buildings provided the bartering merchants only with a roof. Often they consisted of no more than the arcaded ground floor of the town-hall. The seventeenth century Amsterdam Exchange was a sort of cloister, an open court surrounded on four sides by a portico. It had been demolished in 1837 because it was considered dilapidated. The Exchange of 1845 had likewise an open court in the middle. In 1848 this was roofed in. In principle, an Exchange building is a partially or completely covered market. In this the new Exchange did not deviate from the pattern set by the older ones. But it had to differ in another important aspect. In 1836 Morse had built his first telegraph and in 1876 Bell spoke for the first time over the telephone. The new instruments were a boon for traders who wanted to conclude a quick deal; time is of the essence in stockbroking. In 1870 thirty Amsterdam firms submitted a plan to the municipal council for attaching a telegraph office to the existing Exchange. In 1894 the city commissioned its own architect, A. W. Weissman, to draw up an alteration plan. In his design the telegraph and telephone rooms were between the three Exchange halls. This feature was taken over by Berlage in his final plan. Right in the middle of the building lie the offices of telephone and telegraph, adjacent to each of the three large halls. It seems an irony of fate that the increase of business conducted over the telephone has rendered the large Exchange halls obsolete today. The little offices, already so advantageously placed in the centre of the building in 1898, have swallowed the rest.

Next to the three large halls, the stock exchange, corn exchange and produce exchange, lie a small shipping exchange, cloakrooms and a coffee-house. The last could not compete with the older establishments on the other side of the street and soon had to close down. The halls are surrounded on the first, second and third floors by a string of offices and committee rooms, of which the most imposing is the Chamber of Commerce over the main entrance. As in the Houses of Parliament, the layout is clear, logical and convenient, at least judged by the standards of its period. The trapezoïdal site determined the relative position and length and width of the main halls. The offices around the perimeter could receive daylight through ordinary windows, but the interior halls had to be lit by skylights.

XIX. Exterior of the northern end of the Amsterdam Exchange, showing the irregularity and the breaking down of the building block

XX. *Overleaf*: 'Architecture is and will ever be the art of construction' (Berlage). Detail of the interior elevation of the main hall in the Amsterdam Exchange

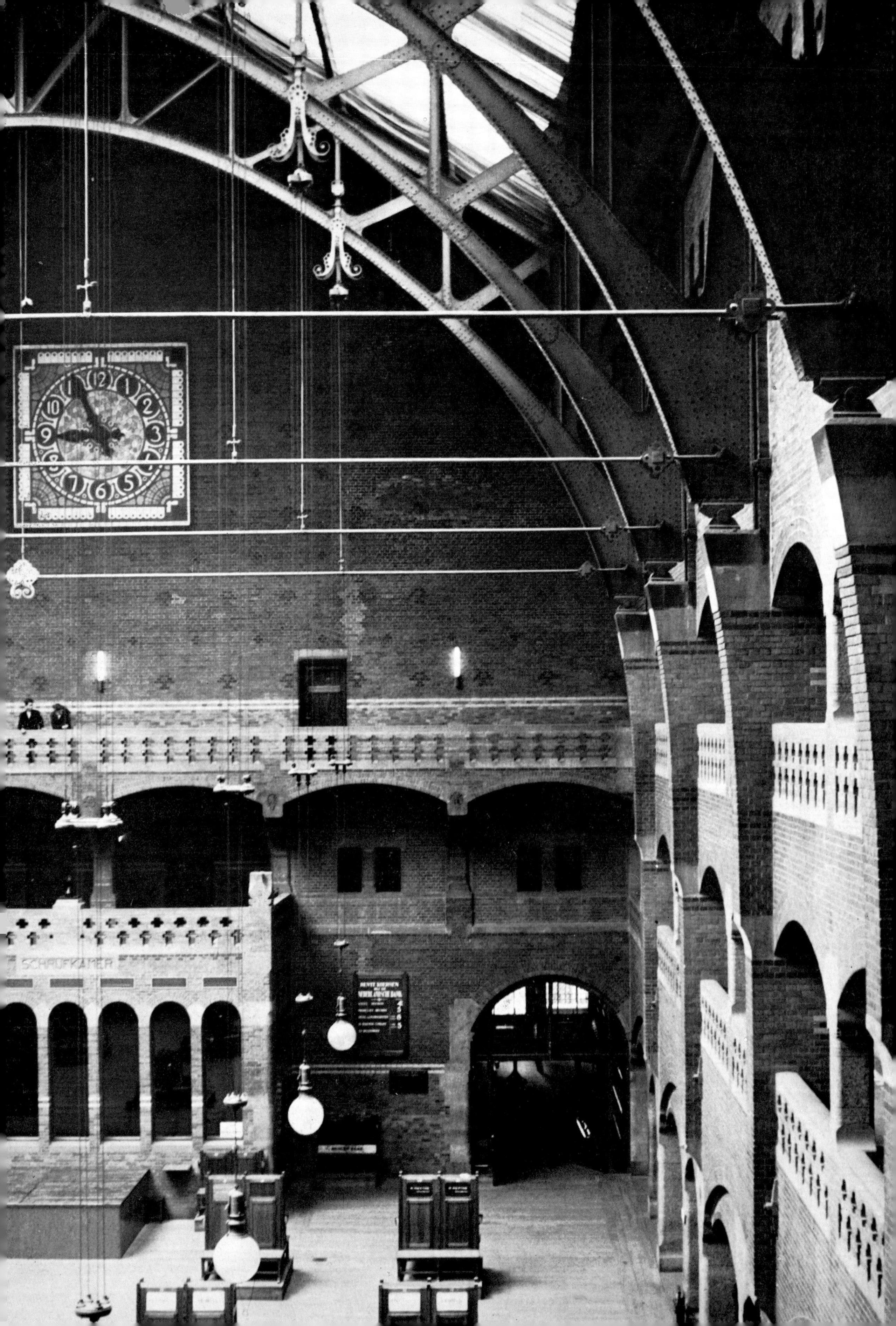
SCHRIJFKAMER

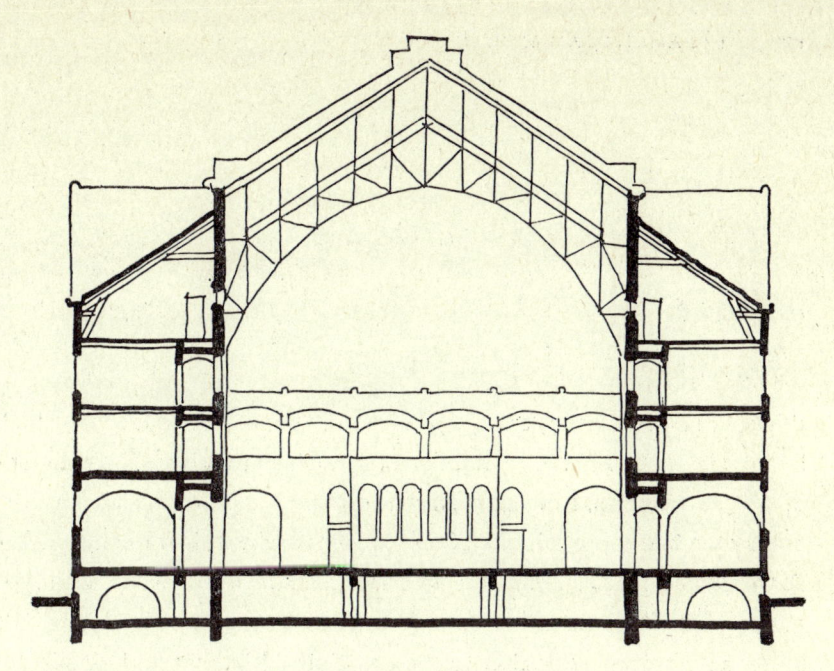

Figure 40. The Amsterdam Exchange; cross-section

Today we are so used to identify modern architecture with an extreme of simplicity, that Berlage's Exchange with its tower, its raised blocks and corners and its row of dormer windows makes a romantic and old-fashioned impression. But simplicity in masses is relative, and the building is already a great deal simpler than the English Houses of Parliament. The time was not yet ripe for endless repetitive elevations. Berlage was sharply attacked for the monotony of his main façade,[1] even though he had broken its length by the standard device of raised pavilions in the middle and at the corners.

Another aspect, easily but incorrectly judged to be old-fashioned is the closed fortress-like appearance. In no matter which architectural book it appears, the picture given of the exterior is always the same and shows the main entrance flanked by a corner pavilion and the tower; it is indeed only from that one particular point that the building can be adequately photographed. The tower contains the liftshaft and the corner pavilion a staircase; therefore only very small windows appear at these points, which gives that part its forbidding appearance. The long elevation next to the tower has fairly large windows and the building is probably just as much or as little isolated as Westminster New Palace. Larger apertures are hardly possible with brick bearing walls.

Moreover, the rear elevation, shown in our photograph (Plate XIX), is broken up in irregular masses. The courtyard on that side opens with an arcade onto the street, in contrast to the inner courtyards of Westminster New Palace. It foreshadows the interlocking of exterior and interior space typical of modern architecture.

Nor is the Exchange as heavy as it looks in the photographs; a glance on the plans should make that clear. The soggy soil of Amsterdam makes it necessary to drive piles beneath every building.[2] Therefore the Dutch have always built extremely light walls, to relieve the foundations as much as possible. The exterior impression of weight is caused, once again, by the entrance front, by the deep window recesses and by the heavy proportions of halls, rooms and window openings. There may be some reminiscence of Romanesque architecture in them, for Berlage writes: 'In my opinion the only style that can have some value for the future, is that which sticks as closely as possible to the principle of honest and simple construction, and in order to achieve that, I have always found medieval art invaluable for preparatory studies.'[3]

In the consistent application of this principle, the Exchange is certainly a modern building. The brickwork—a traditional building material in a country rich in clay and poor in stone—is left exposed not only on the exterior, but inside as well. The great halls show large plain brick walls; only the offices are plastered and panelled. Stone is used for lintels, columns, stair-treads, window-sills and corbelstones, i.e. only for the points exposed to heavy wear or stress. The floors are constructed of jack-arches between iron joists, as in Westminster Palace, but here left exposed in the galleries of the great halls. Likewise exposed are the steel roof trusses, which are accentuated by their conspicuous blue and cream colouring. Wooden doors show every dowel and tenon and are varnished to expose the grain. Berlage seems to have taken a positive delight in revealing his materials and construction; every detail might have come straight from a handbook. Phenomenal and actual construction coincide, in the terminology of this book.

Apart from a few statues and ornamental friezes in coloured tiles, the building is devoid of decoration. It obeys fully Sullivan's dictum 'Form follows function' or Pugin's requirement '...that there should be no features ... which are not necessary for convenience, construction or propriety.' Berlage goes beyond Pugin's demand that 'all ornament should consist of enrichment of the essential construction of the building', for the construction *is* all the ornament of the exchange.

Berlage is quite clear about his artistic intentions: 'We want the substance and not the shadow... Architecture is and will for ever be the art of construction... We have to make natural and comprehensible things again, i.e. things with their actual forms untrammelled by draperies! We must go even further; first we have to study the skeleton, as the painter and the sculptor do, and only then to give a good form to the (full) figure... Thus, for the time being, we have to study the skeleton, that is the sober construction in all its nakedness, to come from that to the full body, but a body which should be unclothed. Even the last cover, even the fig-leaf, has to disappear, for the truth we want is naked.'[4]

2. Analysis

The functions of an exchange, as they were conceived in 1900, determined the layout with the three large halls and the string of offices around them. Construction determined the use of steel trusses for the large spans in the halls, and practically all details. Economy determined the use of brick for all bearing walls and for the jack-arches of the floors. This leaves to art: 1. the slight emphasis on the irregularity of the site in the masses; 2. the use of a geometrical system; 3. the plain appearance and 4. the delight in construction and the use of natural unfinished materials.

On the question of irregular versus regular plans, Berlage took a middle position. When he showed his plans for the first time to his Amsterdam colleagues, he declared that he considered it an advantage that the site for the exchange was irregular and rather restricted. Such irregularity made the work interesting, and gave rise to all sorts of surprising effects, which would probably have looked affected on more regular sites. The given conditions, as they presented themselves to the designer, were agreeable to him, because he could thus arrive at a more picturesque solution.[5] With this argument from the theory of the 'picturesque', Berlage answered the many critics, who had contended that it was impossible to design a monumental building on such an irregular site. Though some of his buildings are irregular and asymmetrical—for instance the First Church of Christ, Scientist and the Municipal Museum in The Hague—he was a 'regular' at heart. Most of his later designs were symmetrical, culminating in the centrally planned Pantheon of Humanity.

These examples were in keeping with his preference for simplicity and modular systems. Berlage has summed up the conditions through which we may arrive at a new style in architecture as follows: 1. architectural composition should be made on a geometrical (modular) system; 2. one should not copy the forms of historical styles; 3. architectural forms should be likewise geometrical, free, but as simple and matter-of-fact as possible, and construed on the same system as the plans and elevations.'[6]

In his preference for simple geometrical forms and in his insistence on structural honesty Berlage shows himself to be an apostle of modern architecture. Geometrical forms and constructive sincerity were two of the three most universally recognized architectural principles of the 1920's, the third being that of spatial integration (of outside and inside or of rooms to one another). Part of the preference for simplicity is a revolt against the existing order in art. In the Western world, competition and individualism have been at a premium ever since the Renaissance, and so some reaction against grandfather's mode of design is inevitable. The Baroque considered the Renaissance outmoded and Neo-Gothic architects looked down on their Classicist predecessors.

But there is far more to the modern movement than a mere change for the sake of change. Pristine geometrical forms appear in the figurative arts too. Modern art is one continuous development from the would-be realism of the Romantics to the abstractionism of the 1950's; from impressionism, cubism, suprematism and the work of Mondriaan to the completely formless paintings of Pollock. Art turns away, not only from a previous style, but from the outside world. According to Abell, the introversion is caused by the unpleasantness of that world.

Ample corroboration for this view can be found in Berlage's own writings. 'Why do we find, in the time in which we live, so much evidence of a great dissatisfaction with the existing institutions and social order?...'[7] 'There is not only an economic, but also a spiritual struggle of all against one, of one against all. Economic cooperation does not exist, nor does spiritual cooperation. It is impossible, because spiritual cooperation demands sacrifice, i.e. subordinating one's own views to those of someone else, and sacrifice is unknown in our cynical time...'[8] 'The greatest sin on its long register of sins is certainly that capitalism sets more store by appearance than by reality, and that it placed not only material but also spiritual ugliness on the throne. With spiritual ugliness in general is meant the absolute lack of a common goal in life, of a cooperation between all of us in one direction.'[9] Berlage sees capitalism as the root of all evil, also in art. He hopes and preaches for an art for all people, which can only come about when the individualistic society of capitalism is replaced by a more equitable one. Though he was the architect of such a temple of capitalism' as the Exchange, Berlage had strong Marxist leanings.

Capitalism prefers electicism to reality, we are told. Art has become isolated from society, hence it has sunk to its present low level. 'And how about the artistic dogma of "l'art pour l'art"? Has it not paled, because it turns out to be nothing else than a far-fetched defense of, on one hand, the unimportant and insignificant, and on the other hand of an isolation of art and artists from the community, a flight from the world of man, just as happens in times of decadence?'[10] If ever we want to arrive again at a great and sincere art, we have to strip architecture of all ornament and to go back to the essentials, i.e. the skeleton and the naked construction. I would be inclined to agree with Berlage's diagnosis, if not entirely with his cure. Eclecticism was indeed all shadow and no substance, a dream which failed to come true. As the gap between dream and reality widened, it became gradually impossible to believe in it, however hard one might try.

With the dream proven false, honesty became the watchword. Never more were we to be fooled by the phantasms of art. But as all art is a question of feeling and values, rather than a physical fact, one deception was only exchanged for another. Architecture had to go back to 'pure' forms; but why should a cube be more 'pure' —or even more geometrical—than a Tudor arch? Is the smooth simplicity of modern buildings really due to function and construction alone? A negative attitude to figurative art produced non-figurative art, but art, all the same.

When classical dreamland lost its credibility, it was exchanged about 1800 for a multitude of historical dreams, whose mutual rivalry made them even less convincing. Attempts were then made to create a dreamland stripped of historical trappings. The illusion of the dream became more apparent and the demand for 'honesty' and 'truth' increased.

So architecture turned abstract, like that of St. Michael. 'One should show, before all else, the naked wall in all its simple beauty.'[11] The exchange shows many such walls, outside and inside. Make-believe was rejected and construction was to become 'honest'; hence the delight in showing every dowel of the doors and each member of the roof-trusses. Besides honesty, there was yet another reason for the coincidence between symbolic and actual structure.

Berlage wrote of 'the hopeless bungling, when an iron construction has to be adapted to historical architecture. The very idea sounds paradoxical, but is the general rule. I saw an example recently of this bungling at the main railway station in Dresden, in itself one of the foremost buildings of its kind. There, without any serious attempt at an architectonic solution, the iron construction is joined onto the stone architecture, in this case it is classical, so that one gets the impression that architect and engineer performed their tasks without any co-operation.'[12]

It will be evident that Berlage, with his belief in the need for cooperation could not accept a split between technology and architecture. All through the nineteenth century people had tried to find a workable attitude towards that most horrible and fascinating of human creations: technics. At first, technology imitated the older handicrafts. Then, machine-production was rejected by art critics like Ruskin and Morris as being ugly by its very nature. Finally, around the turn of the century a more positive attitude appeared, and the machine was seen as a possible friend, not as a born enemy. It could not be combated; so an effort was made to build technology into art. The books of Le Corbusier are full of admiration for aeroplanes, motor cars and bridges, as the 'true works of art' of our time.

Frank Lloyd Wright eulogized the machine age in a lecture in 1901. By showing structure rather than hiding it behind a coat of plaster, and by a meticulously 'correct' construction, Berlage integrated technology with his architecture. And is such an integration not an inspiring ideal for a society which has been divided against itself partly because of the consequences of the division of labour and the Industrial Revolution?

Berlage's expressed preference for simple geometrical forms and a system of proportions adumbrates Elementarism, the *Stijl* and the abstract geometrical style of the twenties. It was caused by the effort to return to fundamentals: visual forms which symbolized a harmonious cosmos. Each of the three major periods of make-believe opened with a recourse to visual fundamentalism: Alberti in the fifteenth century, Ledoux and Boullée on the threshold of the nineteenth century, and Malewitch, Van Doesburg, Lissitzky and Mies in our century. The simple Gestalten (Phileban solids) were invariably used as cosmic symbols.

It is a dreamland, once again. But no effort is spared to make the dream as realistic, as convincing as possible. That is the root of the emphasis on construction and the insistence on 'honesty'.

In conclusion we may try to distinguish again between the different levels of meaning. The first level is that of the parallel between the plain and naked appearance of the Exchange and the business-like character of industrial society and of Berlage's client in particular.

The plain appearance, the construction so emphatically revealed and the 'natural' materials are symbols of the second level. All of them signify 'honesty' as opposed to 'stylistic shamming' or, to put it differently, 'modern reality' in contrast to 'dreams of the past'. The geometrical system of proportions signified 'order'.

The ideals of order and honesty were connected with the social conditions of the period (my third level of meaning). Berlage thought so himself. He believed in the ideal of cooperation. He tried to integrate technology with architecture; therefore he made construction the keynote of his design. Geometrical order should replace artistic chaos, for the same reason that social order should replace social chaos. Our age emphasizes geometric forms (in Phileban solids) rather than *tracés régulateurs*; but the background is the same.

Social disintegration may lie at the root of the preference for the 'abstract', that is: the bare and plain architecture of the Exchange. If Berlage did not go further in this direction, it is due more to the style in which he started working than to any reticence on his part. He had to pave the way for the crystalline geometry of the architecture of the twenties.

Johnson House
New Canaan   1949

1. Description

The little house in New Canaan was designed by the architect Philip C. Johnson for himself. The gently sloping site has been levelled at the far end, and the horizontal portion slightly extended to create a platform on which the main part of the house could be built. Beyond that the ground falls sharply away. Trees surround plot and house on all four sides, with a clearing and lawn on the levelled area.[1]

    The house consists of 2 pavilions, both standing parallel to the road. The largest is Johnson's own abode. Conventional words can hardly be applied to it, but it may perhaps be summed up as a one-roomed bachelor's bungalow. Its most conspicuous feature is the outside wall, which is entirely made up of large sheets of plate-glass. Off centre stands a brick cylinder, rising slightly above the roof, which contains the bathroom and a fireplace. Cabinets subdivide the surrounding room into a sleeping area, a living and dining area and an area for the preparation of food and drinks. The highest cabinets are 6 feet, well below ceiling level, so the concept of one single room is left intact.

    The second building contrast strongly with the first, for its brick walls are pierced by few and small apertures. It serves as a guest house and also for the storage of those accessories which might encumber the glass pavilion. It contains two double bedrooms, a small living-room, a bathroom, the heating plant for both units and storage space.

    The two pavilions are entirely made up of 'pure'—i.e. simple—geometrical forms: rectangles and circles. As might be expected, they are completely devoid of decoration. A magnificent picture by Claude Lorrain standing on an easel and a papier-mâché sculpture group by Nadelman are the only representatives of the figurative arts. The details are structural as in the Exchange, only more formalized.

    Also similar to Berlage's creation are the use of natural unfinished materials and the preference for large unbroken planes. The cabinets are veneered; the steel frame

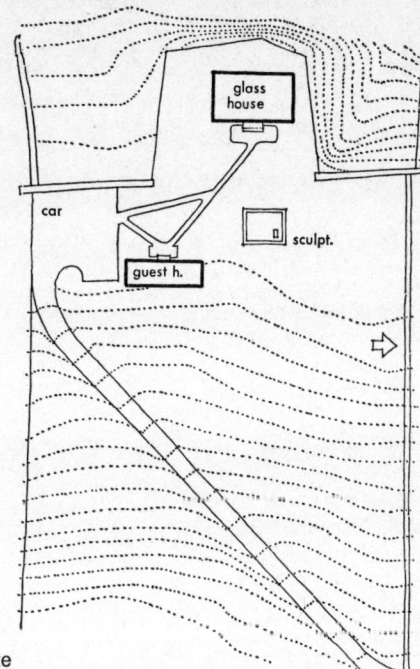

Figure 41. Johnson house; site

and the brickwork of the cylinder and the floor in the glass pavilion are left exposed.

In keeping with the trend in modern architecture, all surfaces are made as large and unbroken as possible. The glass walls reach from floor to ceiling; the brickwork of the guest house rises without a base from the ground to the coping; a brick floor extends from end to end throughout the glass pavilion. I believe this handling of the surfaces can be traced to a predilection for abstract—nearly 'immaterial'—surfaces, to a wish to let nothing distract from the geometrical appearance of the overall design, and to a desire for unification of each surface.

A major point of the design is the isolation. The large pavilion is practically nothing but a glassed-in roof; the guesthouse is nearly completely closed. The solid brick cylinder repeats this contrast on a smaller scale, but even more intensely, being also isolated by its keep-like form. Many modern buildings show such marked contrasts between, say, glass fronts and completely closed end-walls but seldom is the antithesis made so striking.

2. Analysis

Neither construction nor function were controlling factors in the design, though both received adequate attention. The construction is clear and nowhere deceptive, but it is not paraded as in the exchange building. The roof trusses for instance are hidden behind a plaster ceiling.

The influence of the function is far less than in most houses. Johnson is a bachelor and can therefore indulge in the luxury of putting art first and necessity

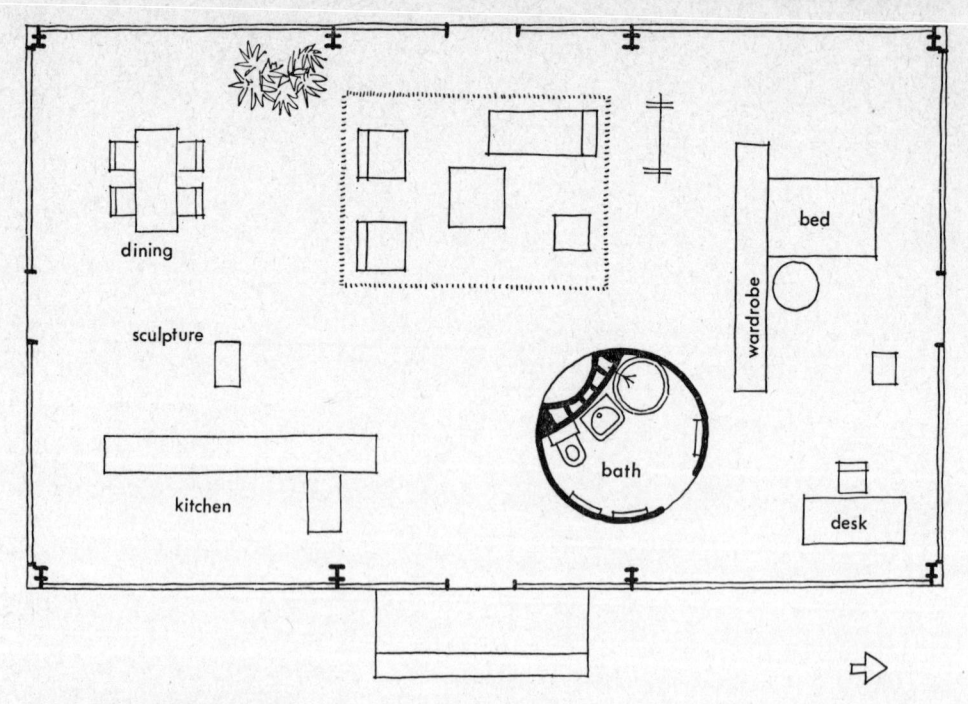

Figure 42. John house; plan

second. A childless couple would already be hard-pressed for sufficient storage space in a one-room apartment without walls, so to speak. Children would spoil the beautiful orderliness of the only inhabitable room even more. Even one person would have a hard task to preserve the simplicity of a permanent 'model apartment'. The great variety of ordinary activities in everyday life can only be lodged in such a simple building when there is some extra to fall back on. Rather than damage the purity of his glass cage by the addition of a wing, Johnson arranged for his guests, and the overflow of his belongings to go into a separate building. And he accepted that his guests had to put on warm clothes to cross 20 feet of lawn in a cold winter, for the sake of architectural perfection. Thus the glass house could remain all glass and all one room.

We are used to seeing a lot of glass in modern architecture, and the idea of letting the bedroom and the kitchen be part of the living room is also familiar. The Johnson house exemplifies principles which are embodied, though far less clearly, in most modern architecture. Here all compromise is left out, and the building owns its perfect clarity to the inexorable logic with which the modern dogmas are carried to their conclusion. Johnson himself has frankly described the many ties by which his house is connected with old and new architecture:[2] 'The arrangement of the two buildings and the statue group is influenced by Mies' theory of organizing buildings in a group. The arrangement is rectilinear but the shapes tend to overlap and slide by each other in an asymmetric manner. The idea of asymmetric sliding rectangles was furthest developed in the *De Stijl* aesthetics of war-time Holland. These shapes, best known to posterity through the painting of the late Piet Mondrian, still have an enormous influence on many other architects besides myself.

'The site-relation of my house is pure Neo-Classic Romantic—more specifically, Schinkelesque. Like his Casino, my house is approached on dead level, and, like his, faces its principal (rear) façade toward a sharp bluff. The eighteenth century preferred more regular sites than this and the Post-Romantic Revivalists preferred hill tops to the cliff edges or shelves of the Romantics.

'The cubic, "absolute" form of my glass house, and the separation of functional units into two absolute shapes rather than a major and a minor massing of parts comes directly from Ledoux, the eighteenth century father of modern architecture. The cube and the sphere, the pure mathematical shapes, were dear to the hearts of those intellectual revolutionaries from the Baroque, and we are their descendants. The idea of a glass house comes from Mies van der Rohe.

'Mies had mentioned to me as early as 1945 how easy it would be to build a house entirely of large sheets of glass. I was sceptical at the time and and it was not until I had seen the sketches of the Farnsworth house that I started the three-year work of designing my glass house. My debt is therefore clear, in spite of the obvious difference in composition and relation to the ground.

'Many details of the house are adapted from Mies' work, especially the corner treatment and the relation of the column to the window. Perhaps if there is ever to be "decoration" in our architecture, it may come from manipulation of stock structural elements such as this (may not Mannerism be next?).

'Except for the cylinder the plan of the house is Miesian. The use of 6 feet closets to divide yet unite space is his. The grouping of the furniture asymmetrically around a coffee table is his. The relation of cabinets to the cylinder, however, is more "painterly" than Mies would sanction.

'The guest house with Baroque plan, central corridor and three asymmetrically placed rooms, was derived from Mies' designs. The three round windows in the rear of the façade are a Renaissance approach to a Miesian motif. Mies uses the round window as a method of admitting light in a brick wall in a manner least to disturb the continuity of the wall. A rectangular hole would compete in direction with the shape of the wall itself. I used the round windows for the same reason, with a totally different compositional effect.'

Four main principles of modern architecture,[3] as I see it, are embodied in the Johnson house: 1. the use of extremely simple geometrical forms, in the pure prisms of the two pavilions; 2. the showing of the materials of the construction, in this case glass, brick and steel; 3. an excessive amount of glass, and 4. the lodging of all living activities in one room in the largest pavilion. Berlage's Exchange was already a great deal simpler than the eclectic architecture that went before; there, too, the raw materials were shown in their 'naked truth'. There is even an indirect connection between the buildings, for Mies, so much admired by Johnson, has repeatedly admitted how much he learned from Berlage's work. In these respects, pure (i.e. simple) geometrical forms and the use of natural materials, contemporary architecture continues along the road taken by the pioneers, and for the same reasons. A hostile world brought, or may have brought, an ever increasing abstraction to art, and the desire to integrate technology with other departments of life has led to the use of naked construction and the use of materials in the raw. The hostility has increased, and therefore, perhaps, the abstraction has increased too.

Living, eating, sleeping and cooking in one room and the extensive use of glass are interrelated principles of design. Both strive for the well-known *spatial integration*. The first aims at the integration of what is usually separate, i.e. a bedroom, a kitchen, a living room, etc.; the second aims at integration of exterior with interior space. Less distinguished solutions may be seen in every home-magazine. The principle has been put in words by Van Doesburg: 'The new architecture has *broken through the wall* and in so doing has completely eliminated the *divorce* of *inside* and *out. The walls are no longer load-bearing*; they are reduced to points of support. And as a result there is generated a new open plan, totally different from the classic because inside and outside space interpenetrate.'[4] Moholy-Nagy wrote: 'In the past, closed spaces were composed out of visible well-proportioned volumes of fixed dimensions; today we experience space in outflowing and inflowing spatial relations, in which outside and inside, above and below, interpenetrate each other.'[5]

What is behind this yearning to symbolically turn man out of his house? Why cannot he have a snug cottage, which does not only materially provide shelter—as the Johnson house does—but which *looks* like a warm lair too? Again, I think, the reason lies in the social conditions. Modern society is emphatically *not* inte-

XXI. Why so much glass? Exterior of the Johnson house, New Canaan

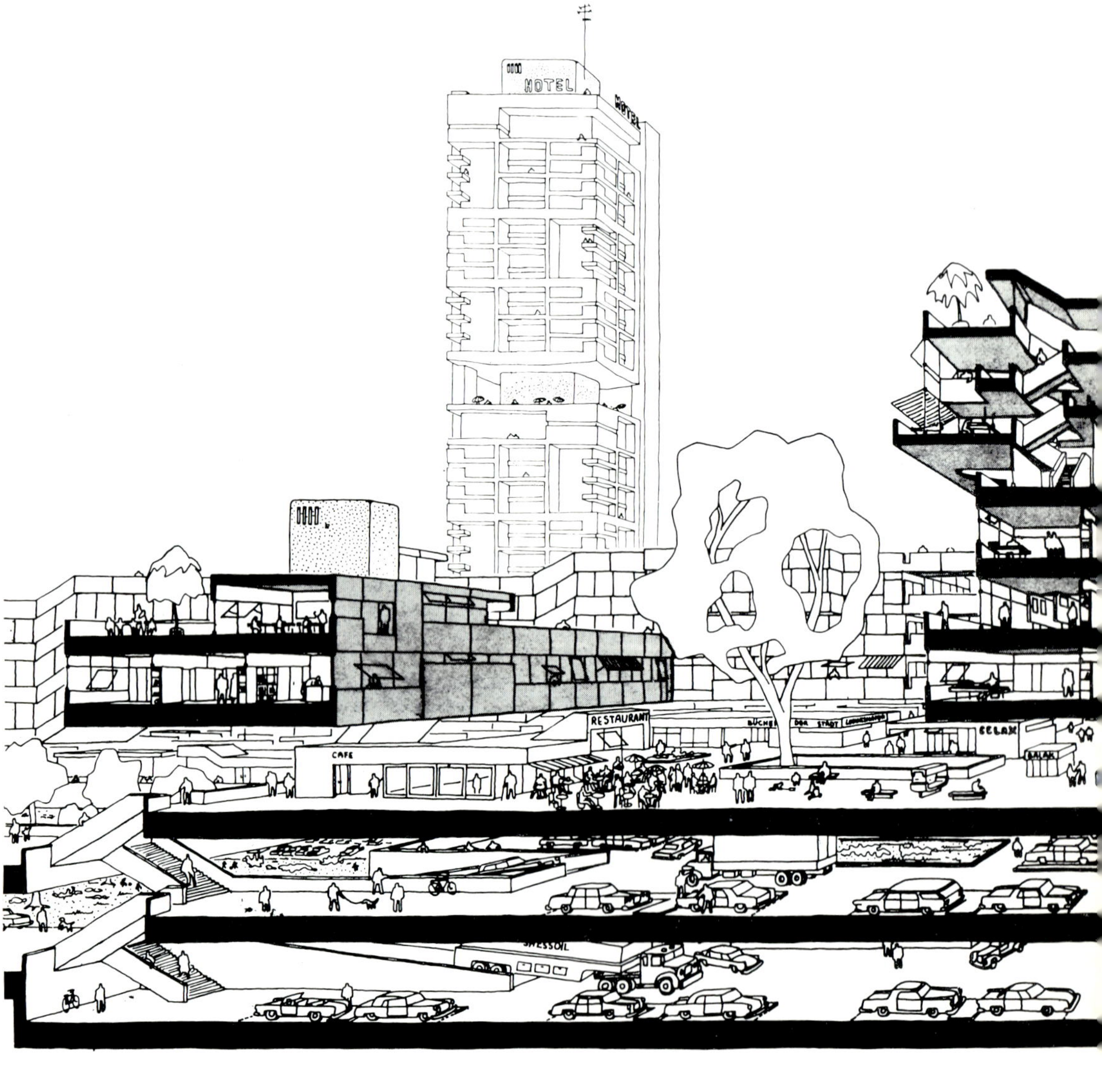
HOTEL
RESTAURANT
CAFE

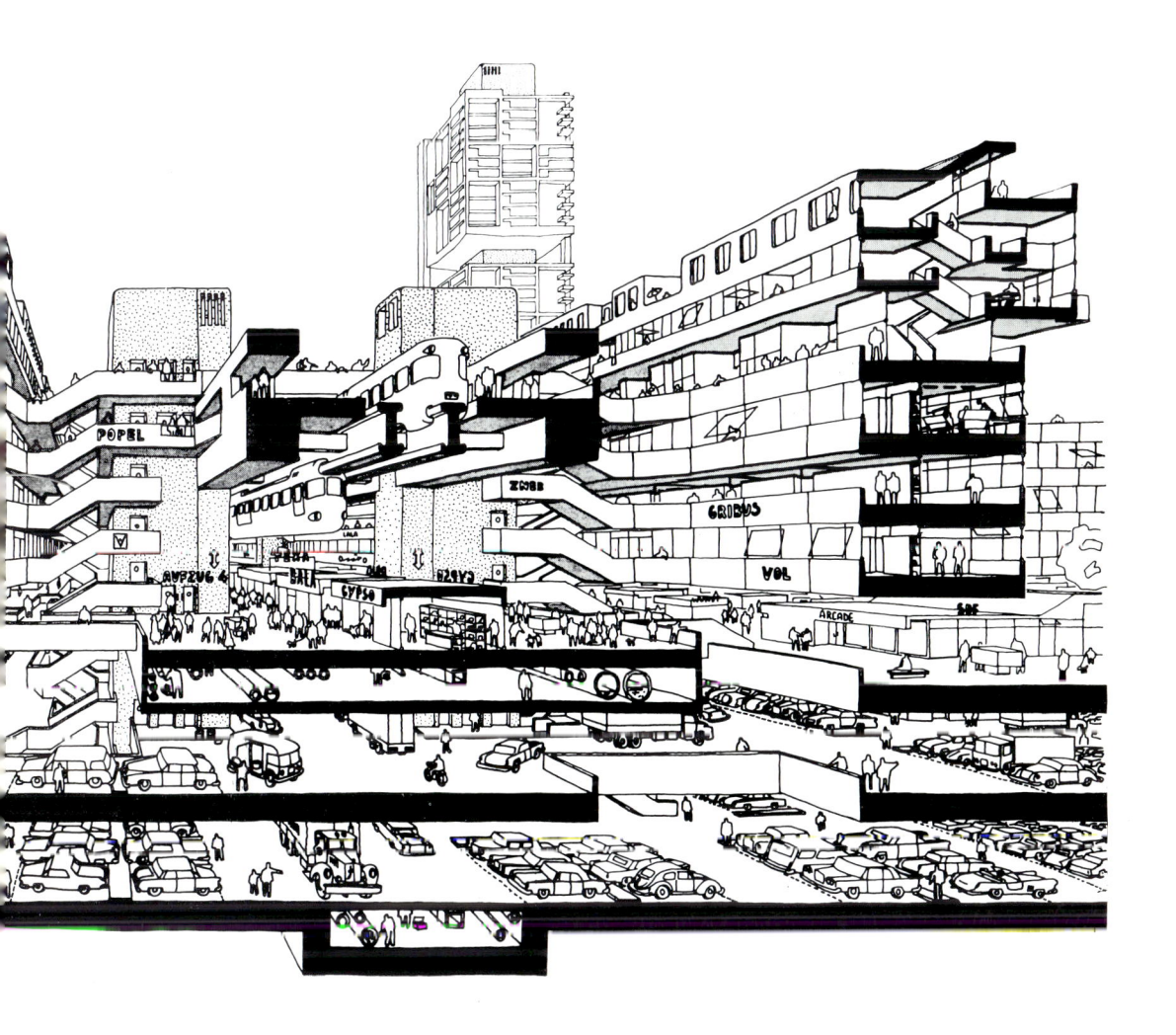

XXII. Towards an integrated environment. Section of the competition project for the replanning of the railway station at Ludwigshafen by Van den Broek and Bakema.

XXIII. 'Visual acoustics in the realm of forms' (Le Corbusier). In this photograph of Ronchamp, even a visible echo

XXIV. Interior of N. Dame du Haut, Ronchamp

grated. Even though social distance between classes is continually diminishing, it has not resulted in a feeling of cooperation and response. Many still feel, just as before, that they do not get their share of the cake. Baker Brownell wrote: 'The peripheries of modern social structure are beyond men's horizons. A man's work in the wholesale grocery, for example, has little or no reference, as far as he knows, to his excursion to the movies in the evening. His lodge meeting has no bearing on the Sunday afternoon drive to Freeport. He listens to the Minnesota game over the radio without reference to the fate of the League of Nations. And war goes on, burning the life of the world, piling terror on terror, but whether he enters or does not, whether he comes back or does not, are rather casual and accidental incidents as far as the other features of his life are concerned. He lives a plural life. Events do not grow out of each other. They are not integrated.'[6]

'On personal life, whatever that may mean, modern society is a disruptive influence. It affects the character and values of people; it affects their expression in the arts, play and work. A pluralism of personal life appears. ... Moral pluralism, cosmic pluralism, aesthetic pluralism are all characteristic of the modern age. Even more significant in the temper of the times is a kind of psychological pluralism. This is, so to speak, the pluralistic assumption; the person no longer takes for granted that he is an integral unit of reality.'[7]

Architecture reveals this plurality and the disintegration in full measure. We do not have one style, but several. The Johnson house is an example of the cubistic school, the Ronchamp chapel belongs to 'organic' architecture. Apart from them, we have Scandinavian Romanticism, and the still wide spread remnants of eclecticism. Disintegration appears in architectural form when all four walls of one room are painted a different colour, when huge rubble fireplaces stand in crisp modern apartments, when small bungalows are faced with clap-board, brick, cement-asbestos, plastic and wireglass, and, in the case of the Johnson house, in the extreme contrast between the open pavilion and its closed counterpart. In the social sense, art has been cut loose from its moorings when, as now, it is no longer comprehended by a fair share of the cultured public, and modern painting, music, and poetry only provoke ridicule.

None are so aware of the social disintegration as the artists themselves. Gropius wrote: 'We all still have before our mind that unity of environment and spirit that prevailed in the horse and buggy time. We sense that our own period has lost that unity, that the *sickness of our present chaotic environment, its often pitiful ugliness and disorder, have resulted from our failure to put basic human needs above economical and industrial requirements*. Overwhelmed by the miraculous potentialities of the machine, human greed has obviously interfered with the biological cycle of human companionship which keeps a community healthy. At the lower level of society the human being has been degraded by being used as an industrial tool. This is the real cause for the fight between capital and labor and for the deterioration of community relations.'[8] And that disintegration is in turn the motivating power behind the use of glass and in- and outflowing space. Materially a house has to be closed against rain and cold, but on the symbolic plane all space is one. The idea of the open plan is to bring the occupant architecturally into contact again with the outside world, the world of his fellow men, of technology and of nature; a world from which he has long been cut off socially.

Mies says: '...we should try to create a unity between nature, houses and people on a more elevated plane. When you look at nature through the glass walls of the Farnsworth house, it takes on a more profound meaning than when you stand outside. More of nature is thus expressed—it becomes a part of a larger whole.'[9] Something like that is behind the one room and the glass walls of the Johnson house, an admitted descendant of the Farnsworth house.

The modern concept of space is that of a continuum, pervading all flimsy partitions, and stretching to infinity. It may be likened to a clear fog, densified at the points of habitation and necessary enclosure, but nowhere divided into distinct and separate parts. Such a concept stands in direct contrast to the finite and clear-cut spatial visions of the Renaissance. Accordingly, as much as the Renaissance loved symmetry, the architects of the 1920's detested it. Symmetry, by equalizing the enclosing walls, focuses on the centre, i.e. inward. Architecture tried to free itself from this introversion, for it wanted to draw the inmates of its glass prisons *out*.

Asymmetry prevails in the arrangement of the two pavilions of the Johnson house, and in the furnishing of the glass house. But its elevation, and the plan *and* elevation of the brick pavilion are as symmetrical as any fifteenth century Italian could wish. Mies has said: 'Why *should'nt* a building be symmetrical? With most buildings on this campus [Illinois Institute of Technology] it is natural that the stairs are located at both sides and that the auditorium or the entrance lies in the middle. So buildings become symmetrical, when it is natural to make them so. But besides that, we do not attach the slightest importance to symmetry.'[10] I cannot believe this to be the full story. Far too many of Mies' designs are symmetrical to ascribe that to the simple demands of function.

Symmetry stresses containment in a building. Its centre or axis marks a special 'place', in contrast to the universe around it. To integrate a building, first with its landscape in the irregular plans of the late eighteenth century, and thereafter with the entire cosmos in the spatial fantasies of Van Doesburg, or in Mies' own Barcelona Pavilion, symmetry was vanquished. It needed an effort, for Gestalt psychology makes symmetrical design all but mandatory. For Mies, all space *is* one, already. His designs are uniform: his chapel for I.I.T. looks exactly like the boiler-house or the auditorium. He uses the same forms for office buildings as for apartments. 'I try', he has said, 'to turn my buildings into neutral frames, in which people and works of art can lead their own existence.'[11]

The Phileban solids of the Johnson house derive from the geometrical style of the twenties. They are visual fundamentals, symbolizing the immutable harmony of the cosmos in contrast to the violent conflicts of society. They meant the same to Ledoux and Boullée. Berlage's process of reduction is carried here to its logical conclusion. As with the earlier dreamlands, the main problem is its credibility. The twenties were content to create an abstract, optically-immaterial white world in architecture. Thirty years later it is necessary again to emphasize the reality of the dream, by exposing the materials.

Some of the Baroque optical tricks, which aimed at involving the spectator, have returned too. The glass house remains invisible from the road and even from its own drive, until you come upon it by surprise (Plate XXI). The careful placing of statuary, inside and out is just as much a 'set stage', as the perspective view down the Imperial Library.

Living, cooking, eating and sleeping all take place in one room. The entire outside wall of the main pavilion is made of glass; its owner lives conceptually a permanent outdoor-life. Both are symbols for a unified cosmos, in opposition to the social divergence of the world of everyday.

Notre Dame du Haut
Ronchamp   1950–1955

1. Description

Ronchamp is a small village in Alsace-Lorraine, close to the German border. A hill in its vicinity, already a place of worship in pagan times, became a Christian sanctuary in the Early Middle Ages.[1] A chapel dedicated to the Virgin Mary was built on its top, and the place acquired some renown for miracles, drawing pilgrims from the region. As the hill top was a natural military observation post in a strip of country contested between France and Germany ever since Charlemagne, it has of course been much knocked about. Today the statue of Mary is the only late medieval remains. The last chapel (Neo-Gothic) was destroyed in 1944 when Ronchamp remained in the frontline for two months. Rebuilding was entrusted to the Protestant architect Charles Edouard Jeanneret, better known as Le Corbusier.

He was commissioned to design a Roman Catholic church seating 200 people; the far larger gatherings of pilgrims on feastdays were to be accommodated outside. An outside altar and pulpit stand at the eastern end of the church, looking out over a sloping lawn. Built into the east wall, between the indoor and outdoor altar areas, is a sort of aquarium, containing the miraculously preserved statue of the Virgin. She can thus be seen from either side; the statue can revolve on its axis with the help of an electric motor, to face whichever altar is being used for mass at the time.

Three small chapels adjoin the church. Each terminates in an apse, which rises in a tower, shedding light over the altar below. Access to the church is given by three doors.

Besides the church, three other buildings stand on the crest of the hill. They are: a simple hostel for the pilgrims with an adjacent coffee shop, the presbytery, and a stepped pyramid which seats a number of the pilgrims at an outside mass and is also intended as a memorial to the French Resistance. All have been designed by

Figure 43. Notre Dame du Haut; site

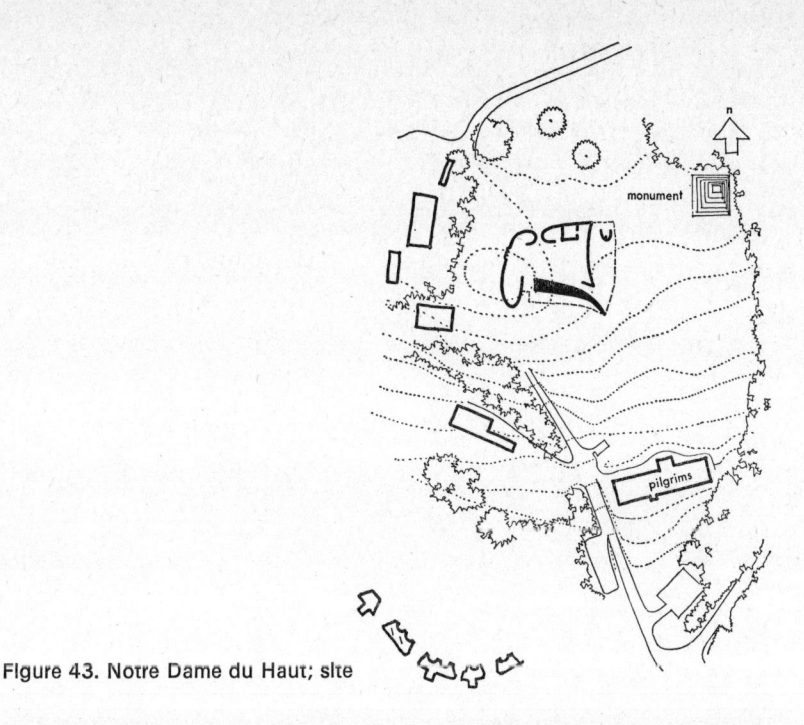

Le Corbusier. In recent years, a string of souvenirshops has sprung up around the back of the church.

The most conspicuous feature of the church is its form. Instead of the transparent simplicity of the Johnson house, we find here complicated curves and highly irregular surfaces. The first modern example is as geometrical as the second is anti-geometrical. Forms like these do not occur in mathematical textbooks; they remind us of rocks, bones or tree trunks, i.e. of the forms of nature rather than of abstraction.

Dominating over the whole building is the heavy awning of the roof. It seems to hover over the walls rather than to rest on them, especially when seen from inside, for a 4-inch clearance remains between the ceiling and the top of the walls. The gap is filled by glass and only interrupted at the points of support.

The southern wall tapers towards the top, with the greatest inclines at the western end. At the easternmost point the wall is perpendicular. A score of windows, greatly varying in size and proportion, have been dug into this wall. Apart from the apertures in the towers, they are the main sources of daylight. The building is rather strongly isolated: approximately 3% of the total outside area is glazed.

The details have none of the elegance of the Johnson house. The stone altars are simple blocks covered by heavy *menseae*; the pulpits are hefty boxes. Massive wooden benches for the faithful stand on crude concrete supports. Except for the stone of the altars, the wood of the benches and some iron chandeliers, all the other surfaces are of cement. The concrete of the roof reveals still the boards of the formwork; the walls have a rough coat of cement plaster. Of course there is no decoration and the concrete is shown in its natural glory. Surfaces are rough in texture, but smooth in the sense of having no projections of any significance.

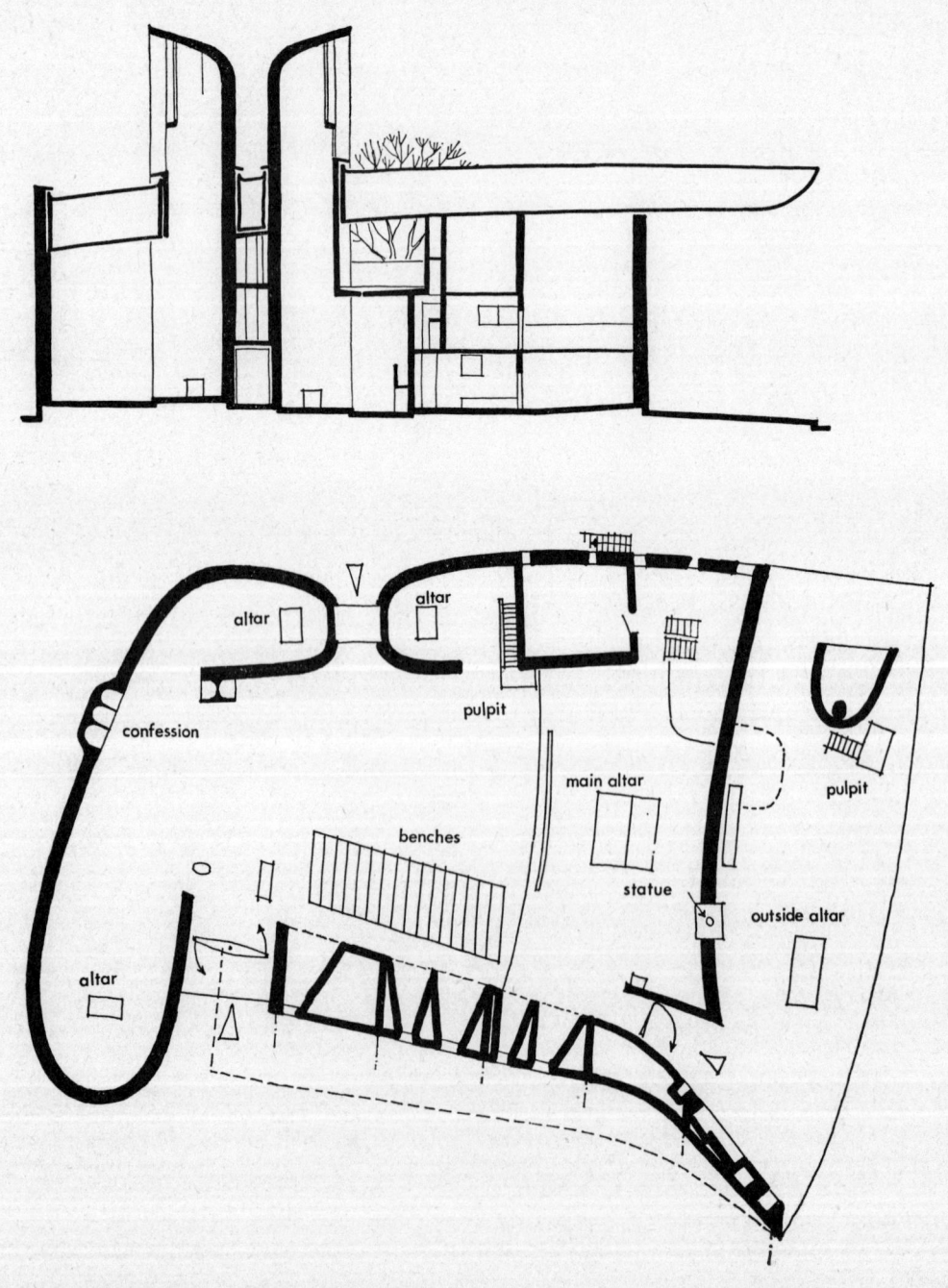

Figure 44. Notre Dame du Haut; section and plan

The chapel was constructed as a reinforced concrete skeleton filled out with the rubble of its ruined predecessor. The heavy roof consists actually of two thin shells of 2.5 inches of concrete, strengthened by purlins and supported on girders 7 feet 5 inches or 2.26 metre high, 15 feet on centre. The girders rest on columns hidden in the walls. The columns and the walls have afterwards been sprayed with the cement gun and white-washed.

Thus actual and symbolic structure do not coincide at all. The walls look monolithic and load-bearing, but consist largely of light filling material. The seemingly heavy chunk of the roof is in reality a thin membrane stretched over a network of joists and girders. To a casual lay observer it may look solid, but it is—of course—hollow. Structural honesty has been sacrificed to monolithic appearance, for the sake of greater unity, just as in the ceiling of the Johnson house.

Compositionally the building consists of one large interior with few adjuncts: the three chapel-towers and the vestry. The space of the small chapels 'grows out of' the main body of the church, with the exception of the north-eastern one. The towers over them are not subdivided by floors into storeys, but one can look up inside to the top. Here, again, we have the spatial continuity so dear to modern architects. The curving walls make it impossible for any sub-space or volume to detach itself as a definite 'Gestalt' from the body of the church proper. In addition, the roof gathers everything together under its massive overhang. Dimensions are all based on the *modulor*, a system of proportions developed by Le Corbusier.[2]

2. Analysis

The programme determined the size of the church, the three chapels and the outside sanctuary. The prominence given to the miraculously preserved statue of Mary made it necessary to put the two altars back to back.

The limitations of the budget dictated the re-use of the rubble of the ruined chapel and the fairly simple mode of construction. All the rest—and that is still nearly everything in and on the building—is due to art.

We can, I believe, bring the main characteristics under 4 headings: 1. the fusion of all parts into one indissoluble whole; 2. the use of irregular, 'organic' forms; 3. the preference for rough surfaces and 4. the heavy appearance.

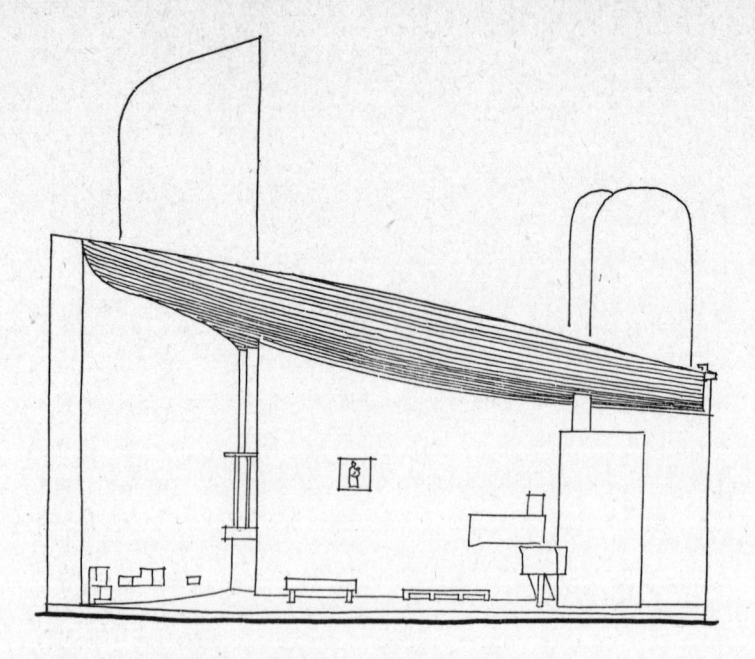

Figure 45. Notre Dame du Haut; east elevation

The following aspects can be ascribed in my opinion to Le Corbusier's desire for unity in the design: the monolithic appearance of the walls; the tent-like roof stretching over everything but the towers, and its likewise apparently monolithic surface; the fusion of two of the three chapels with the main body of the church and the apparent disorder in the window arrangement (there is no façade). We have already delved at length into the possible backgrounds of this craving for unity in the last chapter, and need not go into it again. It may be interesting to note that Le Corbusier has once described social disintegration in much the same way as Baker Brownell. In *Précisions* he writes of: '...an intense and sudden change in the life of the family and the city. Work was no longer divided up in the same way as in the past. The father is no longer the key figure in the family hierarchy. The family was annihilated. Every morning, sons and daughters, father and mother set off, each for a different workshop and a different factory. There they made all sorts of contacts, good and bad. They were tossed about by these new social currents, which day after day and cell by cell transformed the state of society. The dwelling place of their forefathers has lost its soul; the house still stands, but in a state of overwhelming disorder. Each has brought home his own portion of beliefs, ideals and fetishes; these various fetishes create a frightful tumult in the old house and everywhere the family is breaking apart.'[3]

By far the most interesting feature of the Ronchamp chapel is its form. Quite a few other modern buildings show such sinuous architecture: Saarinen's skating rink at Yale university, Aalto's church in Imatra, Utzon's project for the Sydney opera house, and Scharoun's Berlin Philharmonic Hall. They have many points in common with the *Art Nouveau* architecture of the beginning of the 20th century.

of the architects Guimard, Van de Velde, Gaudí and Horta.[4] The old and the new alike find their inspiration in nature. They do not copy natural forms, as Morris did for his flowery wallpapers, but try to make a building look as if it grew by itself rather than was constructed by man.

Le Corbusier has described how he arrived at the form of Notre Dame du Haut: 'The idea was born in my mind, at first unformed, vague, trying to find its shape. On the hill I had carefully drawn the landscape in the 4 cardinal directions... Those drawings were lost; in *them* originated architecturally [the idea of] the acoustic response—*visual acoustics in the realm of forms*... The landscape of these four directions is a powerful reality; it sets the tone. It is to these four directions that the chapel addresses itself...

'The shell of a crab picked up at Long Island, near New York, in 1946, is put on the drawing board. It will become the roof of the chapel; two membranes of concrete, six centimetres thick, at a distance of 2.26 m from each other.'[5]

Once again the theme is integration; integration of building and landscape this time. The building should 'belong' in the landscape and not jar upon the eye as an intrusion of man in the world of nature. Was Le Corbusier so struck by the loveliness of the hills of Alsace that he went out of his way to spare them another desecration? Undoubtedly; but I believe there to be yet a more profound reason.

Immersed in an environment made up of macadam and motorcars, of technics and statistics, modern man has become estranged from his original heritage, the land. Nature is a paradise lost now, and yet man is part of nature, his unnatural abstractions and machines notwithstanding. Technology has isolated man from nature. But does he feel at home in his brave new world, amidst the charts and graphs, the test tubes, the steel furniture of the office and the turning wheels of the factory? Hardly. The smallest blade of grass is more at one with its surroundings than he.

'Flower, plant, tree and mountain stand upright, alive in their own surroundings. If they one day draw the attention with a truly reassuring and sovereign attitude, it is that they seem to be detached from what they are causing all around them to reverberate. We halt, deeply aware of so natural a sound; and we look at them, moved by so much harmony bringing together so much space; and we realize that what we are looking at illuminates its surroundings.'[6] (Le Corbusier)

Organic architecture bridges the gap between the world created by God and the strange world of man's own creation. Buildings in organic form belong to both worlds at once; they have forms also found in nature, yet they are products of technology. Frank Lloyd Wright once wrote: 'Man takes a positive hand in creation whenever he puts a building upon the earth beneath the sun. If he has birthright at all, it must consist in this: that he too, is no less a feature of the landscape than the rocks, trees, bears or bees of that nature to which he owes his being.' And the same feeling has been expressed by Le Corbusier in the following quotation: 'It is urgent to re-establish the conditions of nature, in your body and in your spirit: sun, space, plants and trees. Let us build the roads of the world to render the earth accessible, productive and maternal.'[7]

It is this vision of a building, firmly anchored in the landscape, growing out of it rather than intruding upon it, which I think describes the Ronchamp church most aptly. Hence the sinuous forms and the fusion of all parts: it echoes the fusion between building and the surrounding countryside. Hence structural honesty, once dear to Le Corbusier's heart, is sacrificed to monolithic appearance. Hence, too, the preference for rough and earthy surfaces over the cold and abstract shine of metal from the steel mill or wood from the lathe. And being firmly rooted in the land, the building naturally takes on the heavy look of a rock, which greatly increases the strong sense of isolation.

Organic architecture symbolizes an idealized nature; it is as much a dreamland as that of the Johnson house. Once more, the problem is to make such a paradise convincing, and for that he has used again some of the Baroque devices. All masses are bold and strongly articulated. The sharp and angular forms of the walls and the roof shoot out into space, hitting us full-face, just as the central pavilion of the Imperial Library. Optical trickery again makes its reappearance, in the roof hovering over the walls and in the revolving Madonna. Natural, rough materials add to the impression of reality.

To appear 'real', a building should conform to the perceptual mode of its period. Disintegration affects formal aesthetics; it makes us far more tolerant of contrasts than our fore-fathers. The clash between the various spaces is even greater than in Hildesheim. A limited formal coherence is obtained from the similarity of the towers, the unifying canopy of the roof, the consistent use of angular or sinuous forms and particularly from the unity and simplicity of the cement surfaces.

But the most conspicuous sign of disintegration lies in our numerous modern styles of architecture. When a culture produces buildings so radically different as the Johnson house and the Ronchamp chapel, it can no longer be called homogeneous—even if the two architects have each made designs on the one and on the other set of principles. The pessimist may deplore that we cannot agree on how it should be; a merrier man will rejoice at the variety.

In word and deed modern architects reject whole-heartedly the fanciful shams of nineteenth century historicism. And yet the ideals which they uphold are as historical as any Neo-Gothic office building. The return to a more natural environment by means of an organic architecture goes back to Rousseau; he already believed natural man to be good and true. And the integrated space of the glass palaces is clearly connected with the class-less society, the one-world view of Marx. Neither of these two architectural palliatives seems to be an adequate solution to the difficulties of modern man. For, if my interpretation is correct, he is uprooted and insecure, rather than lonely. Social mobility has accelerated in tempo; crises fall upon him out of the blue; he never knows quite what tomorrow will bring. More 'togetherness' will not remedy this evil. Indeed, according to Riesman and Whyte,[8] there is already far less competition and more friendliness than in the Victorian age; perhaps more than is good for us. But the results are not impressive; insecurity has increased notwithstanding the well-meaning efforts to create 'one big family'. Twentieth century problems evidently cannot be solved by a nineteenth century approach.

Recent developments

After the second world war, modern architecture carried the day. Cities were rebuilt and new towns planned in accordance with the principles of the Charte d'Athènes: housing was removed from the squalor of industrial areas and the congestion of the city-center. In the friendly green suburbs, envisaged by the planners, happy mothers would push their prams over safe wide sidewalks, unhindered by the fumes of motor traffic and children would fly kites on spacious lawns. But in reality only a few old newspapers fluttered over the empty open spaces. Air and sun were gained, as Jane Jacobs has pointed out,[1] at the cost of life.

The old centres of European cities, built for the carthorse and the pedestrian, became cluttered up by cars. Double-deck motorways and underground parking will have to be constructed to keep traffic on the move.[2] The resulting complex buildings (feasible only in the central districts) with their separate levels for public and private transport, pedestrian malls, their high density and integration of functions, contrast sharply with the sleepy suburbs. In the one, people are constantly rubbing shoulders; in the other they can only look at each other over a vast, dull expanse of grass.

Architects, like all other artists, react to the climate of their time and want to reform their surroundings. Their craft, more than almost any other rooted in social necessity and of visible influence on human behaviour, seems to offer them a lever to move the world. As long as modern architecture still had to fight traditionalism it was possible to believe that with its advent the millennium would come. But now it has been victorious, and the dream has not come true 'Instead of the inconvenience of filth and confusion, we have now got the boredom of hygiene. The material slum has gone—in Holland for example it has—but what has replaced it? Just mile upon mile of organized nowhere, and nobody feeling he is "somebody living somewhere". No microbes left—yet each citizen a disinfected pawn on a chessboard, but no chessmen—hence no challenge, no duel and no dialogue.'[3] (Van Eyck)

It is not the ideal which is questioned; that remains the same, i.e. the integrated society. The attack is directed against the means of attaining that ideal, the symbolic apparatus which is now experienced as faded and powerless: 'Architecture should be conceived of as a configuration of intermediary places clearly defined. This does not imply continual transition or endless postponement with respect to place and occasion. On the contrary, it implies a break away from the contemporary concept (call it sickness) of spatial continuity and the tendency to erase every articulation between spaces, i.e. between outside and inside, between one space and another (between one reality and another).'[4] (Van Eyck)

Remedies are sought in two directions. The first attaches itself to the multi-level structures in the city-centres, envisaged in the Buchanan report. This base in reality serves as a springboard for the creation of a new architectural symbol: a cluster of buildings which contain all aspects of life in contrast to the dreary monotony of the dormitory-suburb. In these concentrated buildings people are *forced* to live together. Examples of such projects are the plans for the centres of Frankfurt and Tel Aviv by Van den Broek and Bakema, for an Arctic city by Erskine, for the Free University of Berlin by Candilis, Woods and Josic, and on a more fantastic scale, the sketches of Friedman, Constant and Katavolos. The proposals are often accompanied by texts extolling the virtues of high density and integrated life in slums and primitive communities: 'I believe that so many architects are interested nowadays in the habitat of the Indians (the Pueblos) or in that of the negroes of Africa, it is because here one may still recognize the spatial expression of the whole population. We should not forget, nevertheless, that this population is leading a fierce battle in order to be equipped with modern techniques which were developed in different countries of Europe, of America and Russia. Here is the drama. Here in our society we are attempting to establish for the anonymous client a spatial expression of his way of living. In primitive societies this way of living still exists, but it lacks precisely those techniques which help to get rid of fear and attain total life; we should not forget that those primitive societies are frequently based on the exploitation of this fear. It is extraordinary to think that in the very moment that man and races are confronted with each other every day, there is taking place a confrontation between on the one hand primitive societies with integrated habitat, whose members claim a right to be provided with modern techniques, and on the other hand our society, disintegrated by these very techniques, that seeks new disciplines of integration.'[5] (Bakema)

The inclusion of as many functions as possible in the same building or group of buildings has moreover the advantage of increasing the reality of the architectural symbol, because its roots in the social necessities are more numerous.

Town planning, landscaping and architecture have merged in an indivisible unity in the grand schemes for Frankfurt, Tel Aviv and Amsterdam by Van den Broek and Bakema. The parallel to the large compositions of the Baroque, such as Versailles, Karlsruhe or Bruchsal is obvious.

Other Baroque principles of design have turned up in the Neo-Classical architecture of Pei, Yamasaki, Johnson, Kahn and Arne Jacobsen. Their lay-outs show a predilection for axial planning. Buildings like Kahn's Trenton Bathhouse or Jacobsen's St. Catherine's College at Oxford are rigorously symmetrical. Johnson's Sheldon Art Gallery has a façade which in its symmetry, its emphasis on overwhelming height and the slow rhythm of the pilasters recalls John Wood's Royal Crescent at Bath, Schinkel's Alte Museum at Berlin and Galilei's Lateran façade.

The conscious manipulation of a spatial sequence, ending in a climax, which we met in Vienna and in the Houses of Parliament, has also reappeared. Examples are found in Le Corbusier's Arts Center at Harvard, Aalto's town hall in Säynätsalo and on the outside of Förderer's Economic School at St. Gallen. Such interest in the spatial experiences of the visitor was rare in the functionalistic architecture of the twenties. It occurred only in the work of Loos, and to a small degree also in the work of Le Corbusier.

But the most important parallels to the Baroque and the most fundamental differences with pre-war architecture are found in New Brutalism. The airy, glassed-in cubes are now experienced as 'cold' and 'inhuman'. An aggressive plasticity hits the spectator in his face in Rudolph's Art and Architecture Building in Yale, Kahn's Medical Centre and Förderer's schools in Aesch and St. Gallen. Transparency has been replaced by massiveness and simplicity by complexity. Instead of the immaterial white plaster of the Weissenhof Siedlung we are now confronted with concrete treated as roughly as possible (Rudolph). Concealed windows create a theatrical lighting effect in the library of Förderer's Economic School, in Le Corbusier's monastery church and in Cramer, Jaray and Paillard's church in Zurich.

The expressionistic, emotional architecture of Ronchamp has developed into a whole school of concrete Neo Baroque. The method of overhead lighting of the chapels in Ronchamp is in fact exactly the same as that in Narciso Tomé's 'Trasparente' in Toledo Cathedral of 1732.

The whole evolution is visible in the work of some of the pioneers. Le Corbusier, Aalto and Van den Broek started with the glassy abstract cubes of Functionalism and continually stepped up their plastic intensity in their later work. The relation between the architecture of the sixties and that of the twenties is the same as that between Baroque and Renaissance architecture. There is also a striking similarity between the respective ideals. The chasm between the Neo Platonic harmonic cosmos and the disharmonic social world grew steadily larger; hence the effort to involve the spectator. Architecture turned from philosophy to psychology, from thinking to feeling. Modern architecture ran a similar course. White disembodied cubes such as Poissy, interpenetration of exterior and interior, open planning and acres of glass did not bring the integrated society any nearer. Therefore architects reached for a stronger medicine.

Here ends our story. If my analysis is correct, architects have been trying to express the same concept over and over again during the last five hundred years. To a steadily divergent and competitive society they upheld the ideals of harmony and social unity. Their profession obliges them to synthesize the disparate demands of function, construction and economy; it seems only natural that they transferred this synthetic attitude to the realm of art.

Whether such sermons in stone or concrete are really effective remains to be seen. The influence of planning and building on social life is large indeed, but architects are wont to overrate it.

It may well be that our clients, our society, expect something quite different from our work than we do ourselves. There may be room for a different type of architectural theory: client-directed rather than architect-directed. A theory which assesses as best it can the biological and psychological expectations of the anonymous client, without falling back on a sermon in stone, which—as history shows us—leaves him stone-cold.

An analysis of Van Doesburg's sixteen points

Theo van Doesburg: Towards a plastic architecture

1. FORM. The basis for a healthy development of architecture (and of art in general) is to be found in the suppression of form in the sense of a *preconceived type*.
   Instead of using earlier style-types as clichés, thus to imitate styles, it is necessary to restate the problem of architecture in entirely new terms.

Comment: Historical dreamland has failed. Society drifts further and further away from the idea communities of the past, symbolized in eclectic architecture. Hence the need for a new start and a really convincing symbolism, which will bring about the new society.

2. The new architecture is *elementary*, i.e. it develops from the elements of building in the most comprehensive sense. These elements, such as function, mass, plane, time, space, light, colour, material, etc. are at the same time *elements of plastic expression*.

3. The new architecture is *economical*, i.e. it organizes its elementary means as efficiently as possible without waste of either means or material.

4. The new architecture is *functional*, i.e. it evolves from the accurate determination of practical demands which it establishes in a clear ground-plan.

Comment: Points 2, 3 and 4 aim at the construction of such a truly convincing symbolism. Elementary forms are convincing because they are universal; you cannot go further in reduction than the Phileban solids and Euclidian elements of line and plane. Reduction is also the goal of the statements about economy (3) and the use of the same elements for functional and formal purposes (italicized passage at the end of 2). At the same time a first effort is made to connect the architectural symbols with reality in order to give substance to architectural dreamland: the new architecture is 'functional', 'efficient' and 'practical'.

5. The new architecture is *formless*, yet definite, that is to say, it ignores a preconceived aesthetic formula, a mold (in the sense known by pastry-cooks) in which it casts the functional spaces which have resulted from practical living requirements. Unlike all past styles, the new architectural method knows no self-contained type, no *arche-type*.

Division of functional spaces is strictly determined by rectangular planes. These have in themselves no individual form because, although circumscribed (one plane by the other) they may be thought of as being extended indefinitely. The rectangular planes generate a system of co-ordinates whose points correspond with an equal number of points in universal, open space.

It follows from this that the planes have a direct tensile relationship with open (exterior) space.

Comment: Rectangles are certainly not formless and thus (as Van Doesburg obviously saw also) the third sentence contradicts the first two. The designs of Van Doesburg, Van Eesteren and Rietveld showed too much similarity to deny the existence of a 'preconceived aesthetic formula'. Where eclectic symbolism had failed through dogmatism and the use of archetypes, the new architecture will succeed; that is what inspired the opening lines. Also a rectangle is a simpler and therefore more universal and more neutral form than the forms of eclecticism; in this sense it might be called 'formless'.

'Universal open space' embraces all mankind. It is a symbol for the united society. In architecture this symbol is expressed by the 'exploded cube', more fully described in the points 7 to 11. However, disintegration of the closed forms of the Phileban solids endangers the formal unity of the work of art. The artists of the twenties were well aware of this, and tried to compensate for it by another formal device: repetition. By confining themselves strictly to right angles, and, wherever possible, to complete rectangles, they sought to bring back a formal cohesion which they felt they had to destroy on other points.

6. The new architecture has removed the notion of *monumental* from dependence upon largeness and smallness (the word *'monumental'* is obsolete and must be replaced by the word 'plastic'). It has demonstrated that everything is relationship, relationship of the one to the other.

Comment: We stand in awe before monuments, but we are not directly involved. They belong to a different world and we remain spectators. In connection with its preference for open plans, for involving 'the elements of building in the most comprehensive sense', the new architecture makes a bid for the whole person and his entire life, and in particular for his daily life, which is much more real to him than, say, a Sunday church service. Architecture, for such a long time a mere sham, should partake of that everyday reality. The last sentence once more stresses the unified cosmos, our 'dreamland'.

7. The new architecture knows no *passive moment*. It has conquered the opening in the wall. The *openness* of the window has a *dynamic* meaning in relationship to the *closedness* of the wall surface. Nowhere does there exist merely a hole or a void, everything is strictly determined through contrast. (In order to see this one must compare the different counter-constructions in which the basic architectural elements of plane, line and mass are loosely placed in 3-dimensional relationship.)

8. PLAN. The new architecture has *broken through the wall* and in so doing has completely eliminated the *divorce* of *inside* and *out*. The walls are no longer lead-bearing; they are reduced to points of support. And as a result there is generated a new, open plan, totally different from the classic because inside and outside space interpenetrate.

9. The new architecture is *open;* the whole exists as one space which is divided according to functional requirements. This division is effected by *separating planes* (interior) or through *sheltering planes* (exterior).

The first, which divide the different functional spaces from each other, can be *mobile*. That is to say, the separating planes (the earlier inside walls) can be replaced by movable screens or slabs (doors must also be considered as slabs). In a next stage of its development the groundplan must disappear completely. The two-dimensionally projected spatial composition, fixed in a groundplan, shall be replaced by an exact *calculation of the construction*, a calculation which must reduce the carrying capacity to the simplest but most resistant points of support. For this purpose our euclidian mathematics will no longer be able to serve. Yet with non-euclidian calculations in 4 dimensions this shall be a simple matter.

10. SPACE AND TIME. The new architecture reckons not only with space but also with time as one of its characteristics. The unity of time and space gives the architectonic appearance a new and completely plastic aspect. *(4-dimensional time-spatial plastic aspects).*

11. The new architecture is *anti-cubic*, that is to say, it does not try to freeze the different functional space-cells in one closed cube. Rather *it throws the functional space-cells* (as well as overhanging planes, balcony volumes, etc.) centrifugally from the *core of the cube*, and through this means height, width, depth + time approach a totally new plastic expression in open spaces. In this way architecture gets (insofar as this is possible from a constructional point of view—task of the engineers!) a more or less floating aspect that, so to speak works against the gravitational forces of nature.

Comment: The preceding five points describe explicitly the new symbolic system. All effort is directed at the same goal, i.e. the creation of a unified conceptual space (Elimination of 'the divorce of inside and out'). Van Doesburg realizes that this will be quite difficult in the face of the practical necessity of physically enclosed spaces. Therefore he wants 'separating planes' to be as provisional as possible: preferably they are 'movable screens'. The window is a sheltering plane, and therefore one which cannot be removed or altered at will. But conceptual space ought to flow through the building unobstructedly, regardless of walls and windows. Hence the stress that is laid on the 'dynamic' relationship between opening and wall (7), on movement through space and thereby on the integration between space and time(10). Finally, the thought of a minimal obstruction between inside and outside space leads to a light and airy construction in which the walls are reduced 'to points of support', and which makes a 'floating' impression.

12. SYMMETRY AND REPETITION. The new architecture has nullified monotonous repetition as well as the fixed symmetry of 2 halves, the mirror image, symmetry. It knows no repetition in time, no street wall or standardization. A complex is as much a *whole* as is the independent house. The same laws are required for the complex and for the city as for the independent house. The new architecture, instead of using symmetry, establishes a *balanced relationship of dissimilar parts*, i.e. of parts which, because of their various functions, are different in position, size, proportion

and situation. The equivalence of these disparate parts is established by equilibrium and not through similarity. In addition, the new architecture has made 'front', 'back', 'right', and possibly also 'above' and 'below' of equal value.

13. In contrast with the frontality which results from a fixed, static outlook, the new architecture offers a plastic richness of multi-sided, time-space activity.

Comment: Symmetry creates a closed Gestalt: the rotational symmetry of the central plan even suggests absolute rest and immobility, as was adumbrated already in the Italian Renaissance. These are the exact opposites of the free-flowing conceptual spaces Van Doesburg wanted. With a 'balanced relationship of dissimilar parts' he stated once more his intention to guarantee a minimum of formal coherence. The wholeness of a complex and the equivalence of the various directions underline the essential unity of (conceptual) space again.

14. COLOUR. The new architecture has nullified painting as a separate imaginary expression of harmony, either secondary through representation, or primary through coloured planes.

The new architecture absorbs colour *organically into itself* as an immediate expressional element of its relationships in time and space. Without colour these relationships are not a living reality; they are *not visible*.

The equilibrium of architectural relationships becomes visible first through colour. The problem of the modern painter is to organize colour toward an harmonic whole (not on a surface, not in 2 dimensions, but in the new sphere: 4-dimensional time-space). In a further stage of development these colours will be replaced by synthetic material having its own colour (the task of the chemists). This can be accomplished only when practical demands require the material.

15. The new architecture is *anti-decorative*. Colour (and this colour-shy people must attempt to realize) has become not a decorative or ornamental factor in architecture but rather an *organic, expressive*, architectural element.

Comment: The points about colour reflect Van Doesburg's own work as a painter. The idea of a unified, cosmic space involves also the integration of as many visual elements as possible with the architecture. The building is a 'Gesamtkunstwerk', not in the Wagnerian sense of an addition of the various arts, but in a complete fusion of them. Colour is used by Van Doesburg in his designs with Van Eesteren and in 'la Aubette' as a means to dissociate the various sheltering and separating planes which enclose space, once more with the intention of dissolving masses and creating the impression of a set of independent intersecting planes (see also 5 and 8). Therefore colour is truly a necessity, an 'organic, expressive architectural element'.

The last point summarizes his aesthetic:

16. ARCHITECTURE AS THE SYNTHESIS OF THE NEW PLASTICITY. In the new architecture building is understood as a part, the summation of all the arts in their most elementary manifestation. It presents the possibility of thinking in 4 dimensions, i.e. the plastic architect, and the painter should also be counted as such, must construct in the new sphere of time-space.

As the new architecture admits no imagination (in the form of free painting or sculpture), its intention is to employ all the essential means to create an harmonic whole, a harmony already *present from the very beginning*. In this way every architectonic element helps bring to life a maximum of plastic expression without damaging the practical requirements. (*De Stijl*, 6:6, 7; 1924, pp. 78–83. Translation from: T.M. Brown, *The Work of G. Rietveld Architect*, Utrecht, 1958, pp. 66, 68 and 69.)

Categories of criticism

1. **Function**

1.11 Form and dimensions of one room in relation to the activity for which it is used.
1.12 Location of architectural parts (doors, windows, etc.) in relation to the activity of 1.11.
1.13 Physical and physiological conditions of a room (glare, heat, noise, etc.).
1.14 Psychological conditions of a room (e.g. a room may be cosy, austere, inviting, gloomy, etc.).
1.21 Form and dimensions of the entire set of spaces within a building in relation to its function; in particular the proportion between primary (usable) spaces versus corridors, stairs, etc.
1.22 Location of spaces in relation to each other.
1.23 Psychological aspects of movement through a building.
1.31 Form and dimensions of areas around the building in relation to its and their functions.
1.32 Location of areas around the building in relation to their functions.
1.33 Physical conditions of areas around the building.
1.34 Psychological conditions of the areas around the building.

2. **Construction**

2.11 Performance of a detail in relation to its function.
2.12 The relation between a detail, the materials from which it has been made, and the methods by which it was built.
2.13 Durability and maintenance of details.
2.14 Cost of construction and maintenance of a detail.
2.21 Performance of the structure in relation to its load-bearing function.
2.22 The relation between the structure and materials and methods.
2.23 Durability and maintenance of the structure.
2.24 Cost of construction and maintenance of the structure of a building.

3. **Formal aesthetics**

3.11 Coherence (repetition and similarity, continuity and closure, simple overall form) in: surfaces (materials), detailing, construction techniques, structure, forms of spaces and of masses, site-planning. 'Consistency' in design is a subclass of this: it usually means a repetition of the same compositional element or device.
3.12 Contrast in all the aspects of 3.11.

3.2 System of composition (around a centre or along an axis, symmetrical, etc.). The design of a spatial sequence is a sublcass.
3.3 The creation of atmosphere through lighting, colours, textures.

4. Symbolic aesthetics

4.1 The relation between architectural and other forms through association.
4.2 The relation between architectural forms and the concepts they symbolize (2nd level symbolism).
4.3 The relation between architectural forms and the general social context in which they were created (3rd level symbolism).

5. Interrelations

5.12 The relation between function and structure.
5.13 The relation between function and form in a single building, considered by itself.
5.13 The relation between function and form in connection with the significance of the function in the total urban context (e.g. complex, arresting forms seem more appropriate for a public building than for a private one).
5.23 The relation between construction and form.

Notes

Chapter I. Formal and symbolic aesthetics

1. Sir Henry Wotton, *The Elements of Architecture*, London, 1624.
   Vitruvius, *The Ten Books on Architecture*, Bk I, Ch. III, 2.
2. E. E. Viollet-le-Duc, *Dictionnaire raisonnée de l'architecture française du XIe au XVIe siècle*, Paris, 1854–1868.
   A. W. Pugin, *The True Principles of Pointed or Christian Architecture*, London, 1853.
3. Quoted in: E. Panofsky, *Meaning in the Visual Arts*, Garden City, 1955, p. 202.
4. A. Palladio, *I Quattro Libri dell' Architettura*, Venice, 1570, Bk I, Ch. 21, p. 48.
5. J. Ruskin, *The Seven Lamps of Architecture*, London, 1849, ed. of 1890, p. 230.
6. Le Corbusier, *Vers une architecture*, Paris, 1923, p. 11.
7. R. Arnheim, *Art and Visual Perception*, London, 1956.
   G. Kepes, *The Language of Vision*, Chicago, 1944.
   M. Baugniet, *Essai sur la psychologie des formes*, Brussels, n.d.
8. This arrangement is only the most cursory of summaries of Gestalt psychology, developed by Wertheimer, Köhler and Koffka. Important subjects (as figure-and-ground or the constancies) have been omitted, because they show no appreciable relation to our theme. See: K. Koffka, *Principles of Gestalt Psychology*, New York, 1935.
9. A. Ames, *Nature and Origin of Perceptions*, Hanover, 1949.
10. 'Just as in all other representative arts a single representation is of a single object, so the story (of a drama), being the representation of an action, must be of a single one, which is a whole; and the parts of the scheme of incidents must be so arranged that if any part is transposed or removed, the whole will be disordered and shattered; for that of which the presence or absence makes no appreciable difference is no part of the whole.' Aristotle, *Poetics*, VIII, 4.
11. 'I do not mean by the beauty of form such beauty as that of animals or pictures, which the many would suppose to be my meaning; but, says the argument, understand me to mean straight lines and circles, and the plane and solid which are formed out of them by turning lathes and rulers and measures of angles; for these I affirm to be not only relatively beautiful, like other things, but they are eternally and absolutely beautiful. ...' Plato, *Philebus*, translated by B. Jowett, Oxford, 1953, pp. 610–611.
12. Though the existence of this 'need' in visual perception cannot be demonstrated in experiments, there is some psychological backing for it. See: D. O. Hebb, *The Organization of Behavior*, New York 1949, 1959, pp. 227 f.
13. Th. van Doesburg, 'Tot een beeldende architectuur', in: *De Stijl*, Nos. 6/7, 1924, column 81.

Chapter II. Symbolism

1. A. W. Pugin, *An Apology for the Revival of Christian Architecture*, London, 1843, ed. of 1853, p. 6.
2. See the literature mentioned in the *Preface*, p. viii.
3. J. Ruskin, *The Seven Lamps of Architecture*, ed. of 1890, pp. 375–376: 'In the same way architects would have to be taught to write the accepted style. We must first determine what buildings are to be considered Augustan in their authority; their modes of construction and their laws of proportion are to be studied with the most penetrating care; then the different forms and uses of their decorations are to be classed and catalogued, as a German grammarian classes the powers of propositions; and under this absolute, irrefragable authority we are to begin to work. ... Then when our sight is once accustomed to the grammatical forms and arrangements, and our thoughts familiar with the expression of them all; then we can speak this dead language naturally, and apply it to whatever ideas we have to render.'
4. Ch. Morris, *Signs, Language and Behavior*, New York, 1946.
   C. K. Ogden and I. A. Richards, *The Meaning of Meaning*, London, 1923.
5. Homer, *The Odyssey*, translated by E. V. Rieu, Harmondsworth, 1948, p. 144.
6. S. K. Langer, *Feeling and Form*, New York, 1953, pp. 24 f., 40.
7. E. Panofsky, *Meaning in the Visual Arts*, Garden City, 1955, p. 12.
8. S. Freud, *Die Traumdeutung*, Vienna, 1900; the edition of 1914 has an appendix to Chapter 6 by O. Rank on *Traum und Dichtung*.
   — *Psychoanalytische Studien an Werken der Dichtung und Kunst*, Leipzig, 1924. A summary of Freud's explorations in the field of art in: R. Sterba, 'The Problem of Art in Freud's Writings' in: M. Weitz, *Problems in Aesthetics*, New York, 1959.
9. A. Ehrenzweig, *The Psychoanalysis of Artistic Vision and Hearing*, London, 1953.
   E. Neumann, *Kunst und schöpferisches Unbewusstes*, Zürich, 1954.
10. C. Baudoin, *Introduction à l'analyse des rêves*, Paris, 1949, p. 66.
11. W. Abell, *The Collective Dream in Art*, Cambridge, Mass., 1957.
12. This interpretation in R. Huyghe, *Dialogue avec le visible*, Paris, 1955, p. 304.
13. Abell, *op. cit.*, p. 220. The monsters were still very much alive. See J. Baltrusaïtis, *Réveils et prodiges. Le gothique fantastique*, Paris, 1960.
14. From the 8th to the 13th century there is an increase in naturalism, but it is not at all a rectilinear development. Some Carolingian miniatures exhibit impressionistic realism (Utrecht Psalter). See: E. Panofsky, *Renaissance and Renascences in Western Art*, Copenhagen, 1960.
15. The naturalism of Rheims was influenced by classical examples; see E. Panofsky, *Renaissance and Renascences...*, p. 62. What counts however is not the morphology by itself, but the (possible) reason for copying antique examples.
16. W. Abell, *op. cit.*, pp. 236 f.
17. 'Human beings have probably always seen as they *wanted* to see.' H. Wölfflin, 'Kunstgeschichtliche Grundbegriffe. Eine Revision' in: *Logos* XX, p. 210.

Chapter III. Basic concepts in architecture

1. S. Langer, *Feeling and Form*, New York, 1953, p. 95.
2. The sign of 'Ascoral' in J. Petit, ed., *Le Corbusier, Architecte du Bonheur*, Paris, 1955, Ch. 8.
3. H. E. Winlock, *The Temple of Ramesses I at Abydos*. The Metropolitan Museum of Art, Paper No 5, New York, 1937, pp. 14 and 15.
4. R. Ingarden, *Untersuchungen zur Ontologie der Kunst*, Tübingen, 1962, pp. 257 ff.
5. J. Piaget and B. Inhelder, *The Child's Conception of Space*, London, 1963.
6. P. Rudolph, 'To Enrich our Architecture', *The Journal of Architectural Education*, Vol. XIII, No 1, p. 11.

Chapter IV. Classification of forms

1. The break-down of architecture in small 'elements of composition' stems from the Beaux-Arts teaching and ultimately from Alberti and Palladio. But the elements of the Beaux Arts, as represented in Guadet, are always a mixture of structural concepts and concepts of form; e.g. an arch resting on columns, a vault on piers. I have tried to go further. See: J. Guadet, *Eléments et théories de l'architecture*, Paris, 1902.
2. The use of antithetical concepts as co-ordinates for the clarification of formal problems in art stems from:
H. Wölfflin, *Kunstgeschichtliche Grundbegriffe*, Munich, 1915. My concepts differ from Wölfflin's mainly in being simpler and (therefore) more numerous. I believe in more independent variables than Wölfflin seems to do.
I have also been influenced in my choice of concepts by the Bauhaus primary design course ('Vorlehre') as taught by Itten. (I teach a variant of that course in the Delft School of Architecture.) The term 'co-ordinate' has been first used, as far as I know, by P. Frankl, *The Gothic...* Princeton, 1960, pp. 779, 797, 835.
3. The antithetical concepts of continuity go back to R. Willis, *Remarks on the Architecture of the Middle Ages, especially of Italy*, Cambridge, 1835.

Chapter V. The overall pattern

1. On the levels of meaning, see: E. Panofsky, *Studies in Iconology*, New York, 1939, pp. 3 f.
2. A. Piganiol, *Histoire Romaine*, Paris, 1947, Vol. IV.
A. H. M. Jones, *The Later Roman Empire*, Oxford, 1964.
3. M. Rostovtzeff, *A History of the Ancient World*, London, 1963.
4. C. W. Previté-Orton, *The Shorter Cambridge Medieval History*, Cambridge, 1952.
5. For the typology of societies and the difference between ascriptive (born) social roles and roles based on achievement: T. Parsons, *The Social System*, Glencoe, 1951.
The contrast between traditional static society and modern dynamic and its possible emotive

implications is discussed in F. Alexander, *Our Age of Unreason*, Philadelphia, 1942.
6. J. Burckhardt, *Die Kultur der Renaissance in Italien*, 1860.
   A. von Martin, *Soziologie der Renaissance*, Stuttgart, 1932.
   G. R. Potter, ed., 'The Renaissance', in *The New Cambridge Modern History*, Vol. I, Cambridge, 1957.
7. L. B. Alberti, *Ten Books on Architecture* (Florence, 1485; Leoni Edition 1726), reprint London, 1955, p. 138.
8. Quoted in: E. Kaufmann, *Architecture in the Age of Reason*, Cambridge, Mass., 1955, pp. 96 and 97.
9. C. N. Ledoux, *L'architecture considérée sous le rapport de l'Art, des Mœurs et de la Législation* (Paris, 1804), extract repr. Paris, 1961 (ed. by Y. Christ) p. 103.
10. E. L. Boullée, *Architecture, Essai sur l'Art*, written before 1799, ed. by H. Rosenau, London 1953, pp. 35 and 36.
    On the architecture of Boullée and Ledoux:
    E. Kaufmann, *Von Ledoux bis le Corbusier*, Vienna, 1933.
    — *Architecture in the Age of Reason*, Cambridge, Mass., 1955.
11. J. Summerson, *Architecture in Britain, 1530 to 1830*, Harmondsworth, 1963.
    W. J. Hipple, *The Beautiful, the Sublime and the Picturesque*, Carbondale, 1957.
12. A. W. Pugin, *The True Principles of Pointed or Christian Architecture*, London, 1841.
    — *An Apology for the Revival of Christian Architecture in England*, London, 1843.
    Combined edition of 1853, pp. 39, 1 and 35.
13. See: E. R. de Zurko, *Origins of Functionalist Theory*, New York, 1957.
14. P. Mondriaan, 'Neo Plasticisme – De Woning – de Straat – de Stad', *Internationale Revue*, i 10, 1927, repr. The Hague, 1963, pp. 15 and 18.
15. P. Frankl, *The Gothic-Literary Sources and Interpretations through Eight Centuries*, Princeton, 1960.
    P. Booz, *Der Baumeister der Gotik*, Munich, 1956.
16. L. B. Alberti, *Ten Books on Architecture* (1485) ed. of 1955, pp. XI and 1. The quotation is typical for the new type of architect which appeared in the Renaissance, the learned dilettante, of which Alberti is the earliest famous representative. Palladio, who started as a stone-carver and mason, lays much greater weight on construction. But it is also highly significant that such a new type made its appearance precisely at this time. From the bookish, learned amateur, the line leads over the pupils of the Académie des Beaux Arts to the University trained architect of today.
17. E. L. Boullée, *Architecture* ..., p. 27.

Chapter VI. Santa Costanza

1. Krautheimer originally identified it as the outside wall of an open cemetery. (R. Krautheimer *Corpus Basilicarum Christianarum Romae*, Vol. I, No I, Rome, 1937.) Deichmann identified the wall as the outside wall of the 4th century church: F. W. Deichmann, 'Die Lage der Con-

stantinischen Basilika der heiligen Agnes an der Via Nomentana', *Rivista di Archeologia Christiana*, 1946, Vol. XIII, Nos 1 and 4, pp. 213–234. Excavations have confirmed Deichmann's thesis: R. Perrotti, 'La Basilica di S. Agnese fuori le mura', in: *Palladio. Rivista di storia, dell'architettura*, 1961, Nos III and IV, pp. 157–164. Krautheimer has recently modified his position, and proposed a combination of a funeral banqueting hall, church and covered cemetery: R. Krautheimer, *Early Christian and Byzantine Architecture*, Harmondsworth, 1965, p. 31.
2. A. Grabar, *Martyrium*, Paris, 1946.
3. F. W. Deichmann, *Frühchristliche Kirchen in Rom*, Basel, 1948.
   Particularly on S. Costanza: M. Stettler, 'Zur Rekonstruktion von S. Costanza', *Römische Mitteilungen*, LVIII, 1943, p. 84; K. Lehmann, 'S. Constanza', *Art Bulletin*, Vol. XXXVII, 1955, pp. 193–196 and 291.
4. H. Stern, 'Les mosaïques de l'église de Sainte-Constance à Rome' in: *Dumbarton Oaks Papers*, Vol. XII, Cambridge, Mass., 1958, pp. 159–218.
5. Communicated by P. Singelenberg.
6. Of similar construction: the Pantheon (120), Diocletians mausoleum (300).
7. B. Tamm, *Auditorium and Palatium*, Stockholm, 1963.
8. The double row of columns, necessitated by the weight of the wall, has a precedent in a small temple outside the Porta Portese, reproduced in W. Altmann, *Die Italischen Rundbauten*, 1906, p. 63.
9. The palatial basilicas often had aisles too: thus Split, Tipasa, Oropos and Tivoli. But they lacked probably a clerestory.
10. Quoted and translated in M. Hadas, *A History of Rome*, Garden City, 1956, p. 180.
    On the social conditions in the Later Roman Empire:
    M. Rostovtzeff, *A History of the Ancient World*, London, 1963.
    A. Piganiol, *Histoire Romaine*, Vol. IV, Paris, 1947.
    A. H. M. Jones, *The Later Roman Empire*, Oxford, 1964.

Chapter VII. St. Michael, Hildesheim

1. The principal source is his biography by his teacher Thangmar, *Vita Bernwardi episcop Hildesheimensis;* original text in: *Monumenta Germaniae Historica Scriptorum*, Vol. IV, pp. 754–782. See also: F. J. Tschan, *Saint Bernward of Hildesheim*, Vol. 1, *His Life and Times*, Notre Dame, 1942.
2. See in particular: A. Mann, 'Doppelchor und Stiftermemorie', *Westfälische Zeitschrift*, Vol. 111, 1961, pp. 149–263.
3. On the iconography of St. Michael: L. Réau, *Iconographie de l'Art Chrétien*, Vol. II, Part I, Paris 1956, pp. 44 ff.
4. See: J. Hubert, 'L'église Saint-Michel-de-Cuxa et l'occidentation des églises au Moyen Age', *Journal of the Soc. of Arch. Historians*, Vol. XXI, 1962, pp. 163–170.
5. E. Mâle, *L'Art religieux du XIIIe siècle en France*, Paris, 1919, p. 441.

6. For the description and analysis of the building I have made extensive use of the excellent monograph: H. Beseler and H. Roggenkamp, *Die Michaeliskirche zu Hildesheim*, Berlin, 1954.
7. K. J. Conant, *Carolingian and Romanesque Architecture 800–1200*, Harmondsworth, 1959.
8. In the first half of the 14th century 25 altars are mentioned: Beseler and Roggenkamp, *Die Michaeliskirche...*, p. 24.
9. A. Schmidt, 'Westwerke und Doppelchöre', *Westfälische Zeitschrift*, Vol. 106, 1956 pp. 360 f., 368 f. and 382.
10. J. A. Jungmann, *Missarum Sollemnia*, Freiburg, 1952, p. 293.
11. E. Lehmann, 'Die frühchristlichen Kirchenfamilien der Bischofssitze im deutschen Raum und ihre Wandlungen während des Frühmittelalters' in: *Akten zum VII. Internationalen Kongress für Frühmittelalterforschung, 1958*, Cologne-Graz, 1962.
    — 'Von der Kirchenfamilie zur Kathedrale' in: *Festschrift Friedrich Gerke*, Baden-Baden, 1962, pp. 21–37.
12. C. Heitz, *Recherches sur les rapports entre architecture et liturgie à l'époque carolingienne*, Paris, 1963. Heitz explains the form of St. Michael primarily as a survival from Carolingian church building.
13. J. A. Jungmann, *Missarum Sollemnia*, pp. 89 and 269 f.
    A. Schmidt, 'Westwerke und Doppelchöre ...'
14. A. Mann, *Doppelchor ...*, p. 193, supposes that the main altar of St. Michael was dedicated to the patron; the invocation of the Saviour in the act of consecration would then be a purely formal and habitual gesture. This seems to me far more likely than the very cramped cubicle over the entrance.
15. Many churches of this period show a tendency towards bi-axial symmetry: E. Lehmann, *Der frühe Deutsche Kirchenbau*, Berlin, 1949. The abbey church of Memleben of 979 had also two equal transepts: H. Thümmler, 'Karolingische und Ottonische Baukunst in Sachsen,' in: V. Elbern, ed., *Das Erste Jahrtausend*, Vol. II, Düsseldorf, 1964, p. 890.
16. According to G. Forsyth, 'The Transept of Old St. Peter's in Rome' in: *Late Classical Studies in Honor of A. M. Friend*, Princeton, 1955, pp. 56 f. it occurred first in St. Peter and served to allow pilgrims to circulate around the tomb of the Apostle during mass.
17. R. Krautheimer, 'The Carolingian Revival of Early Christian Architecture', *Art Bulletin*, Vol. XXIV, 1942.
18. F. van der Meer, *Keerpunt der Middeleeuwen*, Utrecht-Brussels, 1950, pp. 41 f.
    A. Schmidt, *op. cit.*
19. On crypts:
    A. Grabar, *Martyrium*, Paris, 1946.
    R. Wallrath, 'Zur Bedeutung der mittelalterlichen Krypta' in: *Beiträge zur Kunst des Mittelalters, Kunsthistorikertagung Brühl 1948*, Berlin, 1950.
    F. Deshoulières, 'Les cryptes en France et l'influence du culte des reliques sur l'architecture' in: *Mélanges à la mémoire de F. Martroye*, 1940.
    On Saxon crypts in particular: H. Claussen, 'Spätkarolingische Umgangskrypten im sächsischen Gebiet' in: *Forschungen zur Kunstgeschichte und christlichen Archäologie*, Vol. III: Karolingische und ottonische Kunst, Wiesbaden, 1957.

20. The usual arrangement in Saxony; see H. Claussen, *loc. cit.*
21. H. Beseler and H. Roggenkamp, *op. cit.*, p. 169.
22. Beseler and Roggenkamp, *op. cit.*, pp. 97 f. and A. Mann, *loc. cit.*
23. R. Wallrath, *loc. cit.* See also:
    G. Bandmann, 'Über Pastophorien und verwandte Nebenräume im mittelalterlichen Kirchenbau' in: *Kunstgeschichtliche Studien für Hans Kaufmann*, Berlin, 1956, pp. 19–59.
24. R. Kautzsch, *Der Mainzer Dom und seine Denkmäler*, Frankfort, 1925.
25. In favour of a Syrian origin, after Strzygowski:
    S. Guyer, *Grundlagen mittelalterlich abendländischer Baukunst*, Einsiedeln, 1950.
    H. Schaefer, 'The Origin of the Two-Tower Façade in Romanesque Architecture', *Art Bulletin*, Vol. XXVII, 1945, pp. 85–108.
    In favour of a relation to medieval city-gates and walls:
    G. Bandmann, 'Früh- und hochmittelalterliche Altaranordnung als Darstellung' in: V. Elbern, ed., *Das Erste Jahrtausend*. Düsseldorf, 1962, pp. 388 and 389.
    See also: G. H. Forsyth, 'St. Martin's at Angers and the Evolution of Early Mediaeval Church Towers, *Art Bulletin*, Vol. XXXII, 1950, pp. 308–319.
26. G. Bandmann, *Mittelalterliche Architektur als Bedeutungsträger*, Berlin, 1951, pp. 90 f.
27. H. Beseler and H. Roggenkamp, *op. cit.*, p. 86.
28. K. J. Conant, *loc. cit.*
29. *Jahrbücher von Hildesheim*, Berlin, 1862, p. 27.
30. Thangmar, 'Vita Bernwardi' in: *Geschichtsschreiber der deutschen Vorzeit*, Berlin, 1858, pp. 11–12.
31. W. Rave, *Corvey*, Münster, 1958. The text, as pointed out by C. Heitz (*Recherches sur les rapports...*) is taken from the Hours read on Tuesdays in November and runs as follows in full:
    P. Civitatem istam tu circumda, Domine, et angeli tui custodiant muros eius.
    A. Exaudi, Domine, populum tuum cum misericordia.
    P. Avertatur furor tuus, Domine, a populo tuo et a civitate sancta tua.
    Possibly it is a paraphrase of Daniel 9: 16-20. Angelic guardians of the heavenly Jerusalem occur also in Apocalypse 21: 12.

Chapter VIII. Notre Dame, Cathedral of Amiens

1. B. H. Slicher van Bath, *De agrarische geschiedenis van West-Europa (500–1580)*, Utrecht-Antwerp, 1960, pp. 86 f.
2. *Ib.*, pp. 147 f.
3. F. L. Ganshof, *Over stadsontwikkeling tussen Loire en Rijn gedurende de Middeleeuwen*, Antwerp, 1941.
4. I owe this explanation of the growth of Amiens to a talk by F. Gorissen, archivist of Cleve.
5. The charter of bishop Geoffrey II of 1236, which says that the parish church of St. Firmin will be demolished to make room for the cathedral (V. Mortet and P. Deschamps, *Recueil des textes relatifs à l'histoire de l'architecture...*, Vol. II, Paris, 1929, pp. 260–261) should probably

not be interpreted as implying a change in the original plan, but as a decision postponed as long as possible to allow the use of St Firmin; see G. Durand, *Monographie de l'église cathédrale Notre Dame d'Amiens*, Amiens-Paris, 1901–1903, p. 29. The later architects, Thomas de Cormont and his son Renaud deserve admiration for the consistency with which they stuck to the initial design. On details, charters, and subsequent history, see G. Durand, *op. cit.* On the chronology: R. Branner, *St Louis and the Court Style in Gothic Architecture*, London, 1965, pp. 138–141. On the proportions and dimensions: N. Luning Prak, 'Measurements of Amiens Cathedral,' *Journal of the Society of Architectural Historians*, Vol. XXV, No 3, October 1966, pp. 209–212.

6. G. Durand, *op. cit.*
7. Ganshof, *op. cit.*
8. H. Jantzen, 'Zur Beurteilung der gotischen Architektur als Raumkunst' in: *Kritische Berichte zur kunstgeschichtlichen Literatur*, Leipzig, 1927, pp. 12 f.
9. E. E. Viollet-le-Duc, *Dictionnaire raisonnée de l'architecture française du XIe au XVIe siècle*, Paris, 1854–1859.
   P. Abraham, *Viollet-le-Duc et le rationalisme médiéval*, Paris, 1934.
   H. Masson, 'Le rationalisme dans l'architecture du moyen-âge' in: *Bulletin Monumental* Paris, 1935.
   H. Focillon, *Art d'occident*, Paris, 1938.
   All four are discussed at length in P. Frankl, *The Gothic. Literary Sources and Interpretations Through Eight Centuries*, Princeton, 1960. This monumental work supersedes all older literature on the subject; it is a history of art besides a history of the history of art. It appeared after the chapter on Notre Dame of Amiens was written; I believe my conclusions to be substantially in agreement with Frankl's more expert opinion. What I call 'unity' he calls 'partiality' in the last chapter (pp. 829 f). He sees a parallel between the Gothic member as part of a larger whole and the Gothic vision of man as a fragment of the universe. On Gothic construction, centering and falsework, see: J. Fitchen, *The Construction of Gothic Cathedrals*, Oxford, 1961.
10. H. Focillon, *Art d'occident*, p. 147.
    P. Frankl, *The Gothic...*, p. 825.
11. E. Gall, *Niederrheinische und normannische Architektur im Zeitalter der Frühgotik*, Berlin, 1915.
12. P. Booz, *Der Baumeister der Gotik*, Munich-Berlin, 1956.
    P. Frankl, *op. cit.*
13. P. Booz, *op. cit.*
14. H. Focillon, *op. cit.*
    P. Frankl, *op. cit.*, pp. 58–60, 811 and 844.
15. A. Kingsley Porter, *The Construction of Lombard and Gothic Vaults*, New Haven, Conn., 1911.
16. A. Choisy, *Histoire de l'Architecture*, 2 vols., Paris, 1899; Vol. I, p. 524; Vol. II, pp. 267–268.
    J. Fitchen, *The Construction of Gothic Cathedrals*, Oxford, 1961.
17. M. Aubert, 'Les plus anciennes croisées d'ogives' in: *Bulletin Monumental*, 1934, pp. 1 f. and 137 f.
18. In the first bays of Rheims, in the chancel, the triforium is also linked with the clerestory

window. On linkage see R. Branner, *St Louis and the Court Style in Gothic Architecture*, London, 1965, pp. 20 f.
19. On the classical revival and the influence of classical models on High-Gothic sculpture: J. Adhémar, *Influences antiques dans l'art du moyen âge français. Recherches sur les sources et les thèmes d'inspiration* (Studies of the Warburg Institute VII), London, 1939; E. Panofsky, *Renaissance and Renascences in Western Art*, Copenhagen, 1960, pp. 62 f.
20. E. Mâle, *L'Art religieux du XIIIe siècle en France*, Paris, 1919.
  The cult of the Virgin is a very intricate affair. Krautheimer stresses her interceding function and has traced the connection of centrally planned churches with a dedication to Mary: R. Krautheimer, 'Sancta Maria Rotunda', in: *Arte del Primo Millennio*, Turin, n.d. about 1950, pp. 21–27. Wallrath has pointed to the frequent dedication of crypts to the Virgin: R. Wallrath, 'Zur Bedeutung der mittelalterlichen Krypta' in: *Beiträge zur Kunst des Mittelalters, Kunsthistorikertagung, Brühl, 1948*, Berlin, 1950. Out of the Lady-Crypts then arose the Lady-Chapels. The official cult of the Virgin dates from the council at Ephesus in 431.
21. E. Mâle, *op. cit.*
22. The concept of class and caste in heaven—the heavenly hierarchy—is far older than the Gothic period. It occurs in Byzantine iconography. See: A. Grabar, *La peinture byzantine*, 1953; in writing in Denys—the pseudo-Areopagite—, *De Caelesti Hierarchia* (±500). But the *influence* of this idea rose to a high point in the later Middle Ages, pervading the iconographical programme as much as philosophy. See: E. Panofsky, *Gothic Architecture and Scholasticism*, London, 1957.
23. E. Panofsky, *op. cit.*
24. Suger' 'De Administratione', XXXIII in: E. Panofsky: *Abbot Suger on the Abbey Church of St. Denis and its Art Treasures*, Princeton, 1946.
25. Suger, *op. cit.*
26. Durandus of Mende, *Rationale Divinorum Officiorum*. Only accessible to me in the French translation in: J. Mason Neale & B. Webb, *Du symbolisme dans les églises du Moyen Age*. Translated from English by M. V. O. Tours, 1847.
27. 'One and the same roof was for Hrabanus Maurus the vita contemplativa and for Hugo de St Victor the vita activa. Obviously there is no value placed on consistency here. The essential is that for this conception every part of the church is seen as two: first, as what it *is* in the tangible foreground, so to speak, and second, as that which it ideally or religiously *means*.' P. Frankl, *The Gothic...*, pp. 212–213.
28. H. Sedlmayr, *Die Entstehung der Kathedrale*, Zürich, 1950.
29. O. von Simson, *The Gothic Cathedral*, London, 1956.
30. Suger, *De administratione*.
31. *Ib.*
32. See for a critical discussion of Sedlmayr's book: P. Frankl, *The Gothic...*, pp. 763 f.
33. Gothic architecture is, I believe, still to be considered as the best example of the morphological development of design, so dear to art historians; *if* this kind of development exists at all, it is in Gothic. According to Frankl, this idea is found as early as 1800 in: J. Anderson, 'Thoughts on the Origin, Excellencies and Defects of the Grecian and Gothic Styles of Architecture'

in: *Recreations in Agriculture, Natural-History, Arts and Miscellaneous Literature*, II and III, London, 1800, 1801.
See for the morphology of Gothic:
E. Gall, *Die gotische Baukunst in Frankreich und Deutschland*, Leipzig, 1925.
F. van der Meer, *Keerpunt der Middeleeuwen*, Utrecht, 1950.
R. de Lasteyrie, *L'Architecture religieuse en France à l'époque gothique*, 2 vols, Paris 1926–1927.
P. Frankl, *Gothic Architecture*, armondsworth, 1962.

34. F. Lesueur, 'St Martin de Tours et les origines de l'art Roman' in: *Bulletin Monumental*, 1949, pp. 7–84.
35. A. Schmidt, 'Westwerke und Doppelchöre', *Westfälische Zeitschrift*, Vol. 106, 1956, pp. 408–409, traces the difference between French churches with exclusively eastern chancels, and the German double-enders to the reform movement of Benedict of Aniane.
36. K. J. Conant, *Carolingian and Romanesque Architecture 800–1200*, Harmondsworth-Baltimore, 1959.
37. See note 33, and:
R. Branner, *La cathédrale de Bourges et sa place dans l'architecture gothique*, Paris-Bourges, 1962.
— 'Paris and the Origin of Rayonnant Gothic Architecture down to 1240', *Art Bulletin*, Vol. 44, March 1962, pp. 39–52.
J. Bony, 'The Resistance to Chartres in Early 13th Century Architecture', *Journal of the British Archeological Association*, 33, Vols. 20 and 21, 1954, pp. 35–52.
38. In detail it is—of course—not as simple as here described; through the powerful lens of art-history the line of development runs not straight, but in a zig-zag. See: E. Panofsky, *Gothic Architecture and Scholasticism*, and the literature of the previous note.
39. See H. Schaefer, 'The Origin of the Two-Tower Façade in Romanesque Architecture', *Art Bulletin*, Vol. XXVII, 1945, pp. 85–108.
Apart from the sources mentioned in this article, the medieval city-gate seems to me also a possible starting point. This is advocated in: G. Bandmann, *Mittelalterliche Architektur als Bedeutungsträger*, Berlin, 1951.
Baldwin Smith believes the two-towered front to be a symbol for the imperial palace: E. Baldwin Smith, *Architectural Symbolism of Imperial Rome and the Middle Ages*, Princeton, 1956.
See also: G. H. Forsyth, 'St. Martin's at Angers and the Evolution of Early Medieval Church Towers', *Art Bulletin*, Vol. XXXII, 1950, pp. 308 f.
40. E. Panofsky, *Gothic Architecture and Scholasticism*, London, 1957. See also for a discussion of this parallel: P. Frankl, *The Gothic...*, p. 700.
41. M. Scheler, *Die Wissensformen und die Gesellschaft*, Leipzig, 1926, pp. 132 f.
42. 'Utex visibili dispositione hominum, invisibilis in notescat dispositio angelorum', Hugh of St. Victor. *Commentaria in Hierarchiam Caelestem II*, quoted in O. von Simson, *op. cit.* p. 139.
43. Suger, 'De Administratione' in: E. Panofsky, *Abbot Suger on the Abbey Church of St. Denis*. The 'cult of the carts' is not restricted to the Gothic period (in which Abbot Haymo of Tutbury's and Archbishop Hugh of Rouen's accounts of Chartres are the most famous examples)

but occurs already as early as 1039 in Rheims and 1055–1082 in Liège; see V. Mortet and P. Deschamps, *Recueil des textes relatifs à l'histoire de l'architecture et à la condition des architectes en France au Moyen Age*, Vol. II, Paris, 1939, pp. 63–66 and 157–158.
44. J. de Joinville, 'Memoirs of Louis IX, King of France' in: *Chronicles of the Crusades*, London, 1914, pp. 505, 506.
45. For instance in the superb St. Ouen in Rouen, begun in 1318.

Chapter IX. Pazzi Chapel, Florence

1. Behaviour observed during three days of measuring in S. Croce and the Pazzi Chapel.
2. W. and E. Paatz, *Die Kirchen von Florenz*, Vol. 1, Frankfort, 1955, p. 507.
3. The date of 1443 has been found painted on the lower portion of the wall adjoining the Castellani Chapel, according to G. Morozzi, superintendent of monuments in Florence.
4. P. Sanpaolesi, *Brunelleschi*, Milan, 1962, p. 82.
5. P. Sanpaolesi, *op. cit.*, p. 84.
6. Communicated to me by J. J. Terwen.
7. The arches are 71 cm, the pilasters 73 cm. The plan in Stegmann-Geymüller shows the arches, *not* the pilasters. See note 9.
8. Late 14th century masonry has been discovered during recent restorations in the lateral wall on the side of the monastery, according to G. Morozzi. The frescos on that wall (one in the vestibule and another quite similar by the same hand above it in the library) afford but little additional material; they *may* be early 14th century, but their mediocre quality might also allow a later dating.
9. Horizontal measurements from J. J. Terwen, vertical dimensions after C. von Stegmann and H. von Geymüller, *Die Architektur der Renaissance in Toskana*, Vol. I, Monaco, 1885. These last measurements, whenever checked, always turned out to be reliable. As the arches do not exactly correspond to the pilasters, Miss Nyberg started on the wrong track to begin with (D. F. Nyberg, 'Brunelleschi's Use of Proportion in the Pazzi Chapel', *Marsyas*, Vol. VII, 1957), but she took also considerable liberties *with* these measurements. Of course my interpretation is pure guesswork too.
10. According to the reasonable interpretation of Moe, Vitruvius always intended his 27, 42, 29,5 or 19,5 modules to be taken along the *entire* width, from outside of column to outside of column. See: C. J. Moe, *Numeri di Vitruvio*, Milan, 1945. Placing them over the centres makes it impossible to add up all the other Vitruvian proportions. But what matters is not Moe's opinion, but Brunelleschi's. The difficulty of interpreting Vitruvius' numbers becomes apparent from the Fra Giocondo edition of 1511, in which 19,5 is changed into 23, and 29,5 into 25 to make them fit in. The manuscript of Vitruvius through which the Renaissance made his acquaintance was dug up in the Library of St. Gallen in 1416.
11. Vitruvius IV—I—2.
12. Some scholars belittle the importance of a knowledge of Roman monuments for Brunelleschi's work (H. Saalman, 'Filippo Brunelleschi, Capital Studies, *Art Bulletin*, Vol. XL, 1958,

pp. 113–137, and E. Luporini, *Brunelleschi*, Milan, 1964). Allowing that Brunelleschi took considerable liberties with the classical orders, and admitting the connection with Tuscan Romanesque capitals, I still cannot see how he could have arrived at such 'correct' classical detailing without a thorough study of the Roman ruins.
13. L. B. Alberti, *Ten Books on Architecture*, transl. by J. Leoni, London, 1751, Bk VI, Ch. II, p. 113.
14. *Ib.*, Bk IX, Ch. VII, p. 201.
15. M. Meiss, 'Masaccio and the Early Renaissance: the Circular Plan' in: *The Renaissance and Mannerism, Studies in Western Art, Acts of the 20th International Congress of the History of Art*, Vol. II, Princeton, 1963, p. 130.
16. A. Venturi, *Storia dell'arte italiana*, Vol. VII, Milan, 1923.
    P. Sanpaolesi, 'Aggiunte al Brunelleschi', *Bolletino d'Arte*, Vol. XXXVII, 1953, pp. 255 f.
    G. C. Argan, *Brunelleschi*, Milan, 1955.
17. See, for instance: M. Aubert, *L'Architecture cistercienne en France*, Paris, 1947, Vol. II, the article on 'Salles capitulaires'.
    And: W. and E. Paatz, *Die Kirchen von Florenz*, Frankfort, 1955, the article on the Spanish Chapel in the green cloister of S. Maria Novella. G. Bandmann in: 'Über Pastophorien...' in: *Kunstgeschichtliche Studien für Hans Kaufmann* goes too far in presupposing a link with Maulbronn and Bebenhausen.
18. P. Sanpaolesi, 'Ipotesi sulle conoscenze matematiche, statiche e meccaniche del Brunelleschi', *Belle Arti*, 1951, pp. 25–54.
    Brunelleschi had a knack for mechanical contraptions and a superior insight in the problems of building practice. Of course he had no inkling of statics in the modern sense of calculations.
19. R. Wittkower, *Architectural Principles in the Age of Humanism*, London, 1949.
20. R. Wittkower, *op. cit.*, ed. of 1952, p. 9.
21. L. B. Alberti, *Ten Books on Architecture*, Bk VII, Ch. V.
22. *Ib.*, Bk VII, Ch. III.
23. *Ib.*, Bk VII, Ch. XII.
24. *Ib.*, Bk VI, Ch. XII.
25. *Ib.*, Bk VII, Ch. X.
26. *Ib.*, Bk I, Ch. X and Bk VII, Ch. XV.
27. R. Wittkower, 'Brunelleschi and Proportion in Perspective', in: *Journal of the Warburg and Courtauld Institutes*, Vol. XVI, 1953, pp. 275–291. Excessive stress on perspective as an explanatory principle in Brunelleschi's architecture in: E. Luporini, *Brunelleschi*, Milan, 1964. The connection between construction and architecture is far closer than that between perspective and architecture. None of Brunelleschi's works after the great Florentine dome shows any marked interest in construction; why, then, could Brunelleschi not invent perspective and never look back thereafter?
28. E. Panofsky, *Galileo as a Critic of the Arts*, The Hague, 1954.
29. See L. B. Alberti, *Ten Books on Architecture*, Bk VII, Ch. IV.
    On Florentine Neo-Platonism:
    N. A. Robb, *Neo-Platonism of the Italian Renaissance*, London, 1935.
    G. Saitta, *La filosofia di Marsilio Ficino*.

E. Cassirer, *Individuum und Kosmos in der Philosophie der Renaissance*, Studien der Bibliothek Warburg, Vol. X, Berlin, 1927.

A convenient summary of the doctrine in:

E. Panofsky, *Studies in Iconology*, New York, 1939.
30. E. S. Piccolomini, *Briefe*, transl. by M. Mell, Jena, 1911. Letter to Andreozio Petrucci.
31. *Ib.*, Letter to Giuliano de Cesarini.
32. W. Goetz, *Das Werden des Italienischen Nationalgefühls*, Munich, 1939.
33. Alberti, *op. cit.*, Bk VI, Ch. III, p. 115.
34. On the term 'Gothic', see:

E. S. de Beer, 'Gothic: Origin and Diffusion of the Term', *Journal of the Warburg and Courtauld Institutes*, Vol. XI, 1948, p. 148. Blaming the Goths for the destruction of the classical tradition perhaps for the first time in: L. B. Alberti, *On Painting* (1435). The *adjective* Gothic first used in 1610; what is called 'Gothic' by us, was called 'tedesco' by the Italian Renaissance authors. The Renaissance sources on the history of art were primarily Florentine: Ghiberti, Manetti, Alberti, Vasari; Florence was traditionally Guelf, i.e. allied with the pope against the emperor. See also: P. Frankl, *The Gothic...*, Princeton, 1960.
35. M. Ficino, 'Five Questions Concerning the Mind', transl. by J. L. Burroughs in: E. Cassirer, P. O. Kristeller and J. H. Randall, *The Renaissance Philosophy of Man*, Chicago, 1948, pp. 198, 199.

Chapter X. Imperial Library

1. W. Buchowiecki, *Der Barockbau der ehemaligen Hofbibliothek in Wien, ein Werk J. B. Fischers von Erlach*, Vienna, 1957, pp. 84, 85, 135. This careful and exhaustive analysis of the building and its iconography is the main source for this chapter.
2. J. Count Mailath, *Geschichte des österreichischen Kaiserstaates*, Hamburg, 1848.
3. W. Buchowiecki, *op. cit.*
4. On Baroque fusion of space: S. Giedion, *Space, Time and Architecture*, Cambridge, Mass., 1941, Part II.

   W. Hager, *Die Bauten des Deutschen Barocks*, Jena, 1942.
5. H. Sedlmayr, *Johann Bernhard Fischer von Erlach*, Vienna-Munich, 1956.
6. The title 'Hercules Musarum' is no dog latin; 18th century scholarship would not have allowed such liberties. Hercules Musarum had a temple in Rome, of 189 A.D. A youth playing a lyre surrounded by the inscription 'Hercules Musarum' is depicted on the verso of coins of Q. Pomponius Musa (C. Daremberg and L. Saglio, ed., *Dictionnaire des Antiquités Grecques et Romaines*, Paris, 1900, Vol. V). This coin is a possible source, for the title was selected by the dignitary specifically in charge of the imperial collection of coins, Carl Gustav Heraeus.
7. The text is reproduced as Figure 140 in: G. Kunoth, *Die Historische Architektur Fischers von Erlach*, Düsseldorf, 1956.
8. Printed in full in W. Buchowiecki, *op. cit.*
9. Codex Albrecht in Buchowiecki, p. 109.

10. *Ib.*, Buchowiecki, p. 93.
11. H. Sedlmayr, 'Die politische Bedeutung des deutschen Barocks', in: *Gesamtdeutsche Vergangenheit, Festgabe für Heinrich, Ritter von Srbik*, Munich, 1938.
12. On Austrian Baroque architecutre:
    H. Sedlmayr, *Österreichische Barockarchitektur*, Vienna, 1930.
    Ib., Johann Bernhard Fischer von Erlach, Vienna-Munich, 1956.
    E. Hempel, *Baroque Art and Architecture in Central Europe*, Harmondsworth, 1965.
    D. Frey, 'Zur Wesensbestimmung des österreichischen Barocks' in: *Festschrift für H. Jantzen* Berlin, 1951.
13. Mailath, *op. cit.*, p. 374.

Chapter XI. Westminster New Palace

1. M. Hastings, *Parliament House*, London, 1950.
2. M. Hastings, *St Stephens Chapel*, Cambridge, 1961.
3. M. Hastings, *Parliament House*, London, 1950.
4. A. Barry, *The Life and Works of Sir Charles Barry*, London, 1867.
5. *Ib.*, p. 238.
6. *Ib.*, pp. 238, 239.
7. That is present opinion. Barry never gave Pugin any official credit for his part in the design; conversely his own (major) contribution to it, i.e. the overall plan and massing, has been minimized too. See: K. Clark, *The Gothic Revival* (1st ed. 1928), London, 1950.
   H. R. Hitchcock, *Early Victorian Architecture in Britain*, 2 vols., New Haven, Conn., 1954.
8. A. Barry, *op. cit.*, p. 257.
9. *Ib.*, pp. 251, 252.
10. A. W. Pugin, *The True Principles of Pointed or Christian Architecture*, London, 1853, p. 1.
11. *Ib.*, pp. 38, 39.
12. A. Barry, *op. cit.*, pp. 241, 242.
13. On 19th century architecture, see:
    H. R. Hitchcock, *op. cit.*
    Ib., Architecture, Nineteenth and Twentieth Centuries, Harmondsworth-Baltimore, 1958.
    C. L. V. Meeks, *The Railway Station, an Architectural History*, London-New Haven, 1957.
    K. W. Luckhurst, *The Story of Exhibitions*, London, 1951.
14. E. Kaufmann, *Architecture in the Age of Reason. Baroque and Postbaroque in England, Italy and France*, Cambridge, 1955.
15. Sir Uvedale Price, *An Essay on the Picturesque as Compared with the Sublime and the Beautiful*, London, 1794.
16. A. Barry, *op. cit.*, p. 241.
17. *Ib.*, p. 245. See also: A. Hyland, 'Imperial Valhalla', *Journal of the Society of Architectural Historians*, Vol. XXI, No 3, pp. 129 f.
18. *Ib.*, p. 257.

19. See: H. R. Hitchcock, *Early Victorian Architecture in Britain*, in particular the illustrations.
20. J. Summerson, *Architecture in Britain, 1530–1830*, Harmondsworth (1953), 1963, p. 283.
21. A. W. Pugin, 'An Apology for the Revival of Christian Architecture in England', appended to: *The True Principles...*, London, 1853, p. 10 f.n.
22. T. Carlyle, *Past and Present* (1st ed. 1843), quote from ed. London, 1895, p. 125.
23. H. Taine, *Notes on England*, quoted in:
    A. Bryant, *English saga (1840–1940)*, London-Paris, 1947, p. 156.
    For details on social history, see:
    G. M. Trevelyan, *English Social History*, London-New York,-Toronto, 1946, Chaps. XV-XVIII.
24. S. T. Coleridge, *The Friend* (1st ed. 1809–1810), 3 vols., London, 1844, Vol II, p. 29.
25. A. W. Pugin, *The True Principles...*, pp. 50, 51.

Chapter XII. The Amsterdam Exchange

1. See A. W. Weissman, *De Beurs te Amsterdam 1835–1903*, Amsterdam, 1904, pp. 112 f. This book also surveys the many changes in opinion and the vacillations of the town-council. Also: *Bouwkundig Weekblad*, 1896, p. 252, and 1903, p. 236.
   P. Singelenberg, 'Enige beschouwingen over de Beurs van Berlage', *Bulletin van de Kon. Ned. Oudheidkundige Bond*, 6th Series, Vol. 12, Column 131–142.
2. Wooden piles are driven in till a lower layer of sand is reached. Unfortunately the supervision on the foundation work has been insufficient: piles of varying lengths have been used, with the result that the shorter ones stand with their tips above the layer of sand. Already in 1906–1907 repairs were necessary because of the cracks which appeared in the building. Functionally the Exchange has become obsolete through the changes in commercial practice. Therefore in 1959 the town council was asked to vote on the choice between demolition and extensive restoration and alteration. In 1961 the latter course was chosen.
3. H. P. Berlage, *Studies over bouwkunst, stijl en samenleving*, Rotterdam, 1910, pp. 68, 69.
4. *Ib.*, pp. 59, 60.
5. *Bouwkundig Weekblad*, Vol. 18, 1898, pp. 109–112.
6. H. P. Berlage, *Grundlagen und Entwicklung der Architektur*, Rotterdam, 1908, p. 107. Interest in studies of systems of proportions revived in Holland around the turn of the century. Berlage mentioned J. H. de Groot in particular as his source. Before Berlage, also P. J. H. Cuypers used modular grids. The source of the system of proportions of the Exchange is E. E. Viollet-le-Duc, *Entretiens sur l'architecture*, Paris, 1863, Vol. I, pp. 386 f. See also: A. W. Reinink, *K. P. C. de Bazel—architect*, Leiden, 1965.
7. H. P. Berlage, *Studies* ..., p. 3.
8. *Ib.*, p. 71.
9. *Ib.*, p. 50.
10. *Ib.*, p. 29.
11. H. P. Berlage, *Grundlagen*..., p. 116.
12. H. P. Berlage, *Studies*..., p. 91.

Chapter XIII. Johnson House

1. Description in: *Architectural Forum*, Nov. 1949.
2. In *The Architectural Review*, Vol. 108, September 1950, pp. 152–159.
3. On modern architecture:
   N. Pevsner, *Pioneers of Modern Design from W. Morris to W. Gropius*, Harmondsworth, 1960 (rev. ed. of *Pioneers of the Modern Movement*, 1936).
   S. Giedion, *Space, Time and Architecture*, Cambridge, Mass., 1941.
   R. Banham, *Theory and Design in the First Machine Age*, London, 1960.
4. T. van Doesburg in an article in *De Stijl*, Vol. 6, *1924*, pp. 78–83.
5. L. Moholy-Nagy, *Von Material zu Architektur*, Munich, 1929, p. 203.
6. B. Brownell and F. Lloyd Wright, *Architecture and Modern Life*, New York-London, 1938, p. 83.
7. *Ib.*, p. 81.
   More factual and scientific, but just as depressing reading makes:
   G. Friedmann, *Le Travail en miettes*, Paris, 1956. For the pessimistic outlook, see R. B. Bailey, *Sociology Faces Pessimism*, The Hague, 1958.
8. W. Gropius, *Scope of Total Architecture* (1st ed. 1943), New York, 1955, pp. 76, 77
9. Interview with C. Norberg-Schulz in: *Baukunst und Werkform*, 1958, p. 615.
10. Interview with C. Norberg-Schulz, *loc. cit.*
11. *Ib.*

Chapter XIV. Notre Dame du Haut in Ronchamp

1. Books on the chapel:
   Le Corbusier, *Chapelle Notre Dame du Haut à Ronchamp*, Paris, 1957.
   Ib., *Ronchamp*, Zurich, 1957.
2. Le Corbusier, *Le Modulor*, Bologne, 1949.
3. *Ib.*, *Précisions sur un état présent de l'architecture et de l'urbanisme*, Paris, 1930, p. 28.
4. On Art Nouveau:
   S. T. Madsen, *Sources of Art Nouveau*, New York, 1956.
   F. Ahlers-Hestermann, *Stilwende. Aufbruch der Jugend um 1900*, Berlin, 1956.
   Significantly, Art Nouveau or the Jugendstil has come in for a reappraisal in the fifties, just when these modern 'organic' buildings were designed.
5. Le Corbusier, *Ronchamp*, Zurich, 1957.
6. *Ib.*, *Chapelle* ..., p. 50.
7. B. Brownell and F. Lloyd Wright, *Architecture and Modern Life*, New York-London, 1938, pp. 19, 20.
8. D. Riesman, N. Glazer and R. Dewney, *The Lonely Crowd*, New York, 1956.
   W. H. Whyte, *The Organization Man*, Garden City, 1956.

Chapter XV. Recent developments

1. Jane Jacobs, *The Death and Life of Great American Cities*, New York, 1961.
2. *Traffic in Towns*, Reports of the Steering Group and Working Group appointed by the Minister of Transport (The 'Buchanan Report'), London, 1963.
3. A. van Eyck, in: A. Smithson, ed., *Team 10 Primer*, London, n.d., p. 15.
4. A. van Eyck, 'The Medicine of Reciprocity', in: *Forum* (Dutch), Vol. XV, No 6/7 (April/May 1961), p. 238.
5. J. B. Bakema, in: *Team 10 Primer*, pp. 6–7.

Index

Aalto, A. 37, 49, 143, 174, 180, 181
Abelard, quoted 96
Abell, W. 20, 21, 23, 41, 42, 158
  quoted 21
Abraham, P. 80, 81, 84
Adam, R. 150
Aesch 180
aesthetics 4f, 41
  architectural 6, 7
  formal 5, 7, 42, 43, 44, 74, 115, 135
  general 7, 11
  particular 7, 11
  symbolic 5, 115
Aigues Mortes 76
Alberti, L. B. 6, 47, 48, 50, 110, 112, 160
  quoted 46, 50, 109, 110, 111, 114
Altamira 22
ambulatory 51, 52, 54, 55, 56, 58, 66, 68, 92
Amiens 76
  cathedral 10, 11, 37, 76–100
  St. Firmin 77
Amsterdam 180
  exchange 143, 152–162, 166
  Algemene Maatschappij van Levensverzekering 152
  De Nederlanden van 1845 152
Angers, St. Martin 70
angularity 34
anisotropy 29, 33
antithetical pair 32, 34
anthroposophy 49

Art Nouveau 29, 49, 174
asymmetry 8, 28, 34, 168
Aubert, M. 84
Avignon, library 122
Bakema, J. B. 179, 180
  quoted 180
Baker, H. 6
Baldwin Smith, E. 15
Balmoral Castle 143
Banham, R. 15
Barcelona Pavilion 3, 29, 169
Baroque 46, 47, 49, 125, 133, 134, 135, 143, 146, 150, 158, 165, 169, 176, 180, 181
  colossality 134
  massiveness 135
  size 134
  unity 125, 134
Barry, A. 139, 140, 141, 142
Barry, Alfred quoted 139, 142, 143
Barry, Ch. 138, 139, 144, 145
basilica, Early Christian 58, 63, 67, 68, 70, 91
Basle 113, 114
Bath, Royal Crescent 180
Baudoin, C. quoted 19
Beauvais cathedral 30, 77, 82, 99
Benevolo, L. 3
Berlage, H. P. 48, 152, 156, 157, 159, 160, 161, 165
  quoted 156, 158, 159
Berlin, Altes Museum 180
  Free University 179

INDEX

Philharmonic Hall 174
Bernward of Hildesheim 61, 62, 69, 72, 73, 74
   quoted 61
Beseler, H. 70
Black Death 76
Blenheim Palace 134
Booz, P. 82
Borgias 113
Botticelli, S. 109
Boullée, E. L. 47, 48, 160
   quoted 47, 50, 169
Bourges, cathedral 85
Brownell, B. 174
   quoted 167
Bruchsal 135, 180
Brunelleschi, F. 50, 101, 103, 104, 105, 107, 110, 111, 112, 127
Buchanan report 178
Buchowiecki, W. 119
Buckminster Fuller, R. 50
Burke, R. 146
Caen 92, 93
Cambrai 93
Candilis, Woods and Josic 179
Canterbury cathedral 81
Capability Brown 47, 143
capitalism 115, 159
Carlyle, Th. 146, 148
   quoted 147
Carroll, L. 148
catholics and protestants 133
Centula, St. Riquier 64, 70, 93
Chambers, W. 150
chapter house 100, 110
Charlemagne 67, 117, 119
Charles V 117, 119, 128, 131
Charles VI 118, 119, 123, 127, 128, 131, 132, 133, 136
Charte d'Athènes 178
Chartres 85, 88, 93
Chiattone, M. 48

Choisy, A. 84
christianity 59
charity 11, 164
Classe, St. Apollinare 77
Classicism 45
Cluny 93
Conant, K. J. 63
concentrated 98
Conques, St. Foy 92, 93
consistency 11
Constantina 51
Constantine 131
construction 49
continuity 9, 98, 115, 141
contrast 9, 10, 11, 36, 42, 74
Coleridge, S. T. quoted 148, 149
Cologne, cathedral 99
composition 36f, 37, 54, 55, 56, 67, 94, 95, 142, 173
concept 26
connection 36
connotation 15
co-ordinate 33, 34, 35, 36
Cordonnier, L. 152
Corvey, abbey church 64, 67, 74, 75
Cramer, Jaray and Paillard 180
Crane, W. 49
crusades 96
crypt 63, 69, 92
Darwin, Ch. 146
de Fouilloy, Evrard 77
de Joinville, J. 96
della Robbia, L. 108, 112
de l'Orme, Philibert 50
de Luzarches, Robert 77, 80
Denis the pseudo Areopagite 90
denotatum 15
Dessau 3
Dickens, Ch. 146, 148
Dijon, St. Bénigne 64
Diocletian 54, 56, 57
discontinuity 67

INDEX

dome 41, 52, 54, 55, 56, 57, 109, 110
dominant contexts 16
Donatello 109
Downton castle 47
dreamland 45, 46, 48, 114, 149, 150, 159, 160
Dresden, railway station 160
Duiker, J. 3, 30
Durandus of Mende quoted 89, 90, 94
Durham, cathedral 92, 93
Early English 139
Eclecticism 45
Edward I 137
Edward the Confessor 137
Ehrenzweig, A. 19
Eiffel, G. 50
El Lissitzky 160
emotion 17, 19
Enea Silvio (Piccolomini) quoted 113, 114
enfilade 46
Erskine, R. 179
Euclidean geometry 8
Eveux, la Tourette 180
Faraday, M. 146
Farnsworth house 165, 168
Ferdinand 117
Ficino, M. 116
  quoted 116
Fischer von Erlach, J. B. 121, 127, 134, 135
Fitchen, J. 84
Florence 114
  Foundling Hospital 109
  Laurention library 122
  Palazzo di Parte Guelfa 103, 105
  Pazzi Chapel 100–117, 125
  S. Croce 100, 101, 103, 107
  S. Lorenzo 103, 104, 110, 111, 112
  S. Maria degli Angeli 112
  S. Spirito 103, 110, 111, 112
Focillon, H. 81, 84
Fonthill Abbey 47, 146
Förderer, W. 180

form 33
Fourier, F. M. C. 148
Fra Angelico 109
Frankl, P. 81, 84
Frankfurt 179, 180
French Revolution 46, 134, 147, 152
Freud, S. 19
Freyssinet, E. 50
Fulda 68
functionalism 25, 48, 145
Gall, E. 81
Galilei, A. 180
Galli-Bibiena, G. 136
Gandy, J. 143
Gaskell Mrs. 148
Gaudí, A. 29, 175
Geneva, Palace of the League of Nations 143
Genoa 113, 114
Gernrode, S. Cyriakus 64, 75
Gestalt 9, 10, 11, 12, 28, 29, 37, 173
Gibraltar 118, 128, 133
Gilbert, C. 6
Gothic 4, 5, 6, 11, 14, 15, 20, 43, 44, 50, 62, 66, 76–100, 113, 139, 140, 145, 146, 147, 150
  Revival 41, 146, 149, 150
  science 82
  structural system 80–84, 92, 98
  universality 87
Gran, D. 129, 136
gravity 29, 30, 49
Great Exhibition 146
Gropius, W. quoted 167
Guarini, G. 50
Guimard, H. 175
Habsburg House, 117, 118, 127, 128, 133
Halberstadt 69
Harlech Castle 27
harmonic cosmos 46, 112, 114, 115, 116, 169, 181
harmony 75
Harvard, Visual Arts Center 37, 49, 180

INDEX

Hautecoeur, L. 15
Heavenly Jerusalem 90, 94
Heitz, C. 64
Henry VIII 137
Heraeus 128
Hercules 127, 129
    Musarum 127, 128, 129
    Pillars of 119
Horland 137
heroon 56, 57
Hersfeld, abbey church 68
hierarchy of heaven 87
hierarchies 95
Highclere Castle 146
Hildesheim 37, 69, 72
    cathedral 74
    St. Michaël 61–76, 78, 80, 84, 85, 87, 88, 91, 93, 95, 98, 115, 176
Holy Roman Empire 117
homogeneity 67, 141
honesty in construction 31, 48, 66, 159, 160, 161, 173
Horta, V. 175
Hugh of St. Victor 95
Imatra, church 174
individualism 115
Industrial Revolution 45, 47, 50, 147, 160
interpreter 15
irregularity 142, 143
isolation 34, 43, 44, 54, 66, 78, 95, 125, 163, 171
Jacob 24, 26
Jacobs, J. 178
Jacobsen, A. 180
Jantzen, H. 80
Joanna of Aragon 117
Johnson, Ph. C. 162, 163, 164, 165, 180
    quoted 164
Jones, I 142
Joseph II 119
Jumièges, abbey church 93
Kahn, L. 180

Karlsruhe 135, 180
Kassel 135
Kautzsch, R. 70
Kitschelt, L. 90
Lactantius quoted 58
Langer, S. 24
language of architecture 14f
Laon, cathedral 81, 85
Lascaux 22
Lear, E. 148
le Corbusier 3, 4, 6, 7, 8, 9, 10, 25, 29, 31, 37, 49, 50, 160, 170, 171, 173, 175, 176, 180, 181
    quoted 6, 8, 174, 715, 176
Ledoux, C. N. 47, 48, 160, 165, 169
Lehmann, E. 64
Le Mans, cathedral 77
Lessay, abbey church 93
levels of meaning 41f, 60, 94, 115, 132, 161
Leopold I 121, 128, 132, 133, 134
Library 121, 122, 123, 128
Livingstone, D. 146, 148
location 36
Lodoli, C. quoted 47
London, Chrystal Palace 150
    Law Courts 143
    Reform club 146
    St. Pancras Hotel 143
    St. Stephen's chapel 137, 138
    Westminster Abbey 137
    Westminster Hall 137, 138, 139, 143, 144, 145
    Westminster New Palace (Houses of Parliament) 37, 137–152, 155, 180
    Westminster Palace 137
Loos, A. 180
Louis XIV 119, 127, 131, 134
Lutyens, E. 6
Mackintosh, C. R. 48
Magnel, G. 50
Mainz, 61

Mâle, E. 62, 87
Malewitch, K. 160
Manetti 101
Mannerism 46, 165
Marlborough 117
Marx, K. 177
Mary, cult of 86
Mary, Virgin 170
Masson 84
mausoleum 51, 55
Maxwell, J. C. 146
meaning 5
Medici 100
Meiss, M. 109
Menai Straits, bridge 150
Mendelsohn, E. 48
Michael the Archangel 62, 69, 74
Middle Ages 22, 44, 45, 49, 51, 70, 73, 76
Mies van der Rohe, L. 3, 4, 11, 29, 143, 160, 165, 166, 168, 169
Mill, J. S. 146
Modern Architecture 45
modulor 173
Moholy-Nagy, C. 166
Moissac, abbey church 93
monasticism 73
Mondriaan P. 158, 165
  quoted 48
monster 20, 21
Mont St. Michel 93
Montano, G. B. 57
Monte Cargano 62
Morienval, abbey church 93
Morris, W. 49, 143, 160
Morse, S. 154
motor activity 30
movement 135
new architecture 9
Nash, J. 150
Nicomachus of Gerasa 82
Nietzsche, F. 11
Neo-Baroque 181

Nero 57
Nervi, P. L. 50
Neumann, B. 19
Neutra, R. 29
New Brutalism 180
New Canaan, Johnson House, 143, 162–170, 171, 176, 177
Neo-Gothic 14, 15, 158
New Haven, Art & Architecture Building 180
  Yale University skating rink
Neo-Platonic philosophy 46, 59, 111, 116
Neo-Renaissance 152
New York, U. N. building 145
Norberg-Schultz, C. 50
Noyon, cathedral 93
organic architecture 29, 173, 174, 176
Otto the Third 61, 74
Oud, J. P. 48
Oxford, St. Catherine's College 180
Odyssey 17
Paleolithic age 22, 23
Palladio, A. 15, 47, 50, 142
  quoted 4, 5, 6
Panofsky, E. 95
  quoted 18, 90
Pantheon of Humanity 157
Paris 85, 88, 93
  Ecole des Beaux Arts 143
  Sainte Chapelle 137
parts 36
Paxton, Sir J. 50, 150
Pazzi 100, 110
Pei, F. M. 180
perception 8, 10, 42, 44
Perpendicular 139, 140
perspective 112
Philadelphia, Richards Medical research centre 180
Phileban solids 6, 10, 28, 29, 37, 45, 66, 74, 104, 114, 115, 135, 160, 161, 169
Philip of Habsburg 117
Philip II of Spain 128

Philip III 118
physical construction 43
Piaget, J. 29
picturesque 47, 87
picturesqueness 142
picturesque asymmetry 49
piliers cantonnés 78, 85
place 24
plasticity 34, 43, 80, 92, 98, 125, 135
Plato 9
pluralism 167
Poissy, Savoie house 181
Pollock, J. 158
Pontigny, abbey church 92
Pope, J. R. 6
Porter, A. Kingsley 84
position 36
Prague, Clam-Gallas palace 126
Price, Sir Uvedale 143
processional service 64
proportion 33, 52, 67, 75, 78, 95, 98, 105, 107, 109, 123
proximity 8
psycho-analysis 19
psychology 19
psychology, Gestalt 7, 34
psychology of perception 7, 10
Pugin, A. W. 4, 14, 48, 140, 142, 156
  quoted 14, 48, 149, 141, 146, 149
Rameses I 25, 26
Raphaël 112
rational and emotional factor 25
reformation 45, 117, 133
Regensburg, cathedral 99
regularity 34, 44, 142, 143, 145
Renaissance 11, 23, 41, 45, 46, 49, 50, 112, 113, 114, 115, 116, 126, 127, 133, 134, 135, 139, 142, 150, 153, 165, 168, 181
repetition 8, 44, 115
Rheims, cathedral 7, 22, 85, 88
Richardson, H. H. 48
Richelieu 117

Riesman, D. 177
Rietveld, G. 29
Roman antiquities 131
  empire 21, 43, 56, 58, 59
Romanesque 43, 44, 62, 91, 113, 156
Rome 64, 114, 115
  Castel Sant' Angelo 56, 62
  Domus Aurea 57
  Pantheon 54, 112
  St. Agnes 51
  S. Costanza 51–61, 112
  St. John in the Lateran 58, 180
  S. Maria Maggiore 58
  S. Peter 46, 51
  S. Stefano Rotondo 112
  temple of Minerva Medica 54
  Thermae 54
Ronchamp 170
  N. D. du Haut 10, 11, 29, 31, 49, 143, 167, 170–178, 181
Roth, A. 3
Rouen, cathedral 77
  St. Maclou 84
Rousseau, J. J. 47, 177
Rudolph, P. 36, 49, 180
  quoted 31
Ruskin, J. 6, 147, 160
  quoted 5
Saarinen, E. 174
St. Benoit-sur-Loire 64, 85
St. Denis 90, 91, 93
St. Gallen, Economic School 180
St. Germain-des-Prés 93
St. Louis 76, 96, 97
St. Savin-sur-Gartempe 92
St. Thomas 95
Sampson quoted 20
Sanpaolesi 101, 103
Savoy, Prince Eugene of 117
Saynätsalo, town hall 180
Scharoun, H. 174
Scheler, M. 95, 96

Schinkel, K. F. 165, 180
Schmitthenner, P. 6
scholastic philosophy 95
Scott, Sir W. 147
Second World War 62
Sedlmayr, H. 90, 94, 126, 131
Senlis, cathedral 93
Sens, cathedral 85, 93
Sethy 25, 26
Shaftesbury, Lord 147
Sheldon Art Gallery 180
Soane, Sir J. 142, 150
Soissons, cathedral 85
Spalato, Diocletians palace 54, 56, 57
Spencer, H. 146
Steiner, R. 49
Stephen, King 137
Stern, H. 55
Strawberry Hill 47
Stuart 146
Stuttgart, Weissenhofsiedlung 3, 180
Stijl 160, 164
Suger 50, 94
 quoted 88, 90, 96
Sullivan L. 48, 142, 156
Summerson, J. 145
Sydney, Opera House 174
Taine, H. 148
Tel Aviv 179, 180
Thangmar quoted 72
The Hague, First Church of Christ, Scientist 157
 Municipal Museum 157
Thoreau, H. D. 148
Toledo Cathedral, Transparente 181
Tomé, N. 181
Torroja, E. 50
Tours, St. Martin 69, 70, 91
tournus, St. Philibert 64, 92
tower 68, 70, 139, 144, 155
Transept 63, 67, 68, 70
Trenton, Bathhouse 180

Treub 152
Triforium 80, 85, 86, 93
two-tower facade, 93, 95
Ulm, cathedral 99
Utzon, J. 174
unity 174
van Albrecht, A. 129
van den Broek, J. H. 179, 180, 181
van de Velde, H. 175
van Doesburg, T. 29, 160, 169
 quoted 9, 10, 166, 182–186
van Eyck, A. quoted 178
van Regteren Altena, J. 103
Venice library 122
Verne, J. 148
Versailles 46, 134, 135, 143, 189
Vézelay, Madeleine 92, 93
Victorian 137–152
Vienna 117
 Imperial library 37, 117–137, 143, 144, 169, 176, 180
 Klesheim palace 126
 Schönbrunn 126, 134, 135
Vierzehnheiligen 37, 46
Villard de Honnecourt 97
Viollet-le-Duc, E. E. 4, 6, 80, 81
Vitruvius 3, 6, 7, 41, 50, 105, 107
von Simson, O, 90, 91, 94
Voysey, C. A. 48
Washington, capitol 27
Weisman, A. W. 154
Werden, abbey church 64
Westwork 64, 70
Whyte, W. H. 177
William Rufus 137
William the Conqueror 137
Wills, R. B. 6
Wittkower, R. 15, 46, 110, 115
Wood, J. 180
Wool trade, 76, 77
Wotton, Sir H. 3
Wren, Ch. 142

Wright, Frank Lloyd 49, 50, 143, 160
  quoted 176
Wyatt, J. 146

Yamasaki, M. 180
Yevele, H. 137
Zürich, Dolderthal flats 3

750